THE SPARTACIST UPRISING

MARQUETTE GERMAN STUDIES

I

The Spartacist

Marquette German Studies, I

Uprising of 1919

and the crisis of the German Socialist Movement: A study of the relation of political theory and party practice

ERIC WALDMAN, Ph.D., *Assistant Professor of Political Science at Marquette University*

THE MARQUETTE UNIVERSITY PRESS · MILWAUKEE

Marquette German Studies are published under the direction
of the Institute of German Affairs of Marquette University.

Library of Congress Catalog Card Number: 58-7265

Manufactured in the United States of America

Acknowledgment

I T IS A well known truism that most books reflect not only the effort of the author but an accumulation of thought and study by many others who have completed research and publication in the same general area of investigation. This book is no exception to the rule, and the author has made extensive use of many excellent studies concerned with German political and historical developments. No effort has been made to repeat descriptive material found elsewhere, although references in the footnotes will direct the reader to more detailed historical studies.

It is impossible to acknowledge our obligations to all of those who have directly or indirectly assisted with the writing of this study. However, the author's intellectual indebtedness to his former teacher, Professor Wolfgang H. Kraus, is of such magnitude that is must be foremost as we acknowledge assistance, advice, and constructive criticism. Many thanks are due to Professor Stefan T. Possony of Georgetown University, Dr. Fritz T. Epstein of the Library of Congress, and Mr. Paul R. Sweet, Chief, German Documents Branch, Historical Division, United States Department of State, who have read the manuscript in its original version and have offered pertinent suggestions for its improvement. Valuable source material in the Library of Congress made it possible that such a study could be carried out within the geographic limits of the United States.

The author is also most grateful to his wife for all she did towards the successful completion of this book. Not only did she type and edit the first draft but her searching questions forced him to present a far clearer presentation than he would otherwise have done. Mrs. Florence Dallin and Dr. Marc Griesbach have earned the author's gratitude for their splendid editorial work. While the author is deeply grateful to these and many others who remain unnamed, the conclusion reached in this book and any interpretations offered are solely the responsibility of the author.

E.W.

Marquette University
Milwaukee 3, Wisconsin

Contents

Introduction

THIS STUDY aims at exploring the crisis of the German socialist movement which grew in intensity from the time of the open split of the Social Democratic Party during the war until its climax in the bloody fighting between the radical left and moderate socialists during the so-called Spartacist Uprising of January 1919. In the course of this primary pursuit, two subsidiary aims are served: an analysis of the relationship existing between the theory and practice of the German Communists during their period of political infancy; and an examination of the impact of the Communists on the course of the German Revolution.

The organization of this study can be summarized as follows: Part I deals with the emergence of the left-wing socialists and Spartacists, the forerunners of the German Communists, prior to the outbreak of the November Revolution of 1918. Part II examines the impact of the November Revolution upon the socialists, and discusses the problems created by the different aims for the revolution held by the various parties and factions of the socialist movement. Part III presents the first major crisis of the German labor movement in the post-World War I period, the Spartacist Uprising. It also deals with the revolution in retrospect, indicating the utilization by present-day German Communists of distorted versions of the revolutionary events of 1918-19 for the sake of contemporary propaganda.

Since the importance of ideological concepts of young revolutionary movements is often underestimated, an effort has been made throughout to relate the political theory of the left-wing socialists and Spartacists (or Communists, as the case may be) to the problems under discussion. It should be remembered that during their early phase almost all revolutionary movements rely heavily on theoretical foundations. The democratic liberal creed was no exception. It is only at a later stage, after consolidation has set in and the revolutionary party or movement acquires maturity, that the pragmatic approach to political problems gains predominance, replacing the earlier ideological guidance and determining party actions.

The translations of German quotations in this study are this writer's own. An effort has been made to keep them as close as possible to the original text in order to retain some of the flavor of the period in which they were written. This holds true particularly for newspaper articles and transcripts of speeches. German words and names appearing in this book were hyphenated, when required, according to German syllabication.

The phase of German political history into which this study falls is marked by an abundance of source material. The author, therefore, was faced with the problem of a proper selection of representative sources and an evaluation of the highly subjective accounts which were written for the most part within a few years after the events. It is probably characteristic of highly controversial issues, such as the one under discussion, that they frequently become the subject of many authors who are less interested in a scholarly treatment of the problem than in proving a particular point of view and in justifying the actions and views of their own affiliations. This lack of objectivity even holds true for such recent publications as Ruth Fischer's *Stalin and German Communism*. Convenient historical oversights and incorrect factual premises are some of the means used frequently by these authors. Fortunately the abundant documentary materials — some in specific collections, but most of them widely dispersed in secondary works — obviate the need to rely on these partisan accounts, except where an analysis of these biased views adds to the over-all understanding of the events under examination.

The Emergence
of the Spartacists

The Left Wing Within the German Social Democratic Party Prior to World War I

1. *The Growth of the German Socialist Movement*

Many of the ideological concepts and organizational characteristics of the Spartacists, the forerunners of the German Communists, have their origin in the period which followed the unification of the Lassallean workers' organization with the Marxian
socialists in 1875. The end product of this fusion was the Social
Democratic Party of Germany (SPD).[1] In the decades following
the union, the SPD developed into a strong mass party and along
with its allied trade unions became a powerful factor in German
political life.

During this period, a number of political factions emerged
within the SPD. These were an outgrowth of basic disagreements
on major political and tactical issues, resulting partly from different interpretations of Marxian doctrines and partly from the
conflicting objectives of an organization which regarded itself as
a proletarian party in a bourgeois state. The perpetuation of
these factions in a period of crisis caused by the outbreak of
World War I led eventually to a division of the German labor
movement into hostile camps, a situation which persists to the
present time.

---

[1] The German designation for the Social Democratic Party of Germany is
Sozialdemokratische Partei Deutsch-
lands, or SPD. This abbreviation will
be used hereafter in this paper.

The purpose of this chapter is to analyze the factors and conditions contributing to the growth of the political thought and revolutionary tactical concepts of the radical left wing of the SPD. This complex later became known, organizationally, as the Spartacist League and eventually, on December 31, 1918, as the Communist Party of Germany (KPD).[2] An attempt has also been made to analyze a selected number of concepts characteristic of the radical left wing of the German socialists.

Socialist ideas were abroad in Germany before 1848, but it was not until that year that a genuine working-class movement came into existence in the form of a number of workers' associations. The growth of organized labor was not impressive, however, until the 1860s, when Ferdinand Lassalle brought life and action into the movement. A group of professed Marxists with a relatively small following was also active among the German proletariat, but it did not succeed in increasing its strength substantially until after the death of Lassalle.[3]

In 1875 the two movements among the German workers combined to form the united SPD, thus providing a more powerful organization to fight for the interests of the increasing number of German workers.[4] Thus, from its very inception the SPD carried within its organization two basically different creeds. Those who held the romantic nationalism and democratic concepts of

[2] The German term is *Kommunistische Partei Deutschlands*. The abbreviation KPD will be used hereafter in this study.

The Spartacist League (*Spartakusbund*) was a loose organization of left wing radicals; under the leadership of Rosa Luxemburg and Karl Liebknecht, it fought against the policies of the SPD and the trade unions which were designed to support the war effort. The group adopted the name "Spartakus," the pseudonym used for their illegal publications. *Spartacus* was the leader of a Roman slave revolt; his name was selected to serve as a symbol for the revolt of the modern "wage slaves." On December 31, 1918, the Spartacists founded the Communist Party of Germany (KPD).

[3] For an excellent account of the early phase of the German socialist movement see Franz Mehring, *Geschichte der deutschen Sozialdemokratie* (4th ed.; Stuttgart; J.H.W. Dietz, 1909). See also Veit Valentin, *Geschichte der deutschen Revolution von 1848-49* (Berlin: Ullstein, [c. 1930-3].)

[4] William S. Halperin, *Germany Tried Democracy* (New York: T.Y. Crowell Co., 1946), p. 16; Joseph A. Berlau, *The German Social Democratic Party, 1914-1921* (New York: Columlin: E. Rowohlt Verlag, 1930), p. 52.

the Lassallean group had complete confidence in the possibility of improving the workers' lot by reforms within the framework of the existing state. The other group accepted the Marxian concepts regarding the historic mission of the proletariat and the ultimate socialist revolution as the final stage of the inevitable class struggle within the capitalist society. It was the second group which gained dominance in the SPD and caused at least a temporary subordination of Lassalleanism.[5]

After the unification of Germany was achieved by Chancellor Bismarck and the subsequent rapid industrialization, the SPD considerably widened its influence among the growing number of German workers. Bismarck's concern with the rapid spread of socialism among the workers prompted his anti-socialist law of 1878 which was intended to stop the growth of the movement. But persecution only resulted in making the SPD stronger, and Bismarck soon realized the futility of the provisions of the anti-socialist law. While keeping the law on the books, in the 1880s he changed his policy toward the workers, in an attempt to give them a definite interest in the perpetuation of the existing state by promulgating progressive social legislation. Marx's famous phrase in the Communist Manifesto that the proletariat has nothing to lose but its chains lost part of its significance for the German workers as a result of the social policies of Bismarck.

After the fall of Bismarck in 1890 — the year which also saw the end of the anti-socialist law — William II sponsored an ambitious program of factory legislation. But even this did not stop the steadily mounting strength of the socialist movement.[6] In the face of this development one could have expected that the German government would follow one of two alternatives. One was the brutal suppression of the socialists. However after 1890 — the year in which the SPD obtained almost one and a half million votes and entered the Reichstag with thirty-five deputies — apparently none of the leading German politicians were in-

---

[5] Berlau, *op. cit.*, p. 329.　　　　[6] Halperin, *op. cit.*, pp.16-17.

clined to use the methods Bismarck had tried with so little success. The other alternative was to pursue a policy based on a compromise with the political aspirations of the middle class and the workers and gradually to transform Germany into a democratic constitutional monarchy. William II and his chancellors (Caprivi, Hohenlohe, and Buelow) followed neither of these courses, but allowed the socialist movement to take its own course.[7]

A few figures will illustrate the rapid strengthening of the SPD and the trade unions during the prewar period. The only figures available for the SPD prior to 1906 are the election results. In 1871 less than three per cent of all votes cast went to the SPD. In 1879 the number had risen to almost nine per cent. During the anti-socialist law period there was a temporary setback and the figure dropped to six per cent in the 1881 election. In 1890 the SPD received almost twenty per cent of all votes cast and in the last election before the war the figure reached 34.8 per cent.[8] In actual votes the number grew from roughly 1,000,-000 to 4,250,329 and the number of representatives in the Reichstag increased to 110. In the elections for the Reichstag on January 12, 1912, every third man over 25 years of age voted for the SPD.[9]

Membership figures for the SPD run as follows: in 1906, 384,327 members; in 1910, 720,038; and in 1913, 982,850. Even more impressive are the trade union figures. Here the information goes back to 1891, the year after the anti-socialist law was discarded. Membership in the trade unions increased from 277,659 in 1891 to 2,548,763 in 1913, and the financial assets of the unions in the same period increased from 425,845 marks to 88,069,295 marks.[10]

[7] Arthur Rosenberg, *Die Entstehung der deutschen Republik* (2d ed.; Berlin: E. Rowohlt Verlag, 1930), p. 52.

[8] Ossip Kurt Flechtheim, *Die KPD in der Weimarer Republik* (Offenbach a.M.: Bollwerk-Verlag, 1948), p. 2.

[9] Gustav Noske, *Erlebtes aus Aufstieg und Niedergang einer Demokratie* (Offenbach a.M.: Bollwerk-Verlag, 1947), p. 37.

[10] Internationaler Arbeiterverlag, *Illustrierte Geschichte der Deutschen*

These figures tell only one part of the story. The SPD had a highly disciplined organization — the first modern mass organization in history — based on a large, thoroughly-trained party bureaucracy, which gave the workers confidence in the strength of their organization. They believed that their party was a bulwark of peace and would make wars completely impossible.

Indeed the SPD had developed into a nationwide party with an organization managed by about 4,100 professional party officials and approximately 11,000 salaried employees. The election results of 1912 had made the SPD a parliamentary power of the first order, and its 94 newspapers assured the party of continuous influence in large segments of the population. By 1914 the SPD had an investment of 20,000,000 Marks and thereby had given evidence of the confidence the party had in the stability of the state and economy.[11]

It has also been asserted that in spite of the great expansion of the party organization and its increased membership, the SPD had lost none of its efficiency.[12] Organizational efficiency is not, however, the only yardstick for measuring the effectiveness of a political party. The tremendous growth of the SPD and the trade unions plus their widespread vested interests were of utmost consequence for many of the changes within the party and for the emergence of a revolutionary opposition faction fighting from within against the increasingly pronounced middle class attitude of the party aristocracy.

2. *The Emergence of Different Factions Within the SPD*

The anti-socialist legislation of 1878 caused considerable difficulties for the SPD. Party leaders were arrested and numerous limitations and restrictions were placed upon party newspapers and other activities. However, the strong-arm methods

Revolution (Berlin: Internationaler Arbeiterverlag, 1929), p. 58 [hereafter cited as *Illustrierte Geschichte*].
[11] William Maehl, "The Triumph of Nationalism in the German Socialist Party on the Eve of the First World War," *The Journal of Modern History*, XXIV (1952), pp. 25, 27. See also: Flechtheim, *op. cit.*, p. 5.
[12] Halperin, *op. cit.*, p. 17

used by the German government to suppress the socialists demonstrated to the workers better than any socialist propaganda could to what extent Bismarck's state served the ruling classes and perpetuated the status quo. Thus, one of the major factors which transformed the SPD into a genuine revolutionary Marxist party was this period of suppression of the socialists.

After the lapse of the anti-socialist law in 1890, the SPD felt a necessity of restating its objectives as well as of clarifying the methods to be used in the Party's coming struggle. At the Party Congress held in Erfurt in 1891, the SPD developed a program which incorporated many more basic Marxist dogmas than had the Gotha Program of 1875, which at one time had been heavily attacked by Marx himself. A materialistic interpretation of history supplied the basis for many parts of the program, which asserted that the class-character of the state determined the political actions of the proletariat. The workers, it was emphasized, must seize political control of the state in order to transform the capitalist economy into a socialist one. The seizure of political power as a prerequisite for the expropriation of the means of production and redistribution of wealth was adopted as a tenet by the Congress.[13]

The formulation of the revolutionary Erfurt Program did not go unchallenged. For example, the Bavarian party leader Georg von Vollmar strongly opposed the revolutionary policies approved by the Congress. He and his followers advocated without much success a program directed at gradual reforms of the existing social, political, and economic institutions. From the fact that the SPD had again become a legal political party within the existing state they concluded that it should fight for reforms in alliance with some of the political parties of the middle classes. Von Vollmar's approach was rejected by the Erfurt Congress; thus defeating this early attempt to revert to some of the reformistic

[13] For a detailed discussion and analysis of the Erfurt Program see Berlau, *op. cit.*, pp. 39-45.

Lassallean concepts — "revisionism" as this school of thought was later called.[14]

Just before the turn of the century another attack was made by the reformists against the adherents of the revolutionary tactical principles inherent in the Marxist theories officially incorporated in the party's program. This time the attack against Marxist dogmas was better organized and more systematized. At least three factors contributed to the success which revisionism was able to achieve as a result. First, there was the substantial attempt by Eduard Bernstein and a number of other socialist leaders to bring Marx's teaching up to date and into harmony with the experiences gained by the SPD. After Friedrich Engel's death in 1895, Bernstein started in the theoretical journal *Neue Zeit* a literary offensive with the purpose of "revising" and "modernizing" Marxism.[15] Bernstein's criticism centered on certain predictions which Marx derived from his analysis of the "bourgeois, capitalist society." He contended that Marx was only partly correct in his prediction concerning the pauperization of the masses and the inevitable cycle of economic crises. The social legislation supported and often initiated by the growing parliamentary faction of the SPD coupled with the tactical successes of the trade unions in the period of general prosperity had materially improved the over-all social and economic situation of the workers.

This improvement of the workers' living standard together with the general optimism caused by the industrial and economic boom form the second reason for Bernstein's eventual success in superimposing the views of the revisionists upon the revolutionary tradition of the party. The revisionists held that society can gra-

[14] *Illustrierte Geschichte,* pp. 61-62.
[15] Bertram D. Wolfe, *Three Who Made a Revolution* (Boston: Beacon Press, 1948), p. 142. See also: Peter Gay, *The Dilemma of Democratic Socialism; Eduard Bernstein's Challenge to Marx* (New York: Columbia University Press, 1952); Vladimir G. Simkhovitch, *Marxism Versus Socialism* (New York: Ginn & Co., 1912); Evan F. M. Durbin, *The Politics of Democratic Socialism* (London: G. Routledge, 1940); and Carl E. Schorske, *German Social Democracy, 1905-1917; The Development of the Great Schism* (Cambridge: Harvard University Press, 1955).

dually grow into socialism and that the improvement of conditions for the workers does not have to wait until the advent of a violent revolution. This view found increased acceptance among a large number of German socialists who came to believe in the SPD as a "democratic-socialist reform party."[16]

A third factor contributing to the success of the revisionist view was the changed social composition of the SPD. After the revocation of the anti-socialist law, the party broadened its base and numerous non-proletarians, bourgeois elements, especially intellectuals, were able to enter the party.[17]

Thus, the concept of evolutionary methods as a means of realizing socialism was the result of the revisionist position. The aim of the party henceforth was to be not armed uprising but the obtaining of a majority in order to take control of parliament.[18]

The revisionists, or reformists, formed the right wing of the SPD. Bernstein and other leading revisionists such as Richard Calwer, Eduard David, and Georg von Vollmar urged the SPD

---

[16] See Berlau, *op. cit.,* pp. 55-66; and *Illustrierte Geschichte,* pp. 62-63; Hugh Seton-Watson, *From Lenin to Malenkov* (New York: Praeger, 1953), p. 17; Wolfe, *op. cit.,* p. 143.

According to Paul Froelich, in order to prove the correctness of their changed interpretation of Marx, the revisionists invoked Engels' introduction to Marx's *The Civil War in France.* Froelich accuses the reformists of falsifying the statements of Engels by omitting certain important phases of the original text. Thus, Engels is quoted as saying that German experience with elections and the great technological advances made in weapons force a change in revolutionary tactics. The struggle for a majority in the legislature replaces the armed uprising. (Paul Froelich, *Rosa Luxemburg, Gedanke und Tat* [Hamburg: Verlag Friedrich Oetinger, 1949], pp. 64-66.)

[17] It has been asserted that skilled workers, of whom the SPD had a considerable number, as a rule influence the nature of a labor party in the direction of a peaceful and democratic movement. By contrast, when the social structure is based on a primitive and poor peasantry and on a small and unskilled labor group, a revolutionary and fanatical labor movement is likely to develop. (Seton-Watson, *op. cit.,* p. 11.)

Professor William Maehl believes that four factors were responsible for the victory of reformism within the SPD. These were: (1) the rapid growth of the party, (2) the rapid growth of the trade unions, (3) the lack of class-consciousness among the workers — the result of a peculiar German historical development, and (4) the successful growth of German capitalism prior to World War I. (Maehl, *op. cit.,* pp. 22-23.)

[18] Walter Tormin, *Zwischen Raetediktatur und sozialer D e m o k r a t i e* (Duesseldorf: Droste-Verlag, 1954), pp. 21-22.

to give up its revolutionary theories and to concentrate instead on objectives within the party's capabilities. These objectives ranged from the abolition of the three-class electoral system in Prussia to a popular control over the formulation and conduct of Germany's foreign policy.[19]

The party center or the so-called orthodox Marxist center led by Karl Kautsky opposed the revisionists' theories. These centrists were well entrenched in the party's Executive Committee and consequently controlled the actual policies of the SPD. As a result, no changes in the official position of the party occurred because of Bernstein's attack upon the revolutionary heritage of the socialist movement, or at least none could be detected in the public utterances of the party leaders.

The initial opposition of the orthodox Marxists to the opportunism of the right wing gradually gave way to a more conciliatory attitude, and the political views of the revisionists were judged by the party leadership on the basis of tactical considerations and not as symptoms of a basic cleavage. Kautsky, for example, regarded Bernstein's revisionism as a purely tactical problem.[20]

This approach to revisionism allowed the party center under certain circumstances to adopt some of the revisionist tactical principles, such as advocating and fighting for specific reforms, without the necessity of justifying these actions with a new set of theories.[21]

Within a few years after the emergence of the reformists in the SPD, another faction appeared. This group was the numerically weak but extremely active radical left which formed itself around those socialists who continued to advocate strict adherence to Marxist principles. The outstanding leaders of the left wing were Rosa Luxemburg, Karl Liebknecht, Clara Zetkin, and Franz

---

[19] Halperin, *op. cit.*, p. 18.

[20] Berlau, *op. cit.*, p. 63.

[21] Berlau analyzes this situation as follows:

"The implications of the SPD attitude toward revisionism indicated that the party was, under certain conditions, ready to jettison not only the practice of political radicalism, but the Marxian essence of its theory as well. All that

Mehring. The radicals of the left accused the so-called orthodox Marxists of the party center of following the opportunist program in practice in spite of their revolutionary terminology and their alleged opposition to the reformists. Thus, the radicals were strictly opposed to the revisionists around Bernstein and to the party centrists led by Kautsky.[22]

The left wing of the SPD was by no means a homogeneous group; important differences in Marxist interpretation were the rule rather than the exception. Nevertheless all of its members held certain views in common. All had the absolute conviction that only a proletarian revolution would end the existing social order and bring about socialism. All were more or less preoccupied with studying the means by which a socialist proletarian party could accelerate the revolution. Finally, all were aware of the contradictions existing between the official socialist theories proclaimed by the SPD and the prevailing tactical moves of the party.[23]

3. *The Influence of the Trade Unions*

Within the trade unions there were tendencies similar to those motivating the revisionist wing of the SPD. The continuous growth of the unions gave their leaders confidence that it was possible to fight for the economic objectives of the worker within the existing framework of the state. Improvement of material conditions for the workers was the main interest of the union leaders, who believed that the achievement of this aim was not intrinsically con-

---

was needed was an impelling external stimulus, a sound need for a change in tactics." (Berlau, *op. cit.*, p. 65.)

[22] Flechtheim, *op. cit.*, p. 6; *Illustrierte Geschichte*, pp. 81-82.

[23] Tormin, *op. cit.*, p. 23.

Otto Grotewohl furnishes a Communist post-World War II interpretation of the reasons behind the emergence of three factions within the SPD in the early part of this century. According to the Communists, the ap-

pearance of the revisionists triggered the threeway split within the party. The strict followers of the Marxist revolutionary doctrines were forced to fight against the heretics and against the conciliatory attitude of the majority of the SPD and its leadership. In the process of this internal party struggle, the three wings developed. (Otto Grotewohl, *Dreissig Jahre Spaeter* [Berlin: Dietz Verlag, 1948], pp. 37-42.)

nected with the revolutionary struggle. Violent revolutionary action might even endanger the economic and social gains made so far. The union leaders thus developed strong opposition to the party's attempt to keep the unions as appendices to the political organization. Gradually they achieved complete independence from the political leadership of the SPD. Union animosity was strongest toward the radical left group within the party, because of their so-called revolutionary romanticism which, it was feared, might disturb the gradual but steady improvement of the workers' lot.[24]

In other words, the immediate interests of the workers were of greater concern to the union leaders than was the emergence of the socialist society of the future. This conservatism was not restricted to political questions; other union decisions took a progressively moderate turn. The unions eventually tried to avoid large-scale strikes in order not to deplete their funds. Simultaneously, internal bureaucracy developed into an autocratic machinery denying the individual members certain democratic rights.[25] Indeed, the union leaders came to regard the SPD as an agency of political interest for the trade unions and not as a movement dedicated to the socialist revolution.[26]

Rosa Luxemburg analyzed the interrelation of the unions' views and those of the revisionists. The reasoning behind the unions' claim for a position of equality, according to her, had a familiar ring; it was based on the illusion that in peaceful periods of the bourgeois society the entire struggle of the workers was re-

[24] Halperin, op. cit., pp. 18-19.

[25] Illustrierte Geschichte, p. 61. The attempt of the unions to reverse the situation and to control the actions of the SPD was ridiculed by Rosa Luxemburg in a speech at the Party Congress in Mannheim in 1906. She compared the union-party relationship with a curious marriage contract of a peasant couple. This contract stated that the will of the husband was to be carried out in all cases in which the wife agreed with him; however, when her will differed from his, then action would have to be taken in accordance with her views. (Rosa Luxemburg, "Reden auf dem Mannheimer Parteitag der SPD, 1906," quoted in Rosa Luxemburg, Ausgewaehlte Reden und Schriften [Berlin: Dietz Verlag, 1951], [hereafter cited as: Ausgewaehlte Reden], II, p. 260.)

[26] John L. Snell, "Socialist Unions and Socialist Patriotism in Germany, 1914-1918," The American Historical Review, LIX (1953-54), p. 67.

duced to the SPD's parliamentary fight for political reforms and the unions' endeavors to obtain economic advantages for their workers.

The theory of "equality" of the unions with the Social Democracy is then not a simple misunderstanding or confusion of terms, but is the expression of the known position of the opportunistic wing of the Social Democracy which indeed wishes to transform the Social Democracy from a revolutionary proletarian party into a middle-class reform party.[27]

The opposition of the radical left to this development proved to be futile. The weight of the unions was felt increasingly not only in the period preceding August, 1914, but also during the war. As a matter of fact, the attitude of the trade unions backed by numerical and financial power proved to be one of the decisive influences in the victory of revisionism over radicalism within the SPD.[28]

4. *Principal Political Concepts of the Left Wing*

The process of challenging revisionist ideas played an important part in the formulation of the political thought of the radical left. However, the claim made by Communist interpreters of the history of the German socialist movement that left wing theories were primarily the result of the emergence and activities of the revisionists cannot be supported by factual evidence. The purpose behind this Communist effort to present the development of theoretical concepts as specific responses to revisionist attempts to falsify and dilute Marxist doctrines was to assert that the Communists alone were true followers of "scientific" Marxism as originated by Marx and Engels.

At least three other major factors contributed to the growth of the left wing faction and its body of revolutionary theories. First, there was the preoccupation of socialists with a number of

---

[27] Rosa Luxemburg, *Massenstreik, Partei und Gewerkschaft,* quoted in Luxemburg, *Ausgewaehlte Reden,* I, pp. 237-38. [28] Halperin, *op. cit.,* p. 19.

theoretical and tactical problems. They were concerned with the type of organization best suited for a socialist party devoted to the idea of changing the existing society. They wondered what part the party was to play in a bourgeois state and what position it should take toward liberal elements. They were further occupied with an analysis of the practical means — available or potential — to be used in the revolutionary struggle aimed at establishing a socialist society. The revolutionary theories resulting from this preoccupation were not caused primarily by polemics against revisionism but by the interpretation given by revolutionary socialists to the teachings of Marx and Engels. It appears, for example, that Marx's doctrine of economic determinism had a much greater influence on these theories than the fight against such concepts of Bernstein's as the gradual or evolutionary change of society.

Secondly, the Russian Revolution of 1905 — especially the mass action of the Russian workers and peasants — had a marked impact on the political thinking of socialists everywhere. The entire problem of the political mass strike or general strike as a modern method in the revolutionary struggle was re-examined. The creation of local revolutionary workers' councils as instruments for conducting revolutionary action was analyzed.

Finally, specific experiences of socialist parties in various countries contributed to the development of radical theories, especially those dealing with tactical methods in the fight for the intermediate and ultimate aims of socialism. For example, in Germany the fight for election reforms and the resistance offered by the German government tended to give emphasis to the tactical doctrines developed by the left wing of the SPD. The radicals were able to conclude that there was no real substitute for the revolutionary struggle as conceived by Marx and Engels as soon as proposed changes affected the prevailing power relations. Continued oppression of the Social Democrats by the German government served to prove the points made by the leftists.[29]

[29] As late as April, 1908, the German Government passed a law prohibiting persons of twenty years or younger to attend political or trade union meet-

The German example also indicated that a study of revolutionary theories must take into account the fact that varying conditions in different countries generate specific problems for the socialist movement. In Russia, the severe oppression and social stratification, particularly the large segment of unskilled laborers and peasants, favored the development of conspiratorial ideas rather than the legal recognition granted the SPD after the repeal of the anti-socialist legislation.

During the first decade of the twentieth century, the left wing of the SPD developed a number of important revolutionary concepts. These concepts were significant for two major reasons. First, they determined to a considerable extent the political actions of the left faction and subsequently those of the Spartacists. Secondly, they had an important impact upon the official policies of the SPD, which at times, at least in resolutions at party congresses and at international conferences, was forced to incorporate revolutionary-sounding principles.

Many of the revolutionary theories of the German left were clarified, formulated, and defended by Rosa Luxemburg, one of the outstanding leftists within the German Social Democracy. Her political thought was characteristic of many of the left-wingers who, as professed revolutionaries, subordinated all tactical and strategic considerations to the final aim of the socialist movement, the realization of socialism. This ultimate aim furnished the yardstick for judging the usefulness of theories and actions. Even the seizure of political power and the socialization of the means of production were regarded only as a means serving the highest possible end, the creation of the classless, socialist society.[30]

Rosa Luxemburg's attitude toward reforms of any kind was clearly influenced by this basic conviction. She strongly opposed Bernstein's view that reform work within a bourgeois democracy

ings. The Social Democratic Youth organization was dissolved, and political work among the youth became illegal from this time until the Revolution of November 1918. (Wolfe, *op. cit.*, p. 600.)

[30] Froelich, *Rosa Luxemburg,* pp. 13-14.

was a substitute for the proletarian revolution, that in fact it was a sort of "slow" revolution. The fallacy of this revisionist approach, according to her, was that the ultimate aim of the socialist movement — the socialist society — was lost in preoccupation with reforming the existing capitalist society. Rosa Luxemburg was not opposed to reforms as a matter of principle; she realized that the fight for reforms could be used as a means of organizing and training the workers. Her position was not reforms *or* revolution but reforms *and* revolution. Important for her was that the daily fight remain organically connected with the ultimate aim.[31]

Karl Liebknecht was equally opposed to substituting for the revolutionary aim the reform of existing conditions. He attacked the so-called new method on three grounds. First, he pointed out that this new method overestimated the benefits which the bourgeois democracy could bestow on the workers; secondly, it underestimated the irreconcilable cleavage between proletariat and bourgeoisie; and finally, it limited the class struggle by the absolute non-violence principle which constituted a surrender of the revolutionary method to the process of gradual reforms. According to Liebknecht, it was foolhardy to believe that the capitalists would ever agree voluntarily to restrictions affecting their vital positions. The so-called peaceful method was dangerous utopianism. He was convinced that as long as the government functioned as "the executive committee of the ruling class" the state would remain an instrument serving the perpetuation of existing power relations.[32]

Completely in agreement with the leftists' position with regard to reforms were their views concerning parliamentarianism

[31] Rosa Luxemburg, *Sozialreform oder Revolution*, quoted in Luxemburg, *Ausgewaehlte Reden*, II, pp. 126-28, 137; Froelich, *Rosa Luxemburg*, pp. 70-74. Luxemburg's strong opposition to Bernstein's conscious intention of transforming the SPD into a liberal reform party led to her futile demands for his expulsion from the party. (Froelich, *Rosa Luxemburg*, p. 96.)

[32] Karl Liebknecht, *Reden und Aufsaetze* (Hamburg: Verlag d. Kommunistischen Internationale, 1921), [hereafter cited as: Liebknecht, *Reden*], pp. 80-87.

as a means for the class struggle. Again it was not absolute opposition which motivated Rosa Luxemburg; she regarded parliamentarianism as one more way for the SPD to propagandize
the workers. Elections for parliamentary representatives were especially suited for this purpose, and parliament itself could be
used as a convenient platform for reaching a great number of
people. But there were some restrictions on how far participation
could go without compromising the revolutionary creed. As a
matter of principle, the party was to remain in opposition under
all circumstances. Participation of socialists in a bourgeois government, as practiced by Alexandre Millerand in France, was
treason to the working class. Representatives of the workers were
permitted to enter a bourgeois government only if they intended
to take over political power.[33] Millerand's entry into the French
government of Waldeck-Rousseau highlighted the problem of
socialist participation in a bourgeois government. For the revisionists this was no problem at all. It was perfectly in agreement with their theory of gradual introduction of socialism
through reforms. Revolutionary socialists who believed that socialism could come only after the breakdown of the capitalist
order could hardly conceive of entering a bourgeois government
for any purpose other than to destroy it from within. The acceptance by a socialist of a position in the executive branch of the
government was considered impossible, because it was held that
oppositional policies could not be pursued within the executive.
This limitation did not apply to the legislature. Rosa Luxemburg's
position toward parliamentarianism was in complete agreement
with her revolutionary concepts: the SPD in a bourgeois society
must remain the opposition party under all circumstances; it may
take over the government only when the bourgeois state breaks
down.[34]

[33] Froelich, *Rosa Luxemburg,* pp.
83-87.
[34] Rosa Luxemburg, "Eine taktische
Frage," quoted in Luxemburg, *Ausgewaehlte Reden,* II, pp. 60-64.

Thus, the invasion of parliament was not a device to replace the necessity of forceful revolution. Rosa Luxemburg followed completely the doctrines of Marx and Engels concerning the revolutionary method of seizing political power by the working class. She claimed that only people like Bernstein wished to accomplish the greatest change in world history, the change from capitalism to socialism, by means of the bourgeois parliament. Rosa Luxemburg's evaluation of parliament was based on her interpretation of the Marxist doctrines pertaining to the nature of society and the state. Any bourgeois state, regardless of its form, was an instrument of the ruling class and therefore directly opposed to the interests of the working class.

Karl Liebknecht insisted on subordination of the parliamentary struggle to the fight of the party and the workers outside the legislature. He held that the party's power came not from the representatives in parliament but from the masses directly.[35] The real power relations operated outside parliament. The legislature could serve as an excellent platform for addressing the masses, but it was dangerous to create among the workers the illusion that the class struggle could be carried on within parliament and thus to replace the need for mass action in streets and factories.[36]

Rosa Luxemburg also stressed these same points. The real power of the SPD was not the effect the representatives had in the Reichstag but the power the people could muster in the streets. She sympathized with the Social Democratic representatives who had the difficult task not only of acting as instruments of an articulate opposition to the bourgeois government but also as representatives of a revolutionary class which intended to upset the existing political, economic, and social arrangements.[37]

---

[35] Karl Liebknecht, "Gegen den Reformismus," quoted in Karl Liebknecht, *Ausgewaehlte Reden, Briefe und Aufsaetze* (Berlin: Dietz Verlag, 1952), [hereafter cited as: Liebknecht, *Ausgewaehlte Reden*], p. 169.

[36] Liebknecht, *Reden*, pp. 22-26.
[37] Rosa Luxemburg, "Sozialdemokratie und Parliamentarismus," quoted in Luxemburg, *Ausgewaehlte Reden*, II, pp. 198-99.

The great power embodied in the masses was demonstrated in the fight for a new Prussian election law. For the first time the SPD mobilized the German workers for a political offensive. The masses responded to the call and held street demonstrations. But the party became afraid of its own enterprising spirit and discontinued the mass action simply by failing to provide further directives. Mass strikes, the logical sequence to the street demonstrations, could have pressed further the demands for election reforms. But they were vigorously opposed by the trade unions which did not sanction using the strike as a political weapon.[38]

An analysis of the Russian Revolution of 1905 provided the leftist, and particularly Rosa Luxemburg, with a basis for re-evaluating the mass strike as a method of furthering the class struggle and the socialist revolution. Prior to 1905, the mass strike was regarded by the international Social Democracy and the SPD as a purely anarchistic and utopian concept.[39] According to Rosa Luxemburg, the Russian Revolution had reversed this view. In fact, the mass strike as used in Russia had opened an entirely new era for the labor movement, because it had placed a new and more powerful weapon in the hands of the workers.[40] Under the impact of the Russian Revolution, discussions on the mass strike as a possible means in the revolutionary struggle became widespread in Social Democratic organizations. This interest proved to Rosa Luxemburg that the methods employed by the SPD up to then had not achieved sufficient results nor satisfied the revolutionary spirit of the party members. New methods were needed to advance the cause.[41]

[38] The inequality of the election law provisions is best illustrated by the election results of 1908 when the SPD received 6 seats with over 600,000 votes while the Conservatives obtained 212 seats with over 400,000 votes. (Rosa Luxemburg, "Was weiter?" quoted in Luxemburg, *Ausgewaehlte Reden*, II, pp. 324-28; Froelich, *Rosa Luxemburg*, pp. 205-06.

[39] Rosa Luxemburg, "Reden auf dem Londoner Parteitag der SDAPR," quoted in Luxemburg, *Ausgewaehlte Reden*, II, p. 275.

[40] Luxemburg, *Massenstreik*, pp. 157-58. Rosa Luxemburg even thought at one time that the mass strike might have replaced the need for fighting at the barricades, the means used by the bourgeoisie in its revolts against feudalism. (*Ibid.*, pp. 227-30.)

[41] Luxemburg, "Der politische Mas-

Many SPD leaders, revisionists, and trade unionists did not share this interpretation of the Russian experience. Labor leaders claimed that a mass strike entailed too many risks for the trade unions. Rosa Luxemburg responded that all actions of a fighting organization involve risks. She reminded the reluctant union leaders that the trade unions gained in strength during the challenging period of the anti-socialist law.[42] Karl Legien's opinion was typical of the union leaders' position. For him mass strikes and general strikes were one and the same. He called them general nonsense and regarded them as undertakings which could endanger the very existence of the unions. Rosa Luxemburg, vigorously opposing this opinion, pointed out that the Russian experience showed that the Russian unions were actually an outgrowth of the revolution.[43]

Liebknecht also endorsed the mass strike as an important weapon for the workers. He asserted that election victories were not enough and that mass actions were also needed. If strikes proved themselves valuable in the economic struggle then there should be no doubt that they could also serve political purposes. He saw in the mass strike, which he believed to be the outgrowth of the realization by the working class of its economic power, the specific proletarian means of combat suitable for all phases of the class struggle.[44]

Rosa Luxemburg gained at least a formal victory when her resolutions concerning mass strikes were adopted at the party congresses in Jena (1905) and in Mannheim (1906) against the opposition of the trade unions. The political strike was thus sanctioned as a weapon of the SPD.[45] Legien claimed that the acceptance of the mass strike resolution was a careless move because it revealed tactical plans to the enemies of the working class.

senstreik," quoted in Luxemburg, *Aus-gewaehlte Reden*, II, pp. 442-43.

[42] Luxemburg, *Was Weiter?* pp. 333-34; and *Massenstreik*, p. 220.

[43] Luxemburg, *Reden auf dem Mann-heimer Parteitag*, pp. 236-57.

[44] Karl Liebknecht, "Ueber den po-

litischen Massenstreik," quoted in Lieb-knecht, *Ausgewaehlte Reden*, pp. 89-90; and Karl Liebknecht, "Fuer den po-litischen Massenstreik," quoted in Lieb-knecht, *Ausgewaehlte Reden*, p. 99.

[45] Froelich, *Rosa Luxemburg*, pp. 124-25, 164, 166-69. In these resolu-

Rosa Luxemburg countered that a modern proletarian mass movement does not decide secretly on its tactics.[46]

From the Russian events of 1905 Rosa Luxemburg inferred the following characteristics of the mass strike. First, a mass strike is not artificially created but comes as the result of a particular situation during a specific phase of the class struggle. A mass strike cannot be called by a decision of the party's executive committee, just as revolution cannot take place upon command. Second, a mass strike is not a substitute should parliamentary action fail. Mass strikes are revolutionary weapons and cannot be made harmonious with policies which place primary emphasis upon parliamentary action.[47] Third, if a mass strike is to be successful, the broad masses must be drawn into the fight in order to make it a real mass movement. It cannot be carried out by organized workers alone. The trade unions must assist the party. The mass strike is also not just a question of discipline and estimated costs but a genuine revolutionary class action. It is unwise to overestimate the role of the party and to underestimate the revolutionary actions of the unorganized masses.[48] The Russian Revolution had shown that the mass strike was influenced by the Social Democratic organizations, but that neither the party nor the masses followed a pre-arranged plan. It was not an organized action but rather a spontaneous uprising of the masses.[49]

Nonetheless, Rosa Luxemburg emphasized the importance of political leadership not only for the period of actual revolutionary mass strikes but also for the valuable training which would pay off in serious revolutionary situations. She synthesized her ap-

---

tions, the mass strike was conceived only as a defense against a possible further limitation of voting rights. Therefore, the mass strike still remained subordinate to the parliamentary work of the party. (Luxemburg, *Massenstreik,* p. 167.)

[46] Luxemburg, *Reden auf dem Mannheimer Parteitag,* p. 258.

[47] Luxemburg, *Massenstreik,* pp. 163-66; and *Der politische Massen-* *streik,* pp. 444-45.

[48] *Luxemburg, Massenstreik,* pp. 220-22; and *Was weiter?* pp. 331-32.

[49] Luxemburg, *Massenstreik,* pp. 179-88. By referring to the Russian events, Rosa Luxemburg even attempted to prove that it was not dialectical to believe that strong organizations must be available before the revolution. In Russia the masses went into the revolution with almost no unions

preciation of the "element of mass spontaneity" with that of the role of the party.[50]

Rosa Luxemburg's confidence in the creative power of the masses, expressed for example in spontaneous mass actions, has provoked many attacks especially from recent Communist interpreters. She was accused of "worshipping spontaneity and negating the role of the party."[51]

Paul Froelich, her biographer, claimed that her ideas were purposely misinterpreted, that she never excluded the conscious political leadership of the party; on the contrary, she desired it. Possibly her mistake was that she did not grasp the extent of the retarding influence which an organization, led by persons opposed to revolutionary methods in the class struggle, could exert. Her overconfidence in the masses is explained by Froelich as a typical mistake of a genuine revolutionary.[52]

Rosa Luxemburg's confidence in mass spontaneity and her opposition to Lenin's ultra-centralism and conspiratorial concepts as guiding principles for the organization of the party led to sharp controversies between the two revolutionary leaders.[53] Her endorsement of the use of force in the revolutionary struggle brought her into sharp opposition with the official policy of the SPD and in particular with the revisionists who, like Eduard David, as-

---

and with only small socialist organizations. (Rosa Luxemburg, *Reden auf dem Jenaer Parteitag der SPD, 1905*, quoted in Luxemburg, *Ausgewaehlte, Reden*, II, p. 246.)

[50] Luxemburg, *Massenstreik*, pp. 205-8, 223-25.

[51] Wolfe, *op. cit.*, p. 257; Rosa Luxemburg, "Nach dem ersten Akt," quoted in Luxemburg, *Ausgewaehlte Reden*, II, pp. 217-18; Fred Oelssner, *Rosa Luxemburg, eine kritische biographische Skizze* (Berlin: Dietz Verlag, 1951), pp. 50-52. Grotewohl, *op. cit.*, p. 41.

[52] Froelich, *Rosa Luxemburg*, pp. 173-76.

[53] *Ibid.*, pp. 107-09. Rosa Luxemburg had fought Lenin's party theory since the split of the Russian party in 1903, believing that this split was detrimental to the furtherance of the Russian Revolution. (Franz Borkenau, *Der europaeische Kommunismus* [B e r n : Francke-Verlag, 1952], p. 25; Luxemburg, *Reden auf dem Londoner Parteitag*, p. 284.) For a brief discussion of the differences between Rosa Luxemburg and Lenin on party organization, see Ruth Fischer, *Stalin and German Communism* (Cambridge: H a r v a r d University Press, 1948), pp. 17-20. Lenin's position is explained fully in his *What Is To Be Done?* (Moscow:

serted that the SPD must use only legal, parliamentary means in its political fight.[54]

5. *Nationalism Versus Internationalism*

Some of the revisionists and many of the trade union leaders had jumped on the German imperialist bandwagon. Their actions were completely in accord with their acceptance of the bourgeois state as the proper framework for their political, social, and economic reform policies. In addition to these nationalistic socialists, many of the other SPD leaders also supported the expansionist foreign policies of the German government. The SPD believed, for example, that there was nothing objectionable to peaceful penetration of colonial areas. Only the leftists retained an internationalist position and continued to oppose the government's nationalism and the nationalistic tendencies within the party. Rosa Luxemburg declared that the Social Democracy must never participate in the foreign affairs of the Great Powers. The working class and its representatives in all countries had their own foreign policies based on revolutionary, international concepts which certainly had nothing in common with the imperialistic plans of their various governments.[55]

The intensification of imperialist designs displayed by the German government and by the governments of several other countries alarmed the international Social Democracy or at least parts of it, and made the socialists aware of the danger of an outbreak of a large-scale European or world war. The Socialist and

Foreign Languages Pub. House, 1947) and *One Step Forward, Two Steps Back* (London: Lawrence & Wishart, Ltd., 1941.) For the views of Rosa Luxemburg, see her *Reden auf dem Londoner Parteitag.* Lenin's concepts on party tactics are contained in his *Two Tactics of Social-Democracy in the Democratic Revolution* (New York: International Publishers, 1935).

[54] Froelich, *Rosa Luxemburg,* pp. 91-93. Luxemburg, *Reden auf dem Mannheimer Parteitag,* p. 261. One of the clearest formulations of the revisionist position toward the bourgeois state and the proletarian revolution is a resolution prepared by Dr. Eduard David and presented for approval to a party meeting in Mainz on September 10, 1906 (Luxemburg, *Massenstreik,* pp. 238-39).

[55] Froelich, *Rosa Luxemburg,* pp. 199-202.

Labor International dealt with the war danger at its international congresses held in Stuttgart (1907) and in Basel (1912).[56]

At the Stuttgart Conference, the position of the international Social Democracy regarding the war issue was debated and clarified considerably. The decision that socialist deputies in the parliaments of all countries were unconditionally pledged to vote against any military expenditure required for colonial expeditions had been on the records of the International since its conference at Paris in 1900.[57] The socialists felt that stronger measures and threats of actions were necessary to prevent an outbreak of a general war. The French and English delegates proposed the calling of a general strike as a countermeasure in case of war. Rosa Luxemburg opposed this motion, insisting that this type of action program would remain only a resolution at best. She maintained that individual Social Democratic parties would undoubtedly fail to act in accordance with the Conference resolutions even though they could expect support from the masses which were much afraid of a war.[58]

The resolution eventually adopted by the Stuttgart Congress called upon all Social Democratic parties to employ every means available to fight against the outbreak of war and for the preservation of world peace.[59] This resolution did not seem adequate nor realistic enough to Rosa Luxemburg. She therefore proposed an important amendment which she had worked out with Lenin and

[56] The correct name for the International was Socialist and Labor International. Only after the Communist International was founded in March, 1919, did the Socialist International become referred to as the Second International and the Communist International as the Third. (Wolfe, op. cit., p. 92.) For a brief sketch of the Second International, see Seton-Watson, op. cit., pp. 15-16, and Paul Froelich, Zehn Jahre Krieg und Buergerkrieg (2d ed.; Berlin: Vereinigung Internationaler Verlags-Anstalten), I, pp. 27-29.

[57] Wolfe, op. cit., p. 598.

[58] Froelich, Rosa Luxemburg, p. 204. For example, in debates at the international conferences many delegates stressed the right to defend themselves against an attack from without. The recognized leader of the German Social Democrats, August Bebel, stated in Stuttgart that he did not see how the SPD could get people for a mass strike if, on the day the war breaks out, six million men would be mobilized immediately. (Froelich, Zehn Jahre, pp. 44-45.)

[59] Illustrierte Geschichte, pp. 79-80.

Martov. After some initial difficulties with Bebel were ironed out, the amendment was adopted. It read as follows:

If a war threatens to break out, it is the duty of the working class and of its parliamentary representatives in the countries involved, supported by the consolidating activity of the International Bureau, to exert every effort to prevent the outbreak of war by means they consider most effective; which naturally vary according to the sharpening of the class struggle and of the general political situation.

Should war break out nonetheless, it is their duty to intervene in favor of its speedy termination and to do all in their power to utilize the economic and political crisis caused by the war to rouse the peoples and thereby to hasten the abolition of capitalist class rule.[60]

The position taken by the radical left of the SPD in regard to the danger of a war and to the means designed to avert it was a matter of record at the international congresses. Rosa Luxemburg included in the immediate tasks of the Social Democracy the propaganda activities directed at the working class in order to make it aware of its historic mission in the class struggle and to prepare it to fight if necessary against war and militarism.[61]

Because the reformists held an opposite view on the issues of nationalism and war, a new type of cleavage developed within the SPD. The nationalistic attitude of some of the SPD leaders had been apparent at the various conferences of the Second International.[62]

William Maehl traces the change of the SPD from its revolutionary and internationalist platform to its identification with the interests of the German nation. At the party congresses of the SPD at Chemnitz in 1912 and at Jena in 1913, the left wing

[60] Wolfe, *op. cit.*, p. 600. For an interesting discussion of the anti-war issue at the Stuttgart Congress, see *ibid.*, pp. 591-600. Cf. also Rosa Luxemburg, "Rede auf dem Internationalen Sozialistenkongress zu Stuttgart," quoted in Luxemburg, *Ausgewaehlte Reden*, II, pp. 308-10. For information on the International Congress at Basel in 1912 see Rosa Luxemburg, *Die Krise der Sozialdemokratie,* quoted in Luxemburg, *Ausgewaehlte Reden*, I, pp. 266-68.

[61] Rosa Luxemburg, "Militarismus, Krieg und Arbeiterklasse," quoted in Luxemburg, *Ausgewaehlte Reden*, II, p. 493.

[62] Maehl, *op. cit.*, pp. 28-29.

radicals (among them Kurt Geyer, Georg Ledebour, Wilhelm Dittmann, Hugo Haase, Karl Liebknecht, Rosa Luxemburg, Clara Zetkin, and Franz Mehring) fought vigorously against the nationalistic trend of the party. They fought a losing battle. In Chemnitz the Party Congress approved the concept of national defense measures because of the "Russian peril." At the Party Congress in Jena, only six years after the International Congress at Stuttgart, the SPD decided that it was not required under all circumstances to vote against military appropriations. This complete reversal of the Stuttgart resolution was adopted by a vote of 336 to 140. The other major issue, the general strike resolution recommended by Rosa Luxemburg, was defated, 333 to 142. Maehl correctly asserts that the SPD had made its great policy change — the adoption of nationalism — long before the fatal August of 1914.[63]

6. General Characteristics of the SPD on the Eve of World War I

In the course of time, reformist concepts and trade union objectives had come to determine the official policies of the SPD. Under this influence, the party had undergone a gradual meta-

[63] Ibid., pp. 32-41. An excellent example of the "patriotic attitude" of the SPD during the pre-war years was a speech made in 1907 by the Social Democratic Reichstag representative Gustav Noske in a debate about the military budget. Noske declared that the SPD recognized the peace policy the German Government was trying to pursue. The SPD also wished to make known that it was not the intent of the party to undermine the discipline of the Germany army. On the contrary, the Social Democrats wished to see Germany militarily strong, and Noske gave the assurance that, in case of war, the Social Democratic workers would take up arms and their patriotism would not be surpassed by that of any other class. A satirical German periodical, the Lustigen Blaetter, published on October 8, 1907, a poem dedicated to the "new patriot," Noske.

Hervé will Soldatenstreik,
Liebknecht spricht so aehnlich,
Ledebour zeigt sich dem Heer
Auch nicht sehr versoehnlich;
Doch der Hoffnung letzten Rest
Soll man nicht verlieren.
Eins steht heute bombenfest:
Noske wird parieren.

Hervé wants a mutiny
Within the army's frame;
Liebknecht talks along this line
And Ledebour's the same.
But do not lose all rays of hope,
One thing stands firm today:
If army orders are sent out,
Then Noske will obey.

morphosis from a revolutionary, proletarian party strictly opposed to the bourgeois class state to a kind of liberal, working-class party content with working for reform and political democracy within the framework of the existing state. It had become a party which had great respect for law and state authority, and even an admiration for force.[64]

Its leaders shunned serious political struggles fearing to destroy the advantages so laboriously acquired. Revolutionary phrases were still heard at party congresses as part of the traditional ritual, but the idea of a violent struggle would have horrified most of the party leaders. The SPD had become a power in its own right. It could reward disciplined followers with positions and promotions, and it could punish violators of party

Geht es mal in ferner Frist Ans Kanonenfuttern, Denkt so mancher Reservist: "Nee,—ick bleib bei Muttern!" Doch das soll uns Kampf und Schlacht Nimmermehr vergaellen, Denn es ist heut' ausgemacht: Noske wird sich stellen.	If cannon-fodder is required At distant time or tide, Quite a few Reservists think: "With mother I shall bide." On this account our battle strength Will not lack in beauty, Because today we're sure that Noske Will report for duty.
Kommandiert der Herr Major: "Feuer vorn und hinten!" Ruft ein arbeitsscheues Korps: "Schmeiss mer fort die Flinten!" Aber dennoch, Mut fuer Mut! Lasst's euch nicht verdriessen, Denn wir wissen absolut: Noske, der wird schiessen!	And if a Major then commands: "Fire front and rear!" But "Throw away the rifles," Shouts a unit filled with fear; Then do not be downhearted, Then do not show dismay, Because we're absolutely sure That Noske'll fire away.
Noske schnallt den Saebel um, Noske geht aufs Ganze, Noske feuert bum bum bum, Noske stuermt die Schanze, Noske schreit: Hurra! Hurra! Noske haelt die Wachen, Noske schiesst Victoria, Noske wirds schon machen.	Noske straps his sabre on, Noske's fire and vim; Noske shoots, bang, bang, bang, bang; He storms the bulwark grim. Noske shouts: Hurrah! Hurrah! He guards us in the night; Noske'll bring the Victory, He'll fix things up all right.
(*Illustrierte Geschichte,* p. 80.)	(translation by Robert Simmons, Modern Language Department, Marquette University)

[64] Maehl, *op. cit.*, p. 15; Carlo Sforza, *Europe and Europeans* (London: Har- rap & Co., 1936), pp. 82-85.

discipline. Leftists such as Mehring and Liebknecht were distrusted, and revolutionaries of the caliber of Rosa Luxemburg were regarded as sources of great annoyance and as alien intellectual trouble-makers.[65]

No public repudiation of the old revolutionary doctrines of the Marxian tradition was made by the party leadership, and the controversies and factional strife were hidden behind a façade of party unity. To the non-socialist world the SPD appeared to be a strong and unified party, while in truth it was composed of three factions of unequal size and influence on party policies. The party center continued to enjoy the unwavering loyalty of the overwhelming number of German Socialists and party sympathizers. It was known neither to them nor to outsiders that the SPD had assumed the characteristics of a reform party and was using revolutionary terminology only to appeal to the workers. The party was not anxious to assume political power, and was content to criticize the existing situation without proposing a political plan of its own.[66] The SPD became the party of the "permanent loyal opposition," actually borrowing this term from British political usage. Some leaders even came to believe that the aims of the Social Democracy could be realized under a monarchical form of government just as well as they could under a republican system.

The tremendous growth in the number of party adherents resulted in the loss of its exclusive proletarian base. It has been suggested that the SPD had developed into the only democratic

[65] Sforza, op. cit., pp. 86-87. Noske's views on the "foreign" influence in the SPD are illuminating:

"The attempt made by a number of foreigners from Poland and Russia to set themselves up as teachers of the German workers caused resentment. . . . It has nothing to do with anti-Semitism when one points out that the 'Marxists' of East European Jewish background had a special aptitude for transforming socialism into a dogma and changing popular views into confessions of faith. They plotted a secret [mysterious] science which always remained incomprehensible to the German workers. Only a few half-intellectuals brought discredit upon the labor movement by their idle talk about Marxism. I do not believe that I have ever mentioned Marxism in a speech or in an article. . . ." (Noske, Erlebtes, p. 27.)

[66] Rosenberg, op. cit., pp. 49-50.

people's party since Germany lacked a genuinely liberal middle-class party.[67]

It has been mentioned above that the SPD also showed considerable nationalistic tendencies. These flourished in spite of SPD approval of resolutions at international socialist conferences expressing opposite views.

Three major reasons have been suggested for the change of character of the SPD during the period preceding August 1914. (1) With the ultimate aim set far in the future, the natural, human reaction was to transform the social revolutionary movement into a reform movement; (2) the realization of some demands inevitably led to a more conciliatory attitude toward the ruling group; (3) the highly institutionalized character of the organization resulted in its becoming the major concern of party officials interested in perpetuating the existing situation and thus it lost much of its revolutionary spirit.[68] All three of these factors exerted influence. Count Sforza on the eve of the European war, interestingly described the SPD as nothing but "a gigantic administrative organization — the body tremendous, but the soul very puny."[69]

---

[67] Maehl, *op. cit.*, pp. 26-27. Count Sforza, the internationally k n o w n Italian statesman, would not honor the SPD with the designation of a genuine democratic people's party. He emphasized that the SPD had absorbed so much Hegelian thought with its characteristic adoration of the state that "the 'rights of man and of citizen' faded into abstract 'principles'. . . ." "Indeed, under the cover of the Marxist formula, considered more revolu-tionary than any others, the German Social Democracy merely continued the special mentality of the old German imperialism. Just like the Liberals who preceded them, the socialists were so full of reverence for the technical bounties of the state that they held any encroachments on the personal rights of citizens to be bearable annoyances." (Sforza, *op. cit.*, pp. 83, 84.)

[68] Flechtheim, *op. cit.*, p. 4.

[69] Sforza, *op. cit.*, p. 85.

The Impact of World War I on the German Socialist Movement

Chapter 2

1. *Support of the War Effort by the SPD and the Trade Unions*

The unanimous vote of the Social Democratic Reichstag faction on August 4, 1914, in favor of granting the war appropriation requested by the German government indicated either that the nationalistic elements within the SPD had succeeded in taking control of the party or that the party had become overwhelmingly patriotic. The vote was a strong declaration of faith in the existing state. It also implied the belief prevalent among Social Democratic leaders that the fate of the German workers was intimately connected with the fate of the national state. The nationalistically inclined socialists were convinced that military defeat would bring disastrous results to the working class.[1]

Prior to the outbreak of the war, the SPD expressed outspokenly anti-war sentiments in its official pronouncements and party newspapers. As late as the end of July, after Austria-Hungary had served its ultimatum on Serbia, *Vorwaerts* — the official organ of the SPD — called on the workers to demonstrate against the war danger and to exert public pressure on the German government to desist from going to the aid of its Austrian ally.[2]

[1] Ludwig Bergstraesser, *Die Geschichte der politischen Parteien in Deutschland* (Munich: Isar Verlag, 1952), pp. 187-88.

[2] For the text of the anti-war proclamation in the July 25, 1914, issue of *Vorwaerts* see, *Illustrierte Geschichte*, p. 91. The Austrian-Hungarian ultimatum to Serbia was dated July 23. It was followed by a declaration of

The International Bureau of the Socialist International met in emergency sessions in Brussels on July 29 and 30. The war had already started in the Balkans. The German socialists were represented at the meetings by Karl Kautsky and Hugo Haase. The assembled delegates unanimously adopted a resolution calling on the workers of all countries to intensify their demonstrations for peace. The International Congress, planned for August 23, 1914, in Vienna, was changed to August 9 and was to meet in Paris. This was the total business accomplished at these meetings.

The last diplomatic meetings of the German and French socialists took place on August 1, 1914. The Executive Committee of the SPD had sent Hermann Mueller to Paris to negotiate with the French socialist leaders on coordinating party action in their respective parliaments in order to prevent an outbreak of war between the two countries.[3] No results were achieved at these conferences either. The French labor leaders requested assurance from Hermann Mueller that the German trade unions and the SPD would call a general strike and thus force the Kaiser to keep Germany out of the war. The French, in turn, promised to do everything in their power to keep the French government from declaring war. Mueller was unable to make these commitments for the trade unions and the SPD. He was fearful that the German government had already succeeded in convincing the German people that their country was threatened by the "Russian peril."[4] Besides not all SPD party leaders were opposed to Germany's going to war. Some of the nationalistic revisionists supported the German war policy even before August 1914.[5]

war on July 28. Germany declared war against Russia on August 1, shortly after Russia had begun to mobilize its military forces. War against France was declared on August 3, and England entered the conflict with a declaration of war against Germany on August 4, after German violation of Belgian neutrality.

[3] Froelich, R o s a Luxemburg, pp.

237-42; Froelich, Zehn Jahre, pp. 63-64.

[4] Albert C. Grzesinski, Inside Germany (New York: Dutton & Co., 1939), pp. 32-33.

[5] Maehl, op. cit., p. 41. Among this group of revisionists were such well-known leaders as Eduard David, Heinrich Cunow, Wilhelm Kolb, Paul Lensch, and Philip Scheidemann.

When Germany declared war against Russia, the anti-war faction within the Social Democratic leadership decreased considerably. The war appropriation question was discussed at a meeting of the Executive Committee of the party on August 2, 1914. Scheidemann, David, and others were for the approval of the government's forthcoming request; Haase and Ledebour opposed it. No decision was reached. The decisive turn came the following day in an executive meeting of the Social Democratic members of the Reichstag. Eduard David argued that the fight against Tsarism must be supported, for it might materially assist the Russian Revolution. Of the one hundred and ten Social Democratic deputies, only fourteen favored a policy of opposition to the war. This minority was led by Hugo Haase, the chairman of the SPD Reichstag faction. The opposition submitted reluctantly to the majority in the interest of party discipline and unity. Thus, on August 4, 1914, the Social Democrats unanimously approved the war appropriation. Even Karl Liebknecht, whose position as an extreme leftist set him apart from the others, voted with the majority. Haase read a statement on the floor of the Reichstag explaining the action of the SPD. He declared that the Social Democrats had worked against the international armaments race and imperialistic policies in general and that the responsibility for the outbreak of the war rested entirely with those who had pursued such policies. The present problem for the Social Democrats was no longer the question of war or peace but the danger which Germany faced because of the threat of foreign invasion.[6]

An example of pre-war nationalist sentiments displayed by leading Social Democrats is an article written by Friedrich Stampfer (later editor-in-chief of *Vorwaerts*) which circulated in many party newspapers on July 31 and August 1, 1914. The article contained the following significant statement: "When the fateful hour strikes, the workers will redeem the pledges given on their behalf by their representatives; the *vaterlandlosen Geselle* will fulfill their duties and will in no respect be surpassed by the patriots." (*Illustrierte Geschichte*, p. 97.) The term *"vaterlandlose Geselle"* means a person without a country. It is used by Stampfer sarcastically. The socialists were frequently accused by their political opponents as "persons without a country" because of their international ties and obligations.

[6] Maehl, *op. cit.*, pp. 40-41; Halperin, *op. cit.*, p. 20; Froelich, *Zehn Jahre,*

The majority of the SPD deputies who decided in favor of the war appropriation may have been influenced by three important factors. First of all, a wave of intense nationalism had seized the German people of all social classes. The population had fallen under a chauvinistic spell. No one seemed willing or able to tell the people the truth about this "defensive" war.[7] August Winnig, the chairman of the construction workers' union and a radical reformist (who eventually was forced out of the SPD), claimed that the attitude of the German workers actually forced the SPD leaders, the Social Democratic Reichstag faction, and the trade unions to support the nationalistic effort.[8]

Secondly, there was the fear that the German government would dissolve the party and the trade unions if the SPD should oppose a war. This was a key argument in Eduard David's efforts to get his fellow deputies to vote for the war appropriation. The loss of legality was the worst thing that could happen to the party bureaucracy. An order to dissolve the Social Democratic organizations was actually under consideration by the government as early as the spring of 1914.[9] Original plans of the War Ministry included the arrest of all Social Democratic deputies at the moment when a state of siege would be proclaimed.[10]

pp. 67-70. For the text of the SPD resolution, see *Illustrierte Geschichte,* pp. 98-99.

[7] Grzesinski, *op. cit.,* p. 33; Maehl, *op. cit.,* pp. 40-41; *Illustrierte Geschichte,* pp. 95-96.

[8] Tormin, *op. cit.,* p. 33. August Winnig, *Das Reich als Republik* (Stuttgart and Berlin: Cotta'sche Buchhandlung, 1930), pp. 99-100. Flechtheim asserts that the action taken by the SPD was not "treason pure and simple" against the working class, as persistently claimed by the left wing radicals, because the patriotic wave had broken down all class barriers. (Flechtheim, *op. cit.,* p. 11.) Indeed, Social Democrats of all ages followed the call to the colors and speedily enlisted. (Grzesinski, *op. cit.,* pp. 33-34.)

[9] *Illustrierte Geschichte,* p. 98; Grzesinski, *op. cit.,* p. 34.

[10] *Illustrierte Geschichte,* p. 96. In spite of their strong aversion to illegality, the Executive Committee of the SPD believed that some precautions should be taken. In August of 1914, it sent the party treasurer, Otto Braun, and Friedrich Ebert to Zurich, Switzerland, with instructions to await further development of the domestic political situation in Germany. Should the party be dissolved and the Social Democratic leaders arrested, these two were free to act on behalf of the party. Ebert and Braun returned to Berlin a few weeks later. (Grzesinski, *op. cit.,* p. 35; Wolfe, *op. cit.,* p. 634.)

The general nationalistic attitude of the trade unions was the third factor. On August 2, 1914, before the SPD had decided on its final position toward the war, an Executive Committee of the trade unions agreed to stop all economic demands on behalf of the workers for the duration of the war. To enforce this policy of economic truce, the union leaders declared that no financial support would be rendered to strikers.[11]

The approval of the war appropriation and the non-strike proclamation of the trade unions in August 1914 were only the first steps made by the German socialists in support of the war. Additional war appropriations were approved as the war progressed.[12]

The SPD proudly proclaimed that it had done everything within its power to support national defense. By its silence the party had acquiesced in the proclamation on August 1, 1914, of a state of siege which entailed such political restrictions as strictest censorship. It had voted on August 4, 1914, for a whole series of emergency laws, suspending the most important labor protection laws, including the regulation of work for women and children. In 1916, Social Democratic deputies voted for the compulsory labor mobilization law (*Vaterlaendisches Hilfsgesetz*) which aimed at forcing into the war economy all men between the ages of seventeen and sixty who were not serving in the army.[13] Most important was the so-called *Burgfrieden,* the voluntary cessation of political party strife for the duration of

---

[11] *Illustrierte Geschichte,* p. 98. Berlau believes that the action of the party was "dictated by the pressure of public opinion, by the fear of governmental retaliation, and by a sincere belief that Germany was faced with foreign aggression." (Berlau, *op. cit.,* p. 135.)

[12] The approval of further war credits on December 2, 1914, was justified by the fact that the borders of the country were still endangered by enemy troops. (Noske, *Erlebtes,* p. 46.) David even claimed that the situation of Ger-many was then more precarious than it had been in August. (Eduard David, *Die Sozialdemokratie im Weltkriege* [Berlin: Vorwaerts Verlag, 1915], pp. 12-13.) War credits were also approved on March 20, 1915, with the justification that neither the aim of security for Germany was reached nor did the enemies show any peace tendencies. (*Ibid.,* pp. 16-17.)

[13] Froelich, *Zehn Jahre,* pp. 94-106; *Illustrierte Geschichte,* p. 128.

the war. For a socialist party this also meant the cessation of the traditional class struggle between bourgeoisie and proletariat.[14]

The trade unions and their leaders also contributed wholeheartedly to the war effort. The early proclamation of the economic truce by the General Commission had a tremendous impact on the nationalistic attitude of the rank-and-file German worker. In the course of the war, the union leaders were able to prove valuable to the German war machine in a variety of ways. During the first weeks of the war an economic crisis developed following the sudden interruption of economic relations with foreign countries. Unemployment rose in spite of the increased draft for the army. The unions stepped in and made payments to workers who were temporarily unemployed because of the war, thus preventing the spread of mass disaffection.[15] The union leaders discouraged economic and political strikes. The fact that the economic truce brought very high profits to the manufacturers did not seem to concern them.[16]

The unions also proved to be one of the most effective instruments in the pro-war publicity campaign designed for domestic consumption. The purpose of the propaganda effort was to keep the workers' morale at the highest possible level in spite of the deprivations imposed by the prolonged war. The *Leitmotif* was the complete interdependence of the outcome of the war and the living standard of the German worker. It was emphasized that a military defeat would bring unemployment, destruction of the trade unions, and reduction or complete loss of all social insurance benefits. In recognition of the contributions rendered by the union leaders, the German government exempted them from military conscription. Their work within the unions was con-

[14] The cooperation of the SPD was the most important single contribution to the establishment of the domestic political and economic truce of the *Burgfrieden*. (Bergstraesser, *op. cit.*, p. 178.)

[15] *Illustrierte Geschichte*, p. 107; Snell, *op. cit.*, p. 69.

[16] Froelich, *Zehn Jahre*, pp. 97-100. The union leaders' lack of attention to the high profits made by the industrialists was possibly caused by ignorance or inexperience.

sidered of greater significance to the over-all war effort than their military service.[17]

The original hostile attitude of the German government toward the trade unions underwent a thorough-going change. An official press communique of November 1915 illustrates this shift in sentiment:

> The free trade-unions have proved a valuable aid . . . and [are] almost indispensable to the economic and communal life of the nation. They have made numerous valuable suggestions in the military, economic, and social fields, some of which were carried out. Their cooperation and advice were placed at the disposal of the military and civil authorities, and were gladly accepted. The gratitude of the nation for the patriotic efforts of organized labor has been frequently expressed by the responsible authorities. . . .[18]

Justifying their support of the German war effort on strictly utilitarian and opportunistic grounds did not satisfy the SPD's right faction which had achieved a position of predominance. Exponents of this group were determined to prove that coopera-

[17] Snell, *op. cit.*, p. 71.

[18] Quoted in Grzesinski, *op. cit.*, p. 35. Another illustration of the pro-war attitude of the trade union leaders is given by *Emil Barth* who asserts that a union functionary of the Berlin Metal Workers, a certain Cohen, declared in October 1914 that war meant salvation for the union. Without war the expected unemployment in the winter of 1914-1915 would have caused the financial ruin of the organization. (Emil Barth, *Aus der Werkstatt der deutschen Revolution* [Berlin: A. Hoffmann's Verlag, 1919], p. 11.) An interesting account on the nationalism of the trade unions comes from John L. Snell who investigated the causes for the well-known patriotic attitude of the SPD during the war. He traced much of this patriotism to the socialist trade unions. There was a very close connection between the unions and the party even though the unions claimed to be independent of the SPD. The General Commission of the trade unions of Germany, the agency which managed most of the activities of its member unions, was composed of thirteen members. Six of the thirteen, including its chairman *Carl Legien* and its vice-chairman *Gustav Bauer*, were Social Democratic Reichstag deputies. Of the 110 SPD deputies, at least 45 had held union positions and 19 were full-time professional union functionaries. The trade unions attempted to take a direct hand in party affairs when anti-war radicalism emerged within the SPD in 1915. Carl Legien requested that union officials be given more functions within the party in order to forestall the spread of anti-war attitudes among the workers. (Snell, *op. cit.*, pp. 66-67.)

tion with the government on many war-time problems was not nationalistic opportunism but was in complete agreement with established Social Democratic principles. For example, by referring to statements made by Marx, Engels, and Lassalle concerning the German cause in the war of 1871, Eduard David attempted to demonstrate that national and international concepts were not mutually exclusive and that internationalism does not necessarily involve anti-nationalism.[19]

Throughout the war the majority of the SPD deputies and high-level party functionaries continued to support the German war effort. They kept repeating the claim that Germany was fighting a defensive war. They assured the workers that various long-postponed domestic political reforms, such as democratization of the government and a badly needed election reform for Prussia, would be forthcoming in the immediate future. However, when dissatisfaction and unrest within the party became increasingly stronger because of the effects of the prolonged war, many of the SPD deputies in the Reichstag became more articulate in their demands for a just peace without annexations.

In 1917, one of the most significant domestic political events in war-time Germany occurred. A coalition of several political parties including the SPD was formed. Its ambitious program was the draft of a peace resolution and proposals for immediate constitutional reforms.[20]

[19] He pointed out further that the Socialist International was organized on the basis of recognition of different nations and was conceived as a defensive organization against the "golden international" of the bourgeoisie. (David, op. cit., pp. 174, 181.) David's entire book is dedicated to the purpose of justifying the actions of the nationalistic elements of the SPD on the war issue. Other socialists of the same type even went so far as to interpret state intervention into the war-time economy as steps in the direction of socialism. (Bergstraesser, op. cit., p. 188; Froelich, Zehn Jahre, pp. 106-08, 137.) For the views of Paul Lensch, see his Drei Jahre Weltrevolution (Berlin: S. Fischer Verlag, 1917).

[20] Bruno Stuemke, Die Entstehung der deutschen Republik (Frankfurt am Main: Ehrig Verlag, 1923), p. 41. This coalition can be considered as the embryonic form of the Weimar Coalition which later was vital in administering the affairs of the new German Republic — SPD, Centrists, and Progressives. For a discussion of the "Peace Resolution of July, 1917," see Halperin, op. cit., pp. 26-31. Professor Friedrich Meinecke also observed that the growing dissatisfaction among the

The German government failed to take action on the proposals of the new parliamentary coalition. The opposition elements took advantage of this situation to enhance their influence among the dissatisfied population.

2. The Opposition to the War Policies of the SPD

Within the framework of this study, it is not possible to trace the genesis of all the groups which were opposed to the war policies of the majority of the SPD leaders. It suffices to recognize that the unanimity of the Social Democratic vote for the war appropriation on August 4, 1914, was the product of party discipline only, and that from the very beginning of the war, dissatisfaction with official policies was prevalent among certain leaders as well as among many local party units.[21]

At the outbreak of the war and for some time thereafter, the oppositional elements within the SPD lacked organization and found it difficult to carry on their work under the state of siege. In the course of the war, however, these groups acquired their own organizational identities, and by 1917, in the third war year, the German socialist labor movement retained little of its former unity. The party had split into three major divisions. In spite of changes in the grouping of personnel, these new divisions were analogous to the three pre-war tendencies within the SPD.[22]

In opposition to the program and actions of the Majority Socialists (as the members of the SPD became known because the majority of the party leaders remained with the original organi-

---

workers required continuous reassurance that Germany was fighting a defensive war and had no annexation plans. Meinecke also stressed that from a psychological point of view drastic changes of the Prussian three-class election system were required. The working class felt that it was intolerable that a rich war profiteer had a more influential vote than a poor combat soldier returning from the front. (Friedrich Meinecke, "Die Revolution; Ursachen und Tatsachen," *Handbuch*

des Deutschen Staatsrechts, ed. by Gerhard Anschuetz und Richard Thoma [Tuebingen: Mohr, 1930], I, pp. 97-98.)

[21] The opposition certainly was not limited during the first few months of the war to a small group of "SPD intellectuals" whose oppositional work "was carried on unnoticed by outsiders," as Berlau claims. (Berlau, *op. cit.*, p. 138) See also Snell, *op. cit.*, p. 72.

[22] Flechtheim, *op. cit.*, p. 24.

zation) were the powerful group of Independent Socialists and various groups of revolutionary radicals. The most important group among these radicals was the Spartacist League. Thus, the left wing radicals were not the only socialists opposed to the war policies of the SPD, and the division of the German Social Democratic movement into anti-militarists and war supporters did not follow the familiar line of demarkation between "revisionist opportunists" and "revolutionary Marxists." This division into "social patriots," pacifists, and revolutionaries was experienced by all socialist parties of the belligerent countries of 1914. The social patriots managed to form the overwhelming majority at the beginning of the war. The pacifists of the left and right wings constituted a much smaller group. However, as the war progressed, this group increased in strength and significance as the population and especially the working class became more and more disappointed with the war. The revolutionaries were a very small and insignificant faction in all countries.[23] To understand the developments within the German labor movement, however, one must realize that the split in the German Social Democracy was not caused by the war alone. This issue only brought the pre-war ideological controversies of the party to a climax.[24]

By the middle of 1917, the SPD war policies were opposed by a new Social Democratic mass organization, the Independent Social Democratic Party of Germany (USPD).[25] This center of opposition developed within the Social Democratic Reichstag faction among the deputies who were against supporting the Government's war policies. Originally these deputies were not opposed to what they thought was a defensive war, but when the imperialistic and annexationist designs of the German government became increasingly obvious, they first abstained from voting and eventually cast their votes against further war credits. It has been observed by some analysts of the German labor movement

---

[23] Seton-Watson, *op. cit.*, pp. 50-51.
[24] Flechtheim, *op. cit.*, pp. 7-8.
[25] *Unabhaengige Sozialdemokratische Partei Deutschlands,* abbreviated USPD. The abbreviation or the term Independent Socialist will be used for this party hereinafter.

that there was really no fundamental difference between the political outlook of the USPD and the SPD except in matters of foreign affairs. Both were revisionists in practice, and neither had repudiated the old Marxist concepts which were still useful in appealing to the German workers.

The Independent Socialists were not a monolithic party but were composed of several groups of various political shadings, and personalities with such different political backgrounds as Haase, Bernstein, and Kautsky.[26]

Even though the break between the Haase group and the SPD was primarily over the war issue, as soon as the USPD developed a program of its own, it expressed not only strong opposition to the government's war policy but also the existing autocratic regime.[27]

[26] Leonore O'Boyle, "The German Independent Socialists during the First World War," *The American Historical Review*, LVI, No. 4 (July, 1951), p. 828; Meinecke, *op. cit.,* p. 100. It is doubtful if these Social Democrats really intended to initiate a split from the SPD, but their determination to vote against the war credits which caused a break in party discipline made this development a necessity. For an example, see the manifesto published in the *Leipziger Volkszeitung* in June, 1915, signed by Haase, Kautsky, and Bernstein, entitled "The Demand of the Hour." In this article, the authors requested a reversal in the policy of war credit approval because of the annexationist plans the government was pursuing. (*Illustrierte Geschichte,* p. 133.) For the development of the voting record of the oppositional Social Democratic deputies, see Stuemke, *op. cit.,* pp. 21-28. The executive committee of the SPD eventually expelled the dissenters who then proceeded to found their own party on April 6-7, 1917, at Gotha. Even before this time, the oppositional deputies under Haase's leadership had activated the Social Democratic Cooperative Group (*Sozialdemokratische Arbeitsgemeinschaft*) in order to protect their right to meet in committees. The importance of this step was that the anti-war protagonists had parliamentary unity for the first time. (Berlau, *op. cit.,* pp. 144-46; Stuemke, *op. cit.,* pp. 30-31; Halperin, *op. cit.,* p. 23.)

Noske did not regard the expulsion of the Haase group as a split in the party, although of course it became that as soon as the USPD was formed. Both Legien, the trade union leader, and he appeared to be satisfied to sever the ties with the oppositional elements. Noske commented on the expulsion as follows: "The German Social Democratic Party did not break into pieces when under the leadership of Haase a part of the [Reichstag] faction left [the party] because of the question of further war credits. The large majority of the deputies remained steadfast to the position [they had taken] in August, 1914. The seed, however, for the destruction of the party had been sown." (Noske, *Erlebtes,* p. 50.)

[27] For a comprehensive account of the history of the USPD, see Eugen Prager, *Geschichte der U.S.P.D.* (Berlin: Verlagsgenossenschaft "Freiheit,"

Because of the growing dissatisfaction among the Social Democratic masses, the USPD rapidly became a second Social Democratic mass party. The growth of the USPD was not greatly influenced by the hostile attitude of the trade unions. After the split occurred, the General Commission quickly declared that the unions would recognize only the old SPD. The USPD was handicapped in its efforts to establish official control over the unions because no general trade union congress was called during the war. The only way it could gain control was from within. It succeeded in this attempt in certain localities; for example, in Berlin and in Leipzig it was able to gain strong influence among the unions. In other places, the hostile union officials managed to keep USPD influence to a minimum.[28]

The anti-war issue had worked within the SPD to break up the unity of the party. The pre-war theoretical and tactical differences among the various factions had not seriously threatened party unity. Once the question of supporting the war had divided the German Social Democracy, however, many other items of disagreement re-emerged and helped create different political plat-

1921). This shift in the domestic policy of the USPD is interesting because as late as December, 1916, when twenty of the oppositional deputies voted against the war credits their justification for the negative vote revealed no revolutionary motivation. They explained that the general war situation was such that Germany was secure from enemy invasion. In other words, it was not their basic anti-war concept which prompted them to vote against the credits but the fact that the borders of Germany were secure. (Bergstraesser, *op. cit.*, p. 185; Rosa Luxemburg, *Entweder-oder*, quoted in Luxemburg, *Ausgewaehlte Reden*, II, pp. 535-36; Karl Liebknecht, "Die Dezembermaenner von 1915," quoted in Liebknecht, *Ausgewaehlte Reden*, pp. 336-43.)

[28] Snell, *op. cit.*, p. 72. There are no reliable figures available for the war period which might permit a comparison of the strength of the SPD and the USPD. The SPD's membership has decreased considerably — primarily because of military service — before the USPD became a competitive organization. Flechtheim collected strength estimates from various sources. According to one source, the SPD had about 248,000 members and the USPD about 100,000 after the split. Another source estimates the respective membership figures as 170,-000 for the SPD and 120,000 for the USPD. The number of newspapers and subscription figures which changed sides after the split relates only part of the shift. The SPD possibly was able to hold on to many more papers than its actual strength because its officials were in strategic controlling positions. Flechtheim relates that from 88 SPD newspapers with 870,000 subscribers, 14 newspapers with about 125,000 subscribers changed to the USPD. (Flechtheim, *op. cit.*, p. 28.)

forms and tactical concepts for the various parts of the former SPD. The critical war-time conditions tended to speed up this process and accelerate the development of pre-war political factions into full-fledged political organizations and parties.

At the time of the break between the oppositional Reichstag deputies and the SPD which led to the founding of the USPD in April 1917, the revolutionary or left wing opposition also emerged as several small organizations. All of them together could not approximate the size of either of the two major Social Democratic mass parties. Throughout the war, these revolutionary groups remained insignificant in membership, and had very little influence upon the masses of the German workers, with the possible exception of the Spartacists and the Revolutionary Shop Stewards.

The left wing opposition to the war policies of the SPD was of a different kind from that of the USPD. The revolutionaries did not regard the actions of the SPD leadership as tactical mistakes. The leftist opposition evaluated the actions of the party and their justifications by people like David as the final and ultimate proof that the SPD had completely accepted the revisionist concepts, even though it still had failed to repudiate its Marxian camouflage. All of these revolutionary groups shared a professed confidence in international socialism in contrast to the narrow nationalism which had taken possession of the SPD leadership. Even after the left wing opposition had recognized this definite change in the SPD, its adherents did not leave in order to form a new party which would be guided by the old revolutionary concepts and by those which developed as the result of the changing situation. They remained, electing to work within the party to bring it back to pre-war platforms which had been codified at the various party congresses. When these attempts failed, however, they either joined the new USPD or remained as unattached revolutionary socialist groups. None of them, with the exception of the Spartacists and the Left Radicals (*Linksradikalen*) who joined the Spartacists in October 1918, ever formed a political party of any significance. Even the Spartacists did not become a party until two months after the German Revolution had started. The failure of the left wing opposition to create a revolutionary mass party prior to that time was later sharply criticized by Communists of the Lenin school. They asserted that this omission deprived the German workers of the leadership of a revolutionary party during the initial period of their social and political upheaval.

Among the revolutionary oppositional groups was the Spartacist League (*Spartakusbund*). In spite of its relatively small numbers, it was a nation-wide organization, and was led by such outstanding pre-war revolutionary leaders as Rosa Luxemburg and Karl Liebknecht. It was probably the most articulate and active of the several leftist oppositional groups. On December 31, 1918, the Spartacist League became the German Communist Party which, in turn, played a decisive part during the period of consolidation of the German Revolution.[29]

The Spartacists met in January 1916 for their first national conference. At this time they adopted a program which subsequently guided their policies and activities.[30] At this conference, it was decided to publish the political tracts which subsequently became known as the Spartacist Letters.[31]

[29] The estimates of Spartacist membership vary from several hundreds to several thousands. (*Ibid.*, p. 29.) The origin of the Spartacists goes back to shortly after the outbreak of the war and the collapse of the Socialist International. On August 4, 1914, a number of revolutionaries gathered around Rosa Luxemburg and decided to continue their fight against the imperialist war, against the war policies of the SPD, and for the principles of the International. One of the first actions of this group was the publication of a declaration signed by Rosa Luxemburg, Karl Liebknecht, Franz Mehring, and Clara Zetkin, in the Swiss Social Democratic press (September, 1914) announcing to the world that not all the German Social Democrats had succumbed to the war policies of the SPD. (Liebknecht, *Reden*, p. 363; *Illustrierte Geschichte*, p. 115.)

[30] *Ibid.*, pp. 135-37; for a discussion of this program see below pp. 55-56.

[31] Flechtheim, *op. cit.*, p. 18. The Spartacist Letters eventually gave the group its name. Before their appearance, the group was called "Group International." This latter designation was derived from the publication, *The Internationale*, which appeared only once in April, 1915 and then was prohibited under the censorship. (Bergstraesser, *op. cit.*, pp. 180-81.) For a description of its contents see *Illustrierte Geschichte*, pp. 130-31, and Froelich, *Zehn Jahre*, pp. 148-49.

Prior to this time, the group around Rosa Luxemburg and Liebknecht attempted to provide political guidance for oppositional elements within local party organizations. The dissemination of propaganda material was a most difficult task considering the restrictions imposed by the state of siege. Nevertheless, some Social Democratic newspapers and periodicals which happened to be under the management of radicals continued for some time to print articles inspired by the opposition.[32] Until the fall of 1915 collaboration with the group around Ledebour and Kautsky was maintained.[33]

The Spartacist League joined the USPD but only because it felt that the new party would afford a protecting roof to the illegal organization of the Spartacists. The League representatives who participated in the founding congress made certain that it was clearly understood that the Spartacists would retain their own organizational identity as well as their freedom of action.[34]

Another group in opposition to the SPD policies was the organization of Julian Borchardt, the International Socialists of Germany (*Internationale Sozialisten Deutschlands* — ISD). Their official organ was the *Lichtstrahlen* which Borchardt started in 1914. In April 1916, it was prohibited.

---

[32] *Illustrierte Geschichte*, pp. 114-16.

[33] This collaboration was not intended to consolidate the opposition to the official war policies of the SPD, but was to provide the left wing radicals with a better opportunity to gain influence among the workers. (*Ibid.*, pp. 131-34.) The practice of penetrating other organizations for the purpose of recruiting members from within is still a standard operating procedure of the Communists.

[34] (Flechtheim, *op. cit.*, p. 23. *Illustrierte Geschichte*, pp. 147-48.) Pertinent are the contents of a letter written by Leo Jogiches, who had taken over the leadership of the Spartacists after the arrest of Rosa Luxemburg and the induction of Liebknecht into the army. The letter was addressed to members of the Spartacist group in Wuerttemberg who were reluctant to join the USPD. Jogiches frankly explained to the Wuerttenberg comrades what advantages the new party provided for the Spartacists. They could work under the cover of the party, undermine its leadership, and submit its members to the influence of the Spartacist League. (*Ibid.*)

Liebknecht was even more blunt in stating why the Spartacists had joined: "We belonged to the USPD in order to drive forth [the party], to keep it within the reach of our whip, [and] to pull the best elements out [for us]." (Karl Liebknecht, *Ausgewaehlte Reden*, p. 522.)

The International Socialists were a small group of radical socialists who never assumed any particular significance in the revolutionary movement in Germany. Borchardt believed that he had views similar to the Bolsheviks led by Lenin; however, his theoretical concepts were much more in line with those of the anarchists. He was convinced of the futility of parliamentarianism and of the inadequacy of any type of political leadership. The masses themselves, he asserted, were capable of handling all political matters. Eventually he despaired because he had become convinced that the masses lacked revolutionary initiative.[35]

Most of his followers moved over to the Left Radicals (*Links-radikalen*), a group very active in Bremen under the leadership of Johann Knief. This group consisted of several hundred members who originally came from a radical faction of the SPD organization in Bremen. Even before the war, they were strongly under the influence of Karl Radek and Anton Pannekoek. In May 1916, Paul Froelich and Johann Knief started the legal weekly publication, the *Arbeiterpolitik*, whose main contributor was Radek. Through Radek, this group maintained close relations with the Central Committee of the Bolsheviks, in particular with Lenin and Zinoviev. The Left Radicals, like the ISD, stressed revolutionary mass action as the means for political and social changes. In contrast to the latter they did not reject parliamentarianism entirely but considered it as auxiliary to mass action. Unlike the Spartacists, who for a long time attempted to influence the party from within, the Left Radicals advocated from the beginning a split of the revolutionary socialists from the reformist SPD. In this respect, their views were much closer to the Bolshevik ideas than those of the Luxemburg-Liebknecht group. (After the Russian October Revolution the Left Radicals immediately declared their approval of the revolutionary practices of the Bolsheviks.) The Left Radicals were opposed to the new USPD and refused to join forces.[36]

[35] Tormin, *op. cit.*, p. 40 Froelich, *Zehn Jahre*, p. 155.

[36] Tormin, *op. cit.*, pp. 40-41; Froelich, *Zehn Jahre*, pp. 155-56; Berg-

The differences between the Spartacists and the Bremen Group did not prevent the two organizations from cooperating. The legal weekly paper of the Bremen Group, the *Arbeiterpolitik* was used by the Spartacists in political discussions. The underground Spartacist Letters were utilized by both groups for active revolutionary propaganda among the masses. In questions of tactics, the numerically weaker Left Radicals subordinated themselves to the Spartacist League.[37]

In contrast to the revolutionary groups discussed above, the Revolutionary Shop Stewards (*Revolutionaere Obleute*) emerged not from the SPD but from the trade unions. As early as 1914, union functionaries in certain Berlin factories who were opposed to the official policies of the SPD and the trade unions organized themselves into small groups. Their purpose was to work from within the unions, mobilizing the workers to fight for a termination of the war. Their membership was highly selective and restricted to union functionaries with adminstrative and political experience.[38]

Experiences gained through the political mass strikes during the war and the spread of the Revolutionary Shop Stewards to other industrial centers resulted in an elaborate clandestine organization which advocated increasingly the use of conspiratorial methods for the coming revolutionary struggle. Until his induction into the German army, Richard Mueller was the leader of the Shop Stewards. In February 1918, he was succeeded by a revolutionary hothead, Emil Barth, who was replaced in the sum-

straesser, *op. cit.*, p. 183; *Illustrierte Geschichte*, pp. 142-45.

Eventually on October 7, 1918, the Left Radicals consolidated with the Spartacists in a "combat partnership" (*Kampfgemeinschaft*) for the forthcoming revolution. (Froelich, *Zehn Jahre*, p. 222.)

[37] Froelich suggests that the differences between the two groups arose from certain characteristics of their respective leaders. The Left Radicals were of the younger generation who had no personal connection with the veteran leaders of the SPD and therefore did not hesitate to sever relations. On the other hand, the leaders of the Spartacists were personalities of the old International who were not ready to break the ties with their comrades so quickly even though they might deeply disagree with them. (*Ibid.*, p. 156.)

[38] Richard Mueller, *Vom Kaiserreich zur Republik* (Berlin: Malik-Verlag, 1925), I, p. 125.

mer of the same year by Ernst Daeumig. The latter was simultaneously a leading member of the USPD and of the Shop Stewards. It was the intention of the Shop Stewards to remain the cadre of leaders for the future socialist revolution and not to become a mass organization.[39]

Politically, the Shop Stewards occupied a position between the USPD and the Spartacist League. Originally they retained their individual memberships in their respective unions; later they also joined the USPD. The Shop Stewards intended to remain the revolutionary activists and therefore avoided (unlike the Spartacists and Independent Socialists) lengthy, theoretical discussions.[40] The differences between them and the Spartacists were primarily of a tactical nature. They were opposed to mass actions and discarded them as useless "revolutionary gymnastics."[41]

In order to strengthen their influence on the USPD and the Spartacists, the Shop Stewards pressed for a common meeting of the revolutionary opposition. The Executive Committee of the USPD delayed such a meeting for some time. Eventually the persistence of the Shop Stewards — and possibly the general revolutionary climate — led certain USPD leaders to participate in the secret meetings of the Shop Steward organization in Berlin. From October 1918, representatives of the Spartacist League also attended these meetings.[42]

[39] *Ibid.*, pp. 125-27. The influence of the Shop Stewards upon the events of November, 1918 has been greatly exaggerated as the result of Emil Barth's *Aus der Werkstatt der deutschen Revolution*. For example, see Erich Otto Volkmann, *Der Marxismus und das deutsche Heer im Weltkrieg* (Berlin: Verlag Hobbing, 1925), pp. 210-13. Volkmann bases many of his views on the information obtained from Barth's book. Barth describes in detail the revolutionary preparations made by his group, the organization of highly disciplined and well-armed shock troops, the procurement of weapons, and the placement of confidence men in sensitive strategic positions. Richard Mueller dismisses Barth's claims as pure nonsense. (Richard Mueller, *Vom Kaiserreich*, pp. 126-27.)

[40] Volkmann, *op. cit.*, p. 210; Halperin, *op. cit.*, p. 79.

[41] Tormin, *op. cit.*, pp. 42-44.

[42] Rosenberg, *Die Entstehung,* p. 245. While Barth's statements must be read with great caution, his description of his attempts to bring unity into the revolutionary movement prior to November, 1918 are of interest: "The most difficult position was in relation to the Spartacists and Left Radicals. They believed that revolutionary per-

3. *The International Anti-War Effort*

Although the Socialist International had collapsed at the outbreak of war, European socialists who continued to oppose their countries' war efforts had not given up hope that some common international action might help bring an early end to hostilities.[43] Nothing ever came of the various international efforts, although discussions at conferences did help clarify the political alignment within the socialist movement and possibly laid the foundation for the Third International.

The anti-war protagonists among the international Social Democracy were divided into the social pacifists and the revolutionary anti-militarists. The pacifists, who included such well-known personalities as Eduard Bernstein (German) and Ramsay MacDonald (British), wished only a return to the peaceful co-existence of nations and classes in order to continue their "peaceful" struggle for social reforms. By contrast, the revolutionaries declared themselves not satisfied with a compromise peace solution between the warring countries since this would only strengthen the bourgeois rule. The revolutionaries intended to exploit the situation created by the war to overthrow the existing power relations and to bring an end to the hegemony of the bourgeoisie.[44]

The "revolutionary anti-militarists" were divided into two factions. The left wing under the leadership of Lenin and Zinoviev advocated the "transformation of the present imperialist war into

ception, motivation, and action can be produced by leaflets and revolutionary gymnastics. . . . Conspiratorial activity was not to their liking." (Barth, *op. cit.*, p. 29.)

[43] Even the social patriots pretended that the International was continuing. Possibly they were satisfied with the explanation offered by Kautsky who stated that the International was an instrument of peace and not war. (Rosa Luxemburg, "Der Wiederaufbau der Internationale," quoted in Luxemburg, *Ausgewaehlte Reden*, II, p. 518.) Shortly after the beginning of hostilities, the Socialist Bureau was moved from Brussels to Amsterdam and claimed that it was continuing the business of the old International. It was headed by the Belgian socialist Vandervelde who became Belgian Minister of War a few weeks later. This new office did not require him to give up his position in the Socialist Bureau. (Volkmann, *Der Marxismus*, p. 114.)

[44] Seton-Watson, *op. cit.*, p. 50.

civil war" aimed at the overthrow of the bourgeoisie.[45] Lenin also proposed severing relations with the social patriots within the national parties as well as with the remnants of the Socialist International as soon as possible.[46] Lenin's opponents among the revolutionary antagonists to the war held views similar to those of Rosa Luxemburg. Luxemburg, like the pacifists, emphasized the fight for peace, although she understood peace as that which would serve the interest of the working class and therefore *ipso facto* would have to be achieved through the proletariat itself. She stressed neither revolution nor civil war as the method to be used in achieving this kind of peace. Her reference was to the revolutionary class struggle only. Rosa Luxemburg found herself in disagreement with Lenin on the question of breaking off relations with the moderate pacifists or even with the social patriots. She believed that as long as the party provided enough internal freedom of action which could be used to enlighten members and make them return to the socialist international concepts, such a break would hurt the revolutionaries. She was convinced that the propaganda work, especially that directed at the Social Democrats, was far more effective from within the party than from outside. On the other hand, she believed the split between war supporters and revolutionaries to be inevitable, although she placed the time of this event after the end of the war.[47]

The three-fold division of the anti-war socialists became quite apparent at the two international conferences held in Switzerland: (1) The social pacifists of the type of the German representatives

[45] Lenin made this statement as early as November 1, 1914, in an article entitled "The War and Russian Social-Democracy," *Selected W o r k s* (Moscow, Leningrad: Co-op. Pub. Society, 1935), V, pp. 123-30.

[46] See V. I. Lenin, *The Collapse of the Second International* (Moscow: Foreign Languages Pub. House, 1949).

[47] In her views concerning the restoration of the International, Rosa Luxemburg also emphasized the fight for peace: ". . . the first step in this direction is action for a quick end to the war . . ." (Luxemburg, *Der Wiederaufbau,* p. 526.) Luxemburg considered the fight for peace the essence of her political actions while Lenin refused to accept this. Luxemburg was thinking in terms of mass appeal, while Lenin restricted his concepts to the small group of revolutionaries trained to deal with theoretical problems. (Froelich, *Rosa Luxemburg,* pp. 248-253.)

from the Ledebour-Bernstein group; (2) the revolutionary anti-militarists of the Lenin-Zinoviev faction (subsequently known as the Zimmerwald Left); and (3) the anti-militarists who placed the class struggle for the proletarian type of international peace at the center of their program. The Spartacist delegates belonged to this last group.

The first of the two international conferences took place at Zimmerwald from September 5 to 8, 1915. The German delegation included Georg Ledebour and Adolf Hoffmann, Social Democratic opposition; Ernst Meyer and Bertha Thalheimer, Luxemburg-Liebknecht group; and Julian Borchardt, International Socialists of Germany. Only Borchardt joined the Zimmerwald Left, the radical group sponsored by the Russian Bolsheviks. The Spartacist delegates did not give their support to the resolution of the Zimmerwald Left which demanded an immediate break from the reformists of the Social Democrats.[48]

At the second Zimmerwald Conference at Kienthal during Easter of 1916 a decisive shift toward the left was apparent. A resolution was adopted making it obligatory for the participating organizations to vote in their respective parliaments against further war appropriations. The main debate, however, centered around the question of whether or not a break should be made with the Socialist International. No final decision was reached.

---

[48] *Illustrierte Geschichte,* pp. 134-37. For part of the resolution of the Zimmerwald Left see *ibid.,* p. 136; Froelich, *Zehn Jahre,* pp. 158-59. According to Liebknecht, the delegates to the Zimmerwald Conference had two important missions to fulfill; (1) to settle accounts with the deserters of the International; (2) to clarify the position of the revolutionary proletariat in regard to the war. In his letter to the Zimmerwald Conference, he expressed his concept of an action program: "Civil war, not *Burgfriede* (armistice)! Practice international proletarian solidarity, fight against the pseudo-nation- alistic, pseudo-patriotic class harmony, utilize the international class struggle to achieve peace and realize the socialist revolution." (Karl Liebknecht, "An die Zimmerwald Konferenz," quoted in Liebknecht, *Ausgewaehlte Reden,* pp. 315-17.)

Also see: Merle Fainsod, *International Socialism and the World War* (Cambridge: Harvard University Press, 1935); Eduard Bernstein, *Die Internationale der Arbeiterklasse und der europaeische Krieg* (Tuebingen: Mohr, 1916); Karl Kautsky, *Die Internationale und der Krieg* (Berlin: Buchhandlung Vorwaerts, 1915); and Ray-

In a compromise solution, the social patriots were severely condemned.[49]

4.   *Characteristic Political Thought of the Spartacists*

In the preceding pages of this chapter an attempt has been made to examine the reactions of the oppositional socialists to the war-time policies and actions of the SPD. This analysis has shown that the fundamental diversity of basic principles eventually destroyed the organizational monopoly of the SPD within the German labor movement. A few new organizations emerged.

For the Spartacists, the question of organization — beyond the point of getting established as an entity of some kind — did not become a problem until almost two months after the beginning of the German Revolution when the Communist Party of Germany was founded. In spite of their distinct revolutionary concepts, they preferred to remain within the fold of a Social Democratic party. (First, the SPD; later, the USPD.)[50]

mond W. Postgate, *The International during the War* (London: The Herald, 1918).

[49] *Illustrierte Geschichte*, p. 148; Froelich, *Zehn Jahre*, pp. 159-60. For the text of the Kienthal resolution see Froelich, *Zehn Jahre*, pp. 238-40. There was a third Zimmerwald Conference at Stockholm in September, 1917. The differences between the pacifists and the revolutionaries could not be resolved any longer. No results could be achieved. In the meantime, the fight in Russia between the Mensheviks and Bolsheviks had almost reached its climax. The Zimmerwald International continued to exist in name only until it was dissolved when the Communist International was founded in March of 1919. The above described Stockholm Conference must not be confused with another international conference held in Stockholm about the same time. The latter conference was arranged by neutral Dutch and Scandinavian socialists and was eventually called by the Executive Committee of the Workers' and Soldiers' Council of Petersburg for the purpose of unifying the international proletariat for a peace without annexation and compensations and based upon the right of national self-determination. None of the aims the conference had set for itself were accomplished. (*Ibid.*, pp. 196-98; Fischer, *op. cit.*, p. 12.)

[50] There were also impatient Spartacists who believed that remaining in the SPD had become intolerable. They wanted to form a new revolutionary party. Rosa Luxemburg was strongly opposed to this. She admitted that the aim must be a revolutionary party, but she emphasized that the Social Democratic masses must not be abandoned and left to the treacherous leaders. Her organizational aim was not the creation of a revolutionary sect separated from the masses but the maintenance of a strong faction comprised of the revolutionary elements working for their aims from within the party. (Froelich, *Rosa Luxemburg*, p. 265.)

An analysis of the political thought of the Spartacists as it crystallized in the course of the war is essential for an understanding of their actions and views in relation both to pre-revolutionary mass events and to the German Revolution. The political concepts of the Spartacists during the war were the product of several factors. First and most fundamental was the revolutionary Marxism of the Spartacist leaders as early as the pre-war period.[51] Second, there was the influence of the war-time experiences. This factor included the support of the war by the SPD as well as the various challenges which a crisis situation presents. Germany experienced an economic crisis resulting from the continuous drain caused by the war. Politically, the country was ruled by a military dictatorship. A growing revolutionary attitude strengthened the desire to change the situation quickly because of deprivations, inefficient management of practically everything, loss of confidence in the government, in military leadership, and in political parties, and finally the abandonment of hope in ultimate victory. The third factor was the impact of international events, primarily the Russian Revolutions of March and October 1917 and the international conferences mentioned before.

Oppositional views were reflected in articles appearing during the early part of the war (e.g., the articles in the *Internationale*), speeches made by Liebknecht in the Reichstag, and leaflets disseminated among the SPD members. As early as August 1914 Liebknecht attacked the axiomatic party unity, declaring that clearness of concepts was more important than unity.[52] In May 1915, the important underground leaflet "The Main Enemy Is In Our Own Country" attempted to explain to the masses that the war must be fought on an international basis.

The main enemy of the German people is in Germany: German imperialism, the German war party, German secret diplomacy. The German people must wage a political fight against this enemy in its

---

[51] Cf. above, chap. I, sec. 4.   [52] Liebknecht, *Reden,* pp. 109-11.

own country in cooperation with the proletariat of other countries whose fight must be directed against their own native imperialists.[53]

For Liebknecht the focal point of revolutionary activity was the struggle against war itself. ". . . the anti-militarist fight is the intensified form of the class struggle against the war and against the violent domestic power politics of capitalism."[54]

The principal political impulses, however, came from Rosa Luxemburg. The fact that she spent most of the war years in prison did not reduce her influence among the left wing radicals.[55] Rosa Luxemburg was strongly opposed to the notion expounded by some Social Democratic leaders that the war had changed the entire concept of the class struggle.

The proletarian tactics *before* and *after* the outbreak of war are supposed to be totally different; they are even to pursue opposite purposes. That presumes that the social conditions [which constitute] the bases for our tactics, are basically different during peace and war. According to historic materialism, as expounded by Marx, history is the history of class struggles. According to Kautsky's revised materialism, it must be added: except during war times. . . . The political class rule of the bourgeoisie does not cease during the war; on the contrary, because of the suspension of constitutional rights it develops into brutal class dictatorship.[56]

[53] Karl Liebknecht, *Der Hauptfeind steht im eigenen Land,* quoted in Liebknecht, *Ausgewaehlte Reden,* p. 301. The great aim of the international proletariat must be the international general strike, at least an international strike in the ammunition and armament industries. (Karl Liebknecht, "Antimilitarismus," quoted in Liebknecht, *Ausgewaehlte Reden,* p. 333.)

[54] Liebknecht, *Antimilitarismus,* p. 323.

[55] Fischer, *op. cit.,* p. 14. A contemporary Communist evaluation of Rosa Luxemburg's historic revolutionary mission during the war summarized it as follows: "Her first task was to tear apart the falsehood of the defense of the Fatherland which the Social Democratic leaders used to cover up their betrayal. . . . The second task consisted of exposing the untruth of the alleged war against Tsarism . . . her third mission was to reveal the betrayal of the *Burgfrieden.* (Oelssner, *op. cit.,* pp. 110-112.)

[56] Luxemburg, *Der Wiederaufbau,* pp. 523-25.

Not until January 1, 1916 when the "Guiding Principles for the Tasks of the International Social Democracy" were adopted at a secret meeting of the opposition in Liebknecht's apartment in Berlin, did the Group International have a program which incorporated their theoretical concepts — as conceived by Rosa Luxemburg.[57]

The Junius pamphlet is the most concise statement of Rosa Luxemburg's anti-war views. In it she also re-emphasized many of her previously expressed political concepts which according to her were confirmed by the experiences of the first war years. She stressed the fact that one of the most important lessons was that the proletariat in this war could not identify itself with any military side. According to her, there was no such thing as a "national" defensive war:

. . . in the present imperialistic milieu, a defensive war fought on a national basis is completely impossible; any socialist policy which disregards this determining [influence of the] historical milieu and which in the midst of the world chaos permits itself to be guided by the isolated point of view of one country, is *a priori* built on sand.[58]

While it might not be possible under the existing circumstances to start a revolution or even to incite mass strikes because "great popular movements are not made with technical recipes from the pocket of the party offices. . . ." the party must provide the masses with clear political directives and make them understand their political mission and interest. Most important is her distinct

---

[57] Flechtheim, *op. cit.,* pp. 16-18. Fischer, *op. cit.,* p. 13. The "'Guiding Principles" were the annex to Rosa Luxemburg's most significant political writing during the war, "The Crisis of the Social Democracy." This piece was written in April, 1915 while she was in prison but was not printed and circulated until one year later. "The Crisis of the Social Democracy" is also known under the pseudonym used by Luxemburg, "Junius," the name of the defender of the English Constitution against the attacks of the absolutist George III. (Froelich, *Rosa Luxemburg,* pp. 257-58; Luxemburg, *Die Krise.*)

[58] *Ibid.,* pp. 359, 386-97. For an explanation of Rosa Luxemburg's concept concerning the historic necessity of imperialism, see *ibid.,* pp. 389-91.

restatement of the interrelation of political mass activity with the over-all situation:

When large mass demonstrations and mass actions in one form or other transpire, they depend upon many economical, political, and psychological factors, upon the prevailing tension [created by] class antagonism, the degree of political understanding [of the masses], and the intensity of the fighting spirit of the masses, something impossible to figure out or to create artificially through party [commands].[59]

The "Guiding Principles" asserted that these were not new concepts but actually "apply the principles of the Erfurt Program to the present problems confronted by international socialism." Thus, the international proletariat must base its revolutionary fight upon the class struggle within each country regardless of peace or war. It must fight against imperialism through parliamentary means and labor union action. In fact, all activities of the labor movement must be synchronized with the international class struggle against imperialism.[60]

The Bolshevik Revolution in Russia in October 1917 transformed many of the theoretical problems of the European socialists into burning issues. All Social Democratic factions felt pressed to take a position toward the events in Russia and toward

[59] *Ibid.*, pp. 374-75. This concept was never repudiated by Rosa Luxemburg. She always remained opposed to any form of *Putsche*. According to her, they were bound to fail because they were isolated events superimposed on existing social, political, and economic realities.

[60] *Ibid.*, pp. 394, 398-99. The mention of parliamentary means in the class struggle against imperialism was clearly a reference to voting against further war appropriations and to making use of parliament as a platform from which the masses could be reached. Liebknecht used both types of parliamentary fight. His basic position in regard to parliamentarianism as a substitute for other means in the revolutionary struggle became apparent in his opposition to the Haase-Ledebour group whom he accused of having too much confidence in the parliamentary approach and of "parliamentary cretenism." (Karl Liebknecht, "Nicht die alte Leier, sondern das neue Schwert," in *Spartakusbrief*, No. 2., November, 1916, quoted in Liebknecht, *Ausgewaehlte Reden*, p. 451.) See also Karl Liebknecht, "Liebknechts kleine Anfrage," in *Politische Briefe des Spartakusbundes*, No. 1a, January, 1916, quoted in Liebknecht, *Ausgewaehlte Reden*, pp. 346-47.

the methods employed by the Bolsheviks in establishing and maintaining their power. For the right wing socialists, this posed no particular problem, since they were opposed to anything connected with violent revolution and dictatorship of the proletariat. Within the left wing groups, however, heated discussions took place on two interrelated questions: the first was to what extent could Bolshevik policies and actions be accepted as valid for Russia; the second was to what extent — if at all — could Bolshevik strategy be used in other countries.[61]

The Spartacists themselves were divided on these issues. Some of the ultra-radical members were eager to give approval to everything the Bolsheviks did; others were more reserved and were reluctant to approve, for example, the dissolution of the Russian Constituent Assembly by the Bolsheviks. Clara Zetkin and Franz Mehring belonged to the first group.[62] Rosa Luxemburg was critical of parts of the Bolshevik program. In the fall of 1918 while still in prison, she started a comprehensive critique of Bolshevik policies. The outbreak of the German Revolution and her own intense participation in it prevented her from finishing it.[63]

Her critique concentrated on four specific issues: (1) the agrarian question, (2) the Bolsheviks' nationality policy, (3) the problem of democracy, and (4) the use of terror. Rosa Luxemburg argued that the distribution of land immediately achieved two things of benefit to the revolution: the destruction of large estates and the support of the peasants. On the other hand, this tactic would make it much more difficult later on to nationalize

[61] Flechtheim, *op. cit.,* p. 26.
[62] *Ibid.,* p. 28.
[63] Paul Levi, who in the spring of 1918 assumed leadership of the Spartacist League after the arrest of Leo Jogiches, published the fragments of the critique in 1922. He was violently attacked for this action by the Communists; they alleged that it helped the charges of the right wing socialists against the Soviet system. The Communists furthermore asserted that Rosa Luxemburg subsequently changed some of the views expressed in this paper when, in the course of the German Revolution, she became convinced of the correctness of the Bolshevik approach. This assertion was made particularly in reference to her opposition to the Bolshevik dissolution of the constitutent assembly, since she eventually fought against the USPD's views of coexistence of the council system with the parliament. (Froelich, *Rosa Luxemburg,* pp. 284-91; Oelssner, *op. cit.,* pp. 125-26.)

the agricultural holdings and, therefore, the original measure was wrong. She ventured to predict that Lenin's agrarian reform created a new and powerful social class which constituted a strong potential enemy to socialism. Its resistance to nationalization would be much more dangerous and tenacious than that encountered from the former aristocratic land owners.

Her opposition to the national self-determination policy of the Bolsheviks was of long standing. She had already fought this doctrine in the program of the Russian Social Democracy.[64]

The most significant part of her critique dealt with the problem of democracy. Rosa Luxemburg was greatly alarmed by the dissolution of the Constituent Assembly and by Bolshevik statements on the uselessness of any popular representation elected during a revolution. The Bolsheviks claimed that democratic institutions were slow and could not keep pace with political developments. Rosa Luxemburg disagreed, and countered that the sluggish mechanism of democratic institutions had a powerful corrector in the constant pressure of the active mass movement: ". . . the cure which Trotsky and Lenin found — putting an end to democracy — is much worse than the evil it is supposed to correct."

Lenin and Trotsky have put the Soviets as the only true representatives of the working masses in the place of representative bodies produced by popular election. However, with the suppression of political life in the entire country, the life within the Soviets, i.e., within the councils must also become weaker and weaker. Without popular elections, unrestricted freedom of the press and assembly, free expression of opinion, life dies in any public institution; it becomes a semblance of life wherein only the bureaucracy remains the active element.[65]

There can be no doubt that Rosa Luxemburg was greatly opposed to the concentration of power in the hands of the few Bol-

[64] Rosa Luxemburg, *Die russiche Revolution* ([Berlin]: Verlag Gesell-

schaft u. Erziehung, 1922), pp. 81-97.
[65] *Ibid.*, pp. 97-117.

shevik politicians (she referred to this situation as "the dictatorship of a handful of politicians") and to the exclusion of the
initiative and control of the masses.[66]

Finally, she turned against the "extensive use of terror by the
Soviet government." She recognized the need for strong measures
during revolutionary upheavals directed against domestic and
foreign counter-revolutionary efforts. However, she considered it
dangerous to make a virtue of necessity and to offer it to the international proletariat as a model of socialist tactics.[67]

Rosa Luxemburg shared the opinion of Lenin and Trotsky
that the Russian Revolution could not survive without the help
of the international proletariat. In the Spartacist Letter No. 8
published in January 1918, this same view was expressed.[68] The
Spartacists readily admitted that the Russian Revolution had
given them considerable moral support and had inspired them to
follow the Russian example.

The acceptance of the Russian pattern also became apparent
at the Reich Conference of Spartacists and Left Radical delegates
held in Berlin on October 7, 1918. Under the impact of the Soviet
example, the delegates decided to work for the establishment of
workers' and soldiers' councils in Germany which, following the
Russian experience, were to serve as the main revolutionary agencies in the period of transition.[69]

---

[66] Froelich, *Rosa Luxemburg*, p. 291.

[67] Luxemburg, *Die russiche Revolu-tion,* pp. 117-18. For a pro-Luxemburg
analysis of her "Die russiche Revolu-
tion," see Froelich, *Rosa Luxemburg,*
pp. 284-97. For an anti-Luxemburg
view, see Oelssner, *op. cit.,* pp. 122-26.

[68] Kommunistische Partei Deutschlands, *Spartakusbriefe* (Berlin, 1920),
pp. 154-55. Hereafter cited as *Spartakusbriefe.* In the Spartacist Letter No.
11 of September, 1918 entitled "The
Russian Tragedy," it was asserted that
only a revolt of the German proletariat
could save the situation in Russia.
(*Spartakusbriefe,* p. 186.) Cf. the text
of a Spartacist leaflet quoted in Walter
Ulbricht, *Der Zusammenbruch*
*Deutschlands im ersten Weltkrieg und
die Novemberrevolution* (Berlin: Dietz
Verlag, 1951), p. 11. While the Spartacists were eager to point out that
they were not imitating the Russian
Bolsheviks, they did look upon the Bolshevik Revolution as the beginning of
the proletarian world revolution. (*Spartakusbriefe,* p. iv.)

[69] A very comprehensive evaluation
of the entire problem of the council
system in Germany and the part it
played in the revolutionary period preceding the military collapse and during
the Revolution proper may be found
in Tormin, *op. cit.* The Reich Conference led to a consolidation of the forces
of the Spartacists and Left Radicals.

5. *The Relation of the Spartacists to the Major Revolutionary Events During the War*

Throughout the war, the Spartacists remained a very small and uninfluential group of revolutionaries who advocated the revolutionary method of bringing the war to an end. They wished to utilize the intensified class struggle, brought about by the crisis conditions, to achieve their next aim, the seizure of political power by the workers. However, because of the great influence of the two major Social Democratic parties, the SPD and the USPD, the Spartacists were able to reach only a relatively small segment of the population.[70] Thus, the major revolutionary events in wartime Germany which became progressively more challenging for the government and the military leaders, were only slightly, if at all, influenced by Spartacist propaganda. These events occurred as the result of such external circumstances as the deterioration of the economic situation or the increasingly hopeless situation at the front, rather than as a result of a revolutionary propaganda.[71]

The anti-war demonstration led by Liebknecht on May 1, 1916, was one of the very few independent Spartacist actions. Even the few protest strikes which followed his arrest were directed not by the Spartacists but by Richard Mueller and a number of Revolutionary Shop Stewards from some large factories in Berlin.[72]

It was generally agreed among the delegates that the revolutionary fermentation in Germany had entered its last phase and therefore the left radical groups should work harmoniously for the revolution. In addition to the adoption of a resolution to create workers' and soldiers' councils all over Germany, the delegates further decided to increase their propaganda among the armed forces and to work out a common program of action. The proclamation of the Reich Conference which was widely distributed contained the action program discussed in Chapter III, Section 1. (*Ibid.*, pp. 193-94; Froelich, *Zehn Jahre*, p. 222; *Illustrierte Geschichte*, pp. 176-78.) For the text of the proclamation of the Reich Conference signed by the Spartacists and the Left Radicals, see *Ibid.*, pp. 176-78. There seems to be a difference of opinion as to when this conference took place. The *Illustrierte Geschichte* places it on October 1, 1918; however, most other sources such as the Spartacist Letter No. 12 give October 7, 1918, as the date.

[70] Bergstraesser, *op. cit.*, p. 182.

[71] Meinecke, *Die Revolution*, p. 100.

[72] Barth, *op. cit.*, pp. 15-16; *Illustrierte Geschichte*, pp. 140-42; Froelich, *Zehn Jahre*, pp. 151-53.

The extensive leaflet propaganda of the Spartacists was intended to familiarize the workers with the political concepts of the radical left. It also served to "enlighten" the people on how the Spartacists interpreted the war and the actions of competitive socialist organizations. Some of the leaflets used current, sharply-debated issues, such as the arrest of Liebknecht or a strike, as a point of departure for a discussion of political concepts.[73] After the Russian Revolution, Spartacist propaganda was further intensified, partly because of the material assistance given by the Bolsheviks.[74]

Spartacist participation in the revolutionary events in Germany was motivated and conditioned by ideological concepts. Those events began in 1915 on a very moderate scale and grew in frequency and intensity until they culminated in the November Revolution of 1918.[75] The first major work stoppage occurred

[73] For examples of Spartacist leaflets see: "2½ Jahre Zuchthaus" and "Aufruf zum Proteststreik" quoted in Froelich, *Zehn Jahre,* pp. 242-43. Rosa Luxemburg, "Was ist mit Liebknecht!" quoted in Luxemburg, *Ausgewaehlte Reden,* II, pp. 563-66. Rosa Luxemburg, "Wofuer kaempfte Liebknecht und weshalb wurde er zu Zuchthaus verurteilt?" quoted in Luxemburg, *Ausgewaehlte Reden,* II, pp. 572-80. Ernst Meyer, *Spartakus im Kriege* (Berlin: Vereinigung Internationaler Verlagsanstalten, 1927), contains a very extensive collection of these leaflets.

[74] Froelich, *Zehn Jahre,* pp. 189-92. For a thorough survey of Bolshevik propaganda disseminated with the assistance of German radical socialists, see E. Drahn and S. Leonard, *Unterirdische Literatur im revolutionaeren Deutschland waehrend des Weltkrieges* (Berlin: Verlag Gesellschaft u. Erziehung, 1920). Included in the Russian activity was a large-scale effort at frontline propaganda by means of newspapers and leaflets. (*Ibid.,* pp. 139-40.) The following are a few examples of this type of literature which reached Germany in considerable quantities: "Thesis about the socialist revolution and the missions of the proletariat during its dictatorship in Russia"; "The councils — the form of government of the workers"; "The bloody monster is dying. Kill it, you German workers, you German Soldiers." (*Ibid.,* pp. 151-58; 167-68; 171-77.) It is also noted that not all revolutionary propaganda from outside Germany came from Bolshevik Russia. The Western Allies resorted to revolutionary socialist propaganda in order to break down German resistance. (*Ibid.,* pp. 188-89.)

[75] Barth reported that as early as 1915 the workers in Berlin had discarded the idea of an economic truce for the duration. He believed that this development was significant because it placed the workers in opposition to their leadership. (Barth, *op. cit.,* p. 12.) In the course of 1915, there were several demonstrations against food shortages: in October the so-called "butter revolt" and in December the "potato unrest." (Froelich, *Zehn Jahre,* p. 185.)

in April 1917, when 300,000 workers went on strike in Berlin alone. The immediate cause was the reduction of the bread ration. The Spartacists tried to capitalize on this strike, formalizing the workers' demands and combining them in a leaflet with political demands:

1. The release of all political prisoners and persons kept in custody for political reasons as well as the abrogation of all political trials.
2. The end of the compulsory labor service law.
3. The end of the state of siege.
4. The restoration of unrestricted freedom of association, press, and assembly.
5. The creation of a representative body composed of delegates of all factories to direct the fight of the workers and to organize the working class in order to enforce peace and genuine political freedom.[76]

The next major revolutionary event in war-time Germany was the revolt of the German navy at Kiel in August 1917. The admiralty dealt most severely with the mutinous sailors. Their two ring leaders were executed. The Spartacists claimed that the sailors had maintained contact with members of the Group International even before Reichpietsch, one of the executed leaders, established liaison with the USPD.[77]

The largest German war-time strike occurred in January 1918. The struggle against the continuation of the war had become a genuine mass movement. In Vienna, a general strike had broken out on January 14. Workers' councils were elected which directed the strike operations. One week later, on January 28, the general strike of the Berlin armament industry started. Over

[76] *Illustrierte Geschichte*, p. 154.
[77] *Ibid.*, pp. 157-59. Professor Meinecke stated that the revolutionary impact of the USPD upon the sailors has not been proved. However, the Russian example and the tendency to lean toward the party with the most radical peace program were of influence. (Meinecke, *Die Revolution*, p. 104.)

500,000 workers participated in Berlin alone. The strike spread quickly to other industrial centers. The organizational preparation was chiefly in the hands of the Revolutionary Shop Stewards and the USPD.[78] The strike had two significant aspects. Politically, it was a protest against German policies in the peace negotiations in Brest-Litovsk and against the official attitude toward the peace feelers extended by the Western Allies. Secondly, the workers struck without consulting their union leaders, who found themselves in a difficult position. They wished to remain neutral but were afraid that they would thereby permanently lose their leadership to the USPD. Eventually union officials managed to take over the strike movement and to push the newly-formed workers' councils aside. The General Commission of the trade unions, however, refused to take part in it and declared its strict neutrality. The strike movement broke down, and by February 3, 1918, the government had the situation well in hand. Large numbers of strikers were drafted and sent to the front where they assisted in spreading defeatist propaganda among the soldiers.[79]

The masses of the German workers had proved that they could start a large-scale mass action without their traditional organizations. It was a demonstration of the changed attitude of the German people toward the war and everything connected with it. It is interesting to note, moreover, that the early resistance move-

---

[78] Flechtheim, op. cit., p. 25.

[79] Snell, op. cit., p. 73; Illustrierte Geschichte, pp. 160-63. In addition to the demands for an immediate peace without annexations and indemnities — as proposed by the Bolshevik peace delegation at Brest-Litovsk — the strikers also requested domestic political changes. For the text of the summons to the general strike, see Froelich, Zehn Jahre, pp. 245-46; and Stuemke, op. cit., pp. 72-73. These demands are similar to those made during the April strike of 1917. It is often asserted that one of the reasons why the strike failed so quickly was that the SPD participated in the strike command. As a matter of fact, Ebert later claimed that the SPD had entered the strike with the express purpose of ending the strike promptly. (Hermann Matern, "Die Politik der KPD und der SPD in der Zeit der Weimarer Republik" [Wissenschaftliche Beilage des Forum (Berlin)], Teil I [September 15, 1952], p. 3); Illustrierte Geschichte, p. 162. Also see Barth, op. cit., pp. 20-23 for an interesting account of the January strike, which could have been interpreted as a warning sign for coming events. (Noske, Erlebtes, p. 76.)

ment in Germany grew independently in form and content from the Russian Bolshevik ideas.[80]

The failure of the strike movement in January 1918 greatly impressed the Revolutionary Shop Stewards and certain leftist elements within the USPD with the fact that other means of class combat were required.[81]

By October, 1918, the revolutionary fermentation had become visible all over Germany. Demonstrations, stormy meetings, and political strikes showed the growing strength of the dissatisfied population and the declining power of the government forces.[82] General opposition to the war had not remained with the socialist workers alone. As early as 1917, the Catholic workers in various parts of Germany (e.g., the Ruhr and the Rhineland), who formed the bulk of the Center Party, had begun to conduct active propaganda for an immediate peace settlement.

The Spartacists did not agree with the conspiratorial preparation of the Revolutionary Shop Stewards. They did not share the belief that a handful of well-armed and well-disciplined revolutionaries could start a revolution. During the various meetings between the Spartacists and the Shop Stewards which occurred with greater frequency throughout 1918, the Spartacists declared themselves for mass actions. The Shop Stewards, in turn, accused the Spartacists of "revolutionary gymnastics."[83]

On the other hand, the Russian Revolution exerted both direct and indirect influences on later revolutionary developments in Germany. It set the pattern of the workers' and soldiers' councils as revolutionary agencies. It also encouraged the German strike movement which gradually changed its emphasis from economic to political issues.[84] Much has been written about the sup-

[80] Fischer, op. cit., p. 16.

[81] Berlau, op. cit., pp. 162-63. For information concerning the preparation for the revolution by the Revolutionary Shop Stewards, see Barth, op. cit., pp. 46-53.

[82] Illustrierte Geschichte, p. 181.

[83] Barth, op. cit., pp. 30, 36-40.

[84] Grotewohl, op. cit., pp. 65, 68. Walter Ulbricht, Zur Geschichte der deutschen Arbeiterbewegung (Berlin: Dietz Verlag, 1953), I, pp. 16-19. A study of the strikes which occurred during World War I was made by the German Labor Front of the Nazi government in 1943. This study examines

port given to the revolutionary groups by the Bolshevik ambassador in Berlin, A. A. Joffe. It appears that Joffe not only distributed revolutionary literature but also allotted considerable sums of money to the USPD.[85] He was formally expelled from Germany on November 5, 1918; he and his staff left the following

the number of strikes in the various industries and locales during the war. For example, in 1917 Berlin led with one-third of all strikers; in 1918, persons who participated in political strikes outnumbered those who engaged in economic strikes. (Arbeitswissenschaftliches Institut der Deutschen Arbeitsfront, *Die Streiks im 1. Weltkrieg 1914-1918* [Berlin: Deutsche Arbeitsfront, January, 1943].)

[85] Arthur Rosenberg. *A History of the German Republic* (London: Methuen & Co., 1936), p. 326; Eduard Bernstein, *Die deutsche Revolution* (Berlin: Verlag fuer Gesellschaft u. Erziehung, 1921), pp. 22-23. Diplomatic relations had been established under the Treaty of Brest-Litovsk. Louis Fischer admits that Joffe's mission was not merely diplomatic. More than ten Social Democratic newspapers were directed and supported by the Soviet embassy in Berlin. (Louis Fischer, *The Soviets in World Affairs* [Princeton: Princeton University Press, 1951], I, p. 75.) Fischer describes the activities of the Soviet Ambassador as follows: "The embassy bought information from officials in various German ministries and passed it on to radical leaders for use in Reichstag speeches, in workers' meetings and in the Press. Anti-war and anti-government literature was sent to all parts of the country and to the front. Tons of literature were printed and clandestinely distributed by Joffe's office. 'It is necessary to emphasize most categorically,' Joffe wrote in an almost unknown memorandum, 'that in the preparation of the German revolution, the Russian Embassy worked all the time in close contact with the German Socialists.' Leaders of the German Independents discussed most matters of revolutionary tactics with Joffe, who was an experienced conspirator. In a radio message, dated December 15, 1918, broadcast by Joffe to the revolutionary soviets of Germany, he admitted having paid 100,000 marks for the purchase of arms for the revolutionaries and announced that he had established in Germany a 10,000,000 ruble fund for the support of the revolution, which was entrusted to Oskar Cohn, a Socialist deputy." (*Ibid.*, pp. 75-76.) For the text of Joffe's radio message see Bernstein, *op. cit.*, p. 69.

Louis Fischer's information about Joffe's activities is partly based on a personal meeting with Joffe and about which Fischer reports in an earlier book.

"Lenin's envoy, Adolf A. Joffe, was new as a diplomat but experienced as a revolutionary, one of the founders of the Soviet regime. According to the cold official formula, he was *persona grata* to the German imperial government. Actually, he endeavored to overthrow it. . . . Years later he told me the story; it was in 1927 when Joffe was forty-four years old. Soviet developments had filled him with anguish and he had decided to commit suicide in demonstrative protest against Stalin's policies. Before he killed himself he asked me to come see him. I had never met him, and had not requested an appointment. But he sent me a message through a mutual friend. He wanted to talk to an outsider for the record. What he revealed was confirmed by his 1919 reports which he took from his files and showed me. His embassy in Berlin, he said, served as staff headquarters for a German revolution. . . . 'We wanted to pull

day.[86] After the November Revolution of 1918, the policy initiated by the Imperial government was continued for some time, and diplomatic relations with Moscow were not resumed until 1922.

down the monarchist state and end the war,' Joffe said to me. 'President Woodrow Wilson tried to do the same in his own way.' . . . 'In the end, however,' Joffe commented ruefully, 'they, we, accomplished little or nothing of permanent value. We were too weak to provoke a revolution.' "

(Louis Fischer, *Men and Politics. An Autobiography*. [New York: Duell, Sloan and Pearce, 1941], p. 26.)

[86] The immediate reason for the expulsion was the discovery of revolutionary literature in a case of diplomatic mail which was purposely broken open at the Friedrichstrasse railroad station in Berlin. The Austrian Social Democratic publication *Klassenkampf* described this incident nine years later, on December 1, 1927: "[the discovered revolutionary circulars] were neither written, nor printed, nor packed, nor dispatched from Russia. They were, in fact, inserted into the diplomatic box by the Imperial (German) police; they were written in Germany by Comrade Levi." Louis Fischer adds: "Many other statements tend to confirm the suspicion that, although Joffe was heavily laden with revolutionary guilt, these particular circulars in his diplomatic mail originated with the Prussian Police." (Louis Fischer, *op. cit.*, p. 77.)

The November Revolution and the Spartacists

The Impact of the November Revolution

1. *Failure of Parliamentarization, October 1918*

During the period immediately preceding the outbreak of the November Revolution of 1918, two major domestic developments took place within Germany. First, under the impact of the military reversals suffered by the German army and the continuous political and economic mismanagement of domestic affairs, large segments of the population became progressively discontented. The majority of the population, weary of the situation which became more hopeless from day to day, desired an immediate termination of hostilities. The masses were convinced that they could not trust their government to bring about the desired peace, since in the past the government had demonstrated its lack of responsiveness to the people's demands. For example, various political promises, such as the one pertaining to the antiquated Prussian election law, had never been fulfilled.[1] As discontentment grew, so did the desire of the masses to see the situation decisively altered, even if this involved the direct participation of the people.

The second important development during this period was caused by the sudden decision of the Imperial authorities to introduce significant changes in the prevailing governmental sys-

---

[1] Reich Chancellor Hertling had given his assurance to trade union leaders that he would stand or fall on the requested change of the Prussian election law. (Stuemke, *op. cit.*, p. 76.)

tem. These changes laid the basis for reforms which transformed Germany into a parliamentary monarchy similar to that in Britain. This action was a conscious attempt to ward off a revolt of the discontented masses by a "revolution from above," as this process was appropriately called by the German Foreign Secretary, Admiral von Hintze.[2]

Germany's military defeat had been accomplished and was so admitted by the two top military leaders, Hindenburg and Ludendorff. They succeeded in convincing the Emperor and von Hintze that two things had to be accomplished without delay: an immediate armistice and a change of the political system within Germany. Ludendorff, in particular, was convinced that the government of Hertling was not able to handle the storm expected from below. For all practical purposes, the government could assume one of two alternative forms: it could establish itself as a military dictatorship — a solution favored by the Conservative Party — or it could become a parliamentary government. The second alternative was adopted after Ludendorff strongly recommended it to the Emperor. Ludendorff believed that parliamentarization would necessarily broaden the popular base of the government and therefore would regain the unity and cooperation of the people so urgently needed to conduct the last phase of the war and the forthcoming peace negotiations. He also emphasized that a democratic form of government would stand a better chance of obtaining easier peace terms from the Allies.[3]

The Emperor accepted the resignation of Hertling and appointed Prince Max von Baden as the new Reich Chancellor. The

[2] Alfred Niemann, *Revolution von Oben — Umsturz von Unten* (Berlin: Verlag fuer Kulturpolitik, 1927), pp. 98ff.

[3] For information on the precarious military situation of Germany following the summer of 1918, see Rosenberg, *Entstehung,* pp. 220-22, and Prinz Max von Baden, *Erinnerungen und Dokumente* (Berlin: Deutsche Verlags-anstalt, 1927), pp. 283-88. The Conservative Party proposed the establishment of a military dictatorship under a General. (Bergstraesser, *op. cit.,* p. 198.) For a discussion of the decision concerning the parliamentarization of the Imperial government, see Rosenberg, *Entstehung*, pp. 226-29, and Stuemke, *op. cit.,* pp. 76-79.

latter enjoyed a reputation of liberal-democratic leanings and was acceptable to liberals and socialists whose cooperation would be needed by the new government.[4] Thus, the first parliamentary government in Germany was, as Rosenberg correctly pointed out, not an achievement of the Reichstag, but the result of a "command" by Ludendorff.[5]

In order for the revolution from above to achieve its first major objective — the broadening of the base of government — it was essential to secure the cooperation of the Majority Socialists. Prince Max made as a condition for his acceptance of the position of Reich Chancellor that the Majority Socialists join his cabinet.[6]

The SPD was not unprepared for this occasion. As early as September 23, 1918, foreseeing the coming crisis of the Hertling government, the SPD Reichstag faction and the Party Committee had met and decided in favor of participating in a future German government, provided that this government would incorporate a number of SPD demands in its platform.[7] Prince Max agreed to

[4] Halperin, *op. cit.,* pp. 56-57. The letter from the Emperor accepting Hertling's resignation contained the following statement which laid the groundwork for the coming parliamentarization: "It is my wish that the German people participate more effectively than heretofore in determining the fate of the Fatherland. It is therefore my will that men who enjoy the confidence of the nation should partake extensively of the rights and duties of government." (*Ibid.,* p. 56.)

[5] Rosenberg, *Entstehung,* p. 227.

[6] Hermann Mueller, *Die November Revolution* (2d ed.; Berlin: Verlag Der Buecherkreis, 1931), pp. 9-10; Stuemke, *op. cit.,* p. 87.

[7] Hermann Mueller, *op. cit.,* pp. 10-11. Some of the Majority Socialist leaders believed that it would be a tactical mistake to join a bourgeois government which most likely would become the caretaker government for the defeated nation. However, Friedrich Ebert, the leader of the SPD, declared prior to the vote on this issue: "If, at this time, you do not wish to come to an agreement with the bourgeois parties and with the government, then we are forced to let matters take their own course. Then we will resort to revolutionary tactics, depend solely upon ourselves, and leave the fate of the party to the outcome of the revolution. Whoever saw what happened in Russia cannot, in the interest of the proletariat, wish to see the same development here. On the contrary, we must throw ourselves into the gap. If it is possible for us to obtain sufficient influence to carry out our demands and also to combine them with the salvation of our country, then it is our damned duty to do it." (Froelich, *Zehn Jahre,* p. 220.) Also see the discussion in Berlau, *op. cit.,* pp. 198-202 pertaining to the SPD views concerning participation in a coalition government prior to the November Revolution. The demands of the Majority Socialists which were formulated on September 23, 1918, are discussed in Prinz Max, *op. cit.,* pp. 321-322.

these demands, and, on October 4, 1918, the Majority Socialists formed a coalition government with the Progressives, the Center, and the National Liberals. The SPD sent Philip Scheidemann and Gustav Bauer, the deputy chairman of the General Commission of the Trade Unions, as their representatives to the cabinet.[8]

Neither Prince Max nor the SPD realized the gravity of the military situation. The Supreme Command had even prepared for the new Chancellor the wording of the request for an armistice.[9]

Therefore, the new government was faced from the beginning with the two difficult problems of effecting an armistice and of accomplishing domestic political reforms. On the day the coalition government was formed, Prince Max forwarded a message to President Wilson, formally accepting the latter's Fourteen Points as the basis for peace negotiations and requesting the armistice as demanded by Ludendorff.[10] Supported by the deputies of the political parties in his coalition, Prince Max set about to accomplish the promised democratic reforms. The reform work commenced on October 8, 1918, and was completed by October 26. The new constitution came into force on October 28, 1918. On that day, Germany became a parliamentary monarchy. Only a few powers remained with the Emperor. The Reich Chancellor became responsible to both houses of parliament (the Reichstag and the *Bundesrat* [Federal Council]),

---

[8] Stuemke, *op. cit.*, p. 87. When the Majority Socialists entered the Government of Prince Max, they demanded, possibly for tactical reasons, that all members of the USPD who were in prison for their radical activities be released. This demand included Liebknecht. (*Ibid.*, p. 101.) The *Vorwaerts* announced shortly and confidently after the coalition government was formed: "The aim of a German democracy will be reached within a short time by means of a peaceful change." (*Illustrierte Geschichte*, p. 172.)

[9] Prinz Max, *op. cit.*, pp. 335-52. Hermann Mueller even doubts that the majority of the SPD leaders would have agreed to the entry of Majority Socialists into the cabinet of Prince Max if they had known how hopeless the military situation was at the end of September, 1918. (Hermann Mueller, *op. cit.*, p. 12.)

[10] Prinz Max, *op. cit.*, pp. 353-509. Prince Max's account of the long exchange of notes between his government and that of the United States is most detailed. His statements concerning the change of the German Constitution is unfortunately extremely brief.

and the military became subordinate to the civilian authorities. On October 27, 1918, Prince Max notified the President of the United States that peace negotiations could now be conducted by a genuine representative government of the German people.[11]

The period immediately preceding the November Revolution witnessed another important event: the development of the SPD into a government party. The entrance of the Majority Socialists as a minority into a bourgeois coalition government headed by a prince can be interpreted as the culmination of the reformist policies pursued by the party throughout the war. The official SPD explanation for this step — that the crisis situation of the German nation required the cooperation of all Germans regardless of party and class — does not change the fact that the Majority Socialists had become a party which participated in the formulation and execution of governmental policies at the highest level.[12]

The SPD, like the other parties represented in the cabinet of Prince Max, had a proprietary interest in the perpetuation of the state organization they helped to create. An evaluation of the

[11] Rosenberg, *Entstehung*, pp. 232-34; Stuemke, *op. cit.*, p. 100.

[12] On October 18, 1918, the following pronouncement of the Executive Committee of the SPD appeared in the *Vorwaerts*:

"At the present time, the situation of our country is extremely serious. The South-East Front has collapsed and on the West Front the mass armies of the Allies . . . storm against our troops with tremendous superiority in manpower and material.

"Germany and the German people are in danger of becoming the victims of the English-French chauvinists' thirst for conquest and of the conquest politicians.

"We have declared on August 4, 1914: 'In the hour of danger we do not leave our fatherland in the lurch' [and that promise] is even more valid today. . . ." (Quoted in Prinz Max, *op. cit.*, p. 451.) Noske stated in his Reichs-tag speech of October 25, 1918: "At the moment we consider the collaboration of the Social Democrats in the government as an emergency action. The people and the country are in the greatest danger. We intend to prevent total collapse by mustering all our strength. We wish to prevent the Germans from fighting against Germans, while the country is being attacked from outside." (Bernstein, *op. cit.*, p. 58.) An illustration of the acceptability of the SPD leaders even by the Emperor after they had joined the coalition government of Prince Max is an alleged statement by the Emperor to the Reich Chancellor: "I would also like to work together with Mr. Ebert. . . . I have absolutely nothing against the Social Democracy, only the name, you know, the name should be changed." (*Illustrierte Geschichte*, p. 171.)

subsequent actions of the SPD must make proper allowances for this fact.

The parties of the coalition were justified in considering October 1918 as the month in which they achieved most of the political objectives which the majority of the German people had been demanding. By the end of October the cessation of hostilities was expected in a matter of days. Traditional military interference in domestic affairs had been removed. Ludendorff had fled the country. The military leaders were divested of their former authority and had been placed under the supervision of the Reichstag. The new election law for Prussia was assured. A general amnesty had liberated many political prisoners, among them Karl Liebknecht.[13]

However, there remained an opposition to the policies of the Reichstag majority: the die-hard Conservatives on the right and the USPD and Spartacist League on the left, which was unalterably opposed to any bourgeois government because of their strong conviction concerning the socialist state. Thus, the revolution against the coalition government could have originated only from these oppositional elements of the right or left. However, since these forces were in a relatively small minority, their revolutionary attempts could have been defeated by the great masses of the middle class and workers who were represented in the coalition government and who had just experienced the realization of their immediate political aims.

Nevertheless, a nation-wide revolution did occur. The very masses which one could have expected to stand behind the political parties of the coalition government, revolted. Unconsciously, they revolted against their own government. For this reason, Rosenberg calls the November Revolution the most amazing of all revolutions.[14] What were the reasons or the motivating forces

---

[13] Liebknecht was released on October 23. Rosa Luxemburg was not affected by the amnesty because she was not a political prisoner at that time. She was held in "protective custody." She was not freed until November 9, 1918, as a result of the revolution. (Froelich, *Rosa Luxemburg,* pp. 303, 305.)

[14] Rosenberg, *Entstehung,* p. 238.

which caused the revolutionary events of November 1918? Several explanations have been offered.[15] Numerous accounts permit the conclusion that, during the month of October 1918, revolutionary propaganda had been intensified but had remained concentrated in Berlin and in the major industrial centers where the radical wing of the USPD and the Spartacists already had their greatest influence.[16]

Revolutionary activities had received impetus and direction from the Reich Conference of the Spartacists and Left Radicals which met on October 7, 1918.[17] The delegates to that conference decided that in view of the situation, created by the growing revolutionary attitude of the masses and by the attempted deception of the people through the parliamentarization process of the government, the German proletariat must fight for the following:

(1) Immediate release of all persons who because of their fight for the interests of the proletariat are suffering in prisons and jails, in protective custody or serving a sentence. . . .

(2) Immediate abrogation of the state of siege.

(3) Immediate cancellation of the compulsory labor law.

Beyond these, the proletariat must request:

(1) Annulment of all war loans without compensation.

(2) Expropriation of the entire bank capital, mines and foundries; substantial reduction of working hours, establishment of minimum wages.

(3) Expropriation of all large estates and middle-sized estates. Transfer of the direction of production to the delegates of agricultural workers and small farmers.

[15] At this point, the validity of the claim that revolutionary activities conducted by the left radical organizations caused the revolution will be evaluated. For a discussion of the causes and driving forces of the November Revolution see Chapter III, Section 2.

[16] See, for example, the extract of the *Tagebuch eines Spartakisten* by Fritz Rueck which contains interesting details about the propaganda work in Stuttgart during October and November, 1918. (*Illustrierte Geschichte*, pp. 182-84.) Rueck also refers to the public meetings which could have been the result of the relaxed domestic policies of the coalition government.

[17] See above, p. 59.

(4) Decisive changes in military affairs, such as:

   a. Granting to soldiers the right of free association and assembly for matters pertaining to official and non-official business.

   b. Abrogation of the right of military superiors to discipline subordinates; discipline will be maintained by soldier delegates.

   c. Abrogation of courts-martial.

   d. Transfer of military superiors by majority decision of the subordinates.

(5) Transfer of the distribution of food to representatives of the workers.

(6) Abolition of individual states and dynasties.

Proletarians, the achievement of these demands does not mean the realization of your aims; this is only the acid test to determine if the democratization which the ruling classes and their agents are telling you about is genuine. The struggle for real democratization does not revolve around parliament, election law or ministers who can simultaneously retain their deputy status in the Reichstag, and other swindles; [the fight] is directed against the real foundation of all enemies of the people: ownership of landed property and capital, control over the armed forces and over the judiciary. . . .[18]

In the intensified propaganda carried out by leaflets, newspapers, workers' meetings, and word of mouth, the Spartacists emphasized more and more the necessity of creating workers' and soldiers' councils as the only type of revolutionary agencies which could serve the interest of the proletariat. In a number of locations, they succeeded in establishing these councils. The Spartacists' demands were directed increasingly toward the transfer of political power from the bourgeois government to revolutionary institutions. For example, in the first issue of *Die Rote Fahne* (The Red Flag) published on November 5, 1918, in Stutt-

---

[18] *Illustrierte Geschichte,* pp. 177-78. Froelich attached so much significance to the Reich Conference of the Spartacists and Left Radicals that he called it the "War Council of the Revolution." (Froelich, *Rosa Luxemburg,* p. 302.)

gart, the Workers' and Soldiers' Council of Stuttgart demanded an immediate armistice and peace to be obtained through the offices of the representatives of the proletariat. The Council also requested the resignation of the Emperor and of other dynasties, the dissolution of all legislative bodies in Germany, including the Reichstag, and the transfer of all power to an assembly composed of the elected representatives of the workers, soldiers, small farmers, and agricultural laborers.[19]

In addition to the propaganda activities carried out by the left wing radical elements, the Revolutionary Shop Stewards also increased their conspiratorial preparation for their planned revolution. They even succeeded in extending their system of confidence men to the military barracks in Berlin. Beginning on November 1, 1918, the Shop Stewards held meetings at which they discussed the day they would "make" the revolution. Liebknecht and Wilhelm Pieck, who represented the Spartacists at these meetings, and a number of USPD functionaries could not agree with the proposal of the Shop Stewards. The USPD wanted to postpone the revolution until after peace had been assured. Liebknecht proposed revolutionary mass actions. The Shop Stewards themselves were divided as to the starting date of the revolution. Their radical elements such as Barth, Daeumig, and Ledebour wanted to set the date for November 4, while Richard Mueller, who represented the moderates among the Shop Stewards, opted for November 11. Only the Shop Stewards were entitled to vote on this issue. A vote of 21 to 19 set the beginning of the revolution on November 11. However, because of the revolutionary events in Kiel and the fact that a number of Revolutionary Shop Stewards were arrested in the midst of their preparatory work, Barth believed himself to be the only leader of the conspirators left on November 8. He called a meeting of the heads of his assault units, temporarily assumed dictatorial powers, and proposed that the revolution begin the next day. None of the per-

---

[19] *Illustrierte Geschichte,* p. 183.

sons present disagreed, and Barth took this as a sign of approval. The next day was November 9, 1918.[20]

There is rather general agreement that neither the revolutionary preparations of the Shop Stewards nor the revolutionary propaganda conducted by the Spartacists had any significance in the developments which led to the revolt in Kiel and from there throughout Germany until it reached the capital on November 9, 1918. Berlau correctly summarizes this aspect of the German Revolution as follows:

. . . The chronological sequence of revolutionary preparation and the event of the revolution is not identical with causality. No causal relation can in fact exist where the actual revolution took place under certain crucial conditions which were outside the control of the groups carrying on the revolutionary activity, and which could not have been foreseen by them.[21]

It has also been argued that if the radical movement had been the decisive element, the revolution would have started in Berlin where preparations had been made. In fact, the capital fell after the revolution had been victorious throughout Germany. The revolt in Kiel which started the revolution was without a leader until Noske was sent there from Berlin.[22]

---

[20] Barth, *op. cit.,* pp. 46-53; Froelich, *Rosa Luxemburg,* pp. 304-05; Richard Mueller, *Vom Kaiserreich,* pp. 138-42; Volkmann, *Der Marxismus,* pp. 206-13. The Majority Socialists did not participate in any revolutionary preparation or propaganda activities. August Mueller, an SPD leader, claimed that he was thoroughly acquainted with the aims of the SPD during the period preceding the fall of the old regime. He declared emphatically that the SPD carried on absolutely no propaganda among the soldiers, did not advocate force, did not participate in the arming of the workers or in any other action which prepares for an uprising. The SPD did nothing to bring about the fall of the government and considered itself completely innocent in regard to revolutionary events. (August Mueller, *Sozialisierung oder Sozialismus?* [Berlin: Verlag Ullstein, 1919], pp. 27-28.) On the contrary, the SPD attempted to use its influence to pacify the workers as many newspaper articles, wall posters, and leaflets indicate. See, for example, *Illustrierte Geschichte,* p. 181. Cf. Rosa Luxemburg's critique on the SPD actions in the Spartacist Letter No. 12, *Spartakusbriefe,* pp. 193-94.

[21] Berlau, *op. cit.,* p. 166.

[22] *Ibid.,* p. 167; Stuemke, *op. cit.,* p. 128; Bergstraesser, *op. cit.,* p. 199.

2. *The November Revolution in the Reich*

The coalition government of Prince Max could have expected the support of the majority of the German people provided the parties which were represented in his government had retained their influence among the electorate. Popular support of the government did not materialize because the people were not convinced that a genuine change in the governmental system had taken place.[23] The fundamental changes in the domestic political situation remained unnoticed by the masses in spite of the fact that many of their demands had been fulfilled or were in the process of being carried out.[24] The attitude of the people toward the new coalition cabinet was the product of several political and psychological factors: (1) The complete confidence of the German people in their military leaders and Supreme Command suddenly vanished under the impact of the military defeat, producing a severe, national shock. The negative sentiments toward the military were transferred to the civilian governmental authorities. Not only the workers but also the middle class and the civil servants lost their confidence in the government and therefore were psychologically unprepared to come to the defense of the old ruling group. (2) For over four years the people had been

Erich Wollenberg is of the same opinion. He wrote: "The revolution which broke out in November, 1918 had only very little in common with the conspiratorial activity [of the Shop Stewards and other left wing radicals]. Imperial Germany broke down under the impact of military defeat which led to a mass revolt of the workers and farmers in uniform. When millions of people march in the streets, storm military barracks and governmental buildings, one cannot do much with a few hundred pistols and a few dozen rifles which were in the secret weapon depots of the conspirators." (Erich Wollenberg, "Der Apparat — Stalins Fuenfte Kolonne," *Ost-Probleme,* 3. Jahrgang, No. 12 [1951], p. 575.) Professor Mei-

necke believed that the influence of propaganda from the radical left began to have some effect after the external conditions, i.e., the conviction that a military victory was impossible, favored the reception of those ideas. However, he thought that the socialist parties contributed more to the revolution through what they represented than what they actually did. (Meinecke, *Die Revolution,* p. 111.)

[23] The diplomatic exchange of notes between the German and United States governments during October, 1918 indicated that the Entente also was not convinced of the basic constitutional changes in Germany.

[24] Tormin, *op. cit.,* p. 54.

totaliy absorbed with the activities of their nation. They had identified themselves intimately and personally with the fate of the state, and had willingly accepted and endured great hardships in its interest. The realization of military defeat drove home the fact that all their sacrifices were in vain. This conviction caused the violent reaction of demanding the immediate termination of hostilities and the removal of any obstacle in the way of peace. The people wanted peace.[25] (3) Until the beginning of the war, the workers' organizations in Germany had been in continuous opposition to the state, and in turn had been distrusted by the government. This mutual lack of confidence had changed during the war, although no closer relations between the workers and the old German state had resulted. In addition to the recognition of military defeat and the conviction that the workers had been deceived, the traditional distrust of the workers toward governmental authorities returned. (4) the firm refusal of the government to carry out domestic political reforms during the war gradually alienated the workers. Reforms could have demonstrated that the workers were a part of the nation with civil and political rights equal to those of other social classes. When political reforms finally were introduced, they came too late. The revolutionary fermentation had by then progressed too far and the government had become politically isolated from the masses.[26]

The government not only failed to convince the masses of the great political changes which had taken place, but it actually aggravated the situation by making numerous mistakes. The enumeration of constitutional achievements in the press and in proclamations alone did not suffice to prove to the people that political transformation had occurred. The masses could be impressed

[25] Hermann Mueller, op. cit., p. 16; Konrad Haenisch, "Die Ursachen der deutschen Revolution," Handbuch der Politik (Berlin: W. Rothschild, 1920), II, pp. 256-57.

[26] Ibid., pp. 257-58. Konrad Haenisch, who later in 1918 became the Prussian Minister for Education and a leading SPD official, was convinced that a timely modernization of the German constitutional system would have brought an organic evolution instead of a forceful revolution.

only by actions which would bear out these claims. The people saw only that Count Hertling, the Reich Chancellor, had been replaced by a prince. Vice-Chancellor von Payer and the Prussian ministers remained in office. The Minister of War was a general as in the past. No apparent changes had been made in either the army or navy. The successor of Ludendorff was General Groener who was hated by the Berlin workers from the time of the strike in the armament industry because of his rigorous actions which were evaluated by most of the Socialists as "labor-hostile" and not merely the acts of a policeman maintaining order. Matters which the people could observe daily had changed little. The state of siege was not abolished and censorship and political restrictions continued as before. In the Prussian provinces and in the constituent states, the commanding generals were still the highest authorities. In Berlin, the commanding general was von Linsingen, who continued to control domestic affairs, pass ordinances, prohibit workers' meetings, order arrests, and apply censorship regulations to the press until November 9, 1918.[27]

Considering the ill effects of these aspects of the rule by the "people's government" upon the population and especially the workers, one might conclude that it was a mistake to continue the state of siege with all its restrictive provisions. It is also difficult to understand why the new government permitted the long adjournments of the Reichstag during this transitional period. A Reichstag in permanent session would have added power to the cabinet's position.[28]

[27] Hermann Mueller, who was known as a moderate Social Democrat, refers to the political rule by these commanding generals, who implemented the provisions of the state of siege, as military dictatorship. (Hermann Mueller, *op. cit.*, p. 15.) An example of the method used by the commanding general of the Greater Berlin District, General von Linsingen, is the following official announcement, dated Berlin, November 7, 1918: "Following the Russian example, certain circles intend to create workers' and soldiers' councils in violation of the law.

"These institutions are in contradiction to the existing State institutions and constitute a threat to public safety.

"By authority of paragraph 9b of the Law Concerning the State of Siege, I, herewith, prohibit the organization of such associations and participation in them."

(Froelich, *Zehn Jahre,* p. 224.)

[28] After the coalition cabinet was formed, the Reichstag adjourned from

Thus, the masses were not encouraged to expect radical changes in the prevailing domestic conditions. In regard to the termination of the war, the conviction developed that the people must take matters into their own hands the same as during the great strikes in January of the same year.[29]

"Germany was like a powder-keg — one spark was needed to set off the explosion."[30] The revolt of the sailors in Kiel in the first days of November 1918 provided this spark. In spite of the peace offers made by the government of Prince Max, the German Naval Command assembled the German fleet in late October for an operation against the British ships off the coast of Flanders. The naval command officers decided to die fighting rather than surrender the fleet. The sailors' revolt climaxed their refusal to participate in this futile and costly military gesture. A general strike of the workers in Kiel came in support of the mutinous sailors. On November 4, the elected workers' and soldiers' councils seized political power from the officials of the imperial regime who offered very little resistance.[31] The Majority Socialists still

October 5 to October 22; and again after the passing of the constitutional changes, it adjourned from October 26 until November 9. (Rosenberg, *Die Entstehung*, pp. 239-42.)

[29] Bergstraesser believed that the government had lost confidence in itself in view of imminent military defeat. (Bergstraesser, *op. cit.*, p. 199.)

Troeltsch blames Prussian militarism as one of the most significant contributory factors in the formation of the revolutionary attitude from below. He suggests that the development of militarism into a dominant political institution was one of the main reasons for the lack of flexibility of the entire Imperial system and its resistance to democratization. When reforms were finally initiated to counteract the increased pressure from below, it was too late to stop the growing revolutionary sentiments. (Ernst Troeltsch, *Spektator-Briefe* [Tuebingen: Verlag J.C.B. Mohr, 1924], pp. 1-12.)

Wilhelm Keil's description of the situation in Wuerttemberg at the end of October, 1918 is a good example for this period which was characterized by an increase in revolutionary mass action. (Wilhelm Keil, *Erlebnisse eines Sozialdemokraten* [Stuttgart: Deutsche Verlags-Anstalt, 1948], II, pp. 27-40.)

[30] Richard Mueller, *Vom Kaiserreich*, p. 134.

[31] Harry R. Rudin, *Armistice 1918*, pp. 246-54; Rosenberg, *Die Entstehung*, pp. 249-50; Bernstein, *op. cit.*, pp. 14-16; Noske, *Erlebtes*, pp. 8-54; Prinz Max, *op. cit.*, pp. 572-79 and 584-88; *Das Werk des Untersuchungsausschusses der Verfassunggebenden Deutschen Nationalversammlung und des Deutschen Reichstages 1919-1928* (Berlin: Deutsche Verlagsgesellschaft fuer Kultur u. Geschichte, 1928), X, pp. 198-207 and 282-315.

remained strictly opposed to the revolutionary actions in Kiel; they believed that a revolution in Germany would be a great misfortune.[32] The coalition government sent the Social Democratic Reichstag deputy Gustav Noske and the leading member of the Democratic Party, Secretary of State Conrad Haussmann to Kiel to re-establish order and to prevent the spread of the movement. But it was too late. The military revolution spread rapidly throughout Germany. On November 5, it had reached Hamburg; on the following day, general strikes started in Bremen and Luebeck. Newly formed workers' and soldiers' councils assumed political power everywhere and encountered no real resistance.

The revolutionary movement spread like a fire out of control. Dresden, Leipzig, Chemnitz, Magdeburg, Brunswick, Frankfurt, Cologne, Duesseldorf, Hanover, Nuremberg, and Stuttgart were in the hands of workers' and soldiers' councils on November 7 and 8. Everywhere the revolution took place without serious fighting. The police and military authorities surrendered without resisting and the bourgeoisie, who seemed paralyzed with fear, remained idle in the face of events. In Munich the movement went beyond [the scope of the revolution elsewhere] under the leadership of Kurt Eisner. During the night of November 7-8, the dynasty of the Wittelsbach was disposed of, the republic proclaimed, and the Workers', Soldiers', and Peasants' Council installed.[33]

The revolution, however, could not be regarded as complete so long as the central imperial authorities had not been replaced by revolutionary institutions. On November 9, the revolution finally reached Berlin.[34] The rapid spread of the revolution, its uniform organizational pattern, and the orderly nature of the

[32] Troeltsch, op. cit., p. 14.

[33] Prinz Max, op. cit., p. 137; Gustav Noske, Von Kiel bis Kapp (Berlin: Verlag fuer Politik u. Wirtschaft, 1920), pp. 8-50. For a detailed account of the revolutionary events during the period from November 4 to 9, see Hermann Mueller, op. cit., pp. 23-41. See also Illustrierte Geschichte, pp. 190-94.

[34] Ulbricht believed that Berlin was "behind schedule" because of the concentration of imperial forces in the capital. He also believed that the Majority Socialists were more effective in Berlin than elsewhere in delaying the outbreak of the mass uprising. (Ulbricht, Zur Geschichte, p. 24.)

transfer of political and military powers might lead to the conviction that it was a centrally directed and controlled mass operation. In reality, the opposite was the case. It was a spontaneous mass movement lacking any central leadership. Its systematic creation of workers' and soldiers' councils which took possession of the executive power everywhere did not follow any pre-conceived plans.[35] The Spartacists and radicals of the left wing of the USPD would have liked to superimpose their revolutionary concepts on the mass movement during the initial phase of the revolution, but their influence was as negligible then as it was during the period immediately preceding the revolution, with the exception of a few localities. The position of the Majority Socialists, who might have been the only party with a sufficiently large following to bring about a mass uprising, was a matter of record. The SPD was a government party and remained absolutely opposed to revolutionary methods. After it had failed to prevent the outbreak of the revolution, its leaders did everything possible to re-establish law and order quickly.[36] Grzesinski, who held a leading party position in Kassel, summed up the situation as follows:

Sheer absurdity to assume, as has so often been claimed, that the revolution of 1918 had been carefully planned! No agreement whatsoever existed between the leaders of the Social Democracy and of the trade-unions regarding the proper procedure to be followed. Nothing was prepared. Everything happened unexpectedly. Not even the leaders of the Social Democracy, the most advanced political movement of Germany, had thought of an overthrow of the entire governing

[35] Berlau, op. cit., p. 193; Flechtheim, op. cit., p. 33.

[36] For example, in a proclamation of the Executive Committee of the SPD dated November 4, 1918, the party pleaded with the workers not to undertake rash actions. (Richard Mueller, Vom Kaiserreich, pp. 218-19.) Prince Max wrote in his memoirs: "Day after day, the 'Vorwaerts' pleaded with the workers not to be drawn into revolts." (Prinz Max, op. cit., p. 569.) Also see a leaflet addressed to the sailors and workers prepared by the Vorwaerts and signed by Prince Max as Reich Chancellor, Philip Scheidemann, as Secretary of State, and Ritter von Mann, as Secretary of State in charge of naval affairs. (Ibid., pp. 572-73.)

system and of its replacement by a democratic republic. In truth they had not even desired it.[37]

The lack of political leadership also explains the vague and minor part political demands played during the mass uprising, a fact which Communist interpreters of the events completely disregard. The German Revolution was definitely not inspired by socialist ideas. As has been pointed out before, its purpose was to secure peace; only as a secondary issue was it ready to destroy those institutions which were regarded as obstacles to the realization of its primary goal. Gradually, the masses came to believe that the Emperor himself was one of the main obstructions and, therefore, must be removed.[38] A proclamation of the Workers' and Soldiers' Council at Kiel, dated November 7, 1918, clarified its aims as follows: "Our aim is a free, social people's republic. . . . Our main task is to secure peace and to make up for the damages inflicted by the war."[39] As seen in this light, the German Revolution assumes the character of a military revolt of sailors and soldiers, who, under the impact of the military defeat, seized the initiative in order to terminate the war.[40]

The German Revolution was strangely enough a very orderly process. As soon as the workers' and soldiers' councils had established themselves in place of the former imperial authorities, they used their power to re-establish and maintain law and order. The Soldiers' Council of Luebeck announced on November 5, 1918:

. . . the power in Luebeck is in our hands. . . . It had become necessary to clean up the corrupt conditions and remove the military dic-

[37] Grzesinski, op. cit., p. 49.
[38] Prince Max remarked about the demands of the revolting sailors:
"Only a minor part of the demands of the people were of a political nature. They requested right of assembly, permission to receive all newspapers, abolition of the duty to salute superior ranks when not on duty, same rations [for officers and enlisted personnel], and a revision of the penal order . . ." (Prinz Max, op. cit., p. 603.)

[39] Hermann Mueller, op. cit., pp. 37-38.

[40] Troeltsch, op. cit., p. 26. "The break-down of October and November was in a sense a general strike of a hopelessly defeated army against the madness of its leaders." (John W. Wheeler-Bennett, The Nemesis of Power [London: MacMillan, 1953], p. 15.)

tatorship of yesterday. The purpose of our action is immediate armistice and peace. We shall not interfere with the organs in charge of maintaining order. Everything will continue in its usual manner. We are expecting the co-operation of the population of Luebeck. Military authority was transferred without bloodshed, and we hope this will continue. We give warning that rioting, plundering, and robbery will be punished by death. The distribution of food remains the task of the civil administration.[41]

[41] Bernstein, *op. cit.,* p. 17. The Workers' and Soldiers' Council of the town of Stendal publicly announced that "The council accepts its obligation to maintain law and order." (Hermann Mueller, *op. cit.,* p. 40.) The orderliness of the transfer of power in Kassel is also the *leitmotif* of Grzesinski's description of the November events. Because of the lack of an overall plan and in the absence of any directives from SPD leadership, the local party functionaries were forced to use their own initiative. A workers' and soldiers' council was also formed in Kassel. It was composed of 600 delegates, half of them representing the SPD, USPD, and trade unions and the second half comprised of soldiers' delegates. The workers' and soldiers' council was intended to function as the law-making body. A Workers' and Soldiers' Committee with Grzesinski as chairman was formed as its executive organ. SPD and USPD shared on an equal basis the responsibilities in the revolutionary d i s t r i c t government. (Grzesinski, *op. cit.,* pp. 49-52.)

Also see Keil, *op. cit.,* pp. 84-122 for an account of the peaceful changes in Wuerttemberg. A provisional coalition government was formed there which, beginning with November 11, even included members from the bourgeois parties. There was also a workers' and soldiers' council in existence. However, the Provisional government did not give much attention to its activities.

See also the description of the November events in Bielefeld by Carl Severing. Severing suggested the name "People's and Soldiers' Council" for the new revolutionary administrative body in order to indicate dedication to democratic principles and negation of the dictatorship of the proletariat. Severing also stated that the new revolutionary agency did not create difficulties for the regular administrative offices. All civil servants remained in office. The People's and Soldiers' Council acted less as an administrative agency than as a controlling or supervisory authority. (Carl Severing, *Mein Lebensweg* [Koeln: Greven Verlag, 1950], I, pp. 225-29.

A recent evaluation of the character of the councils was made by Walter Kleen, the director of the Special School (*Sonderschule*) "Rosa Luxemburg" of the Socialist Unity Party SED located at Erfurt. Kleen also supports the concept that the councils were not socialistic institutions inspired with revolutionary zeal. Based on a study of documentary records of the council of Erfurt and that of Arnstadt and vicinity, Kleen comes to the conclusion that the councils were "power instruments of the bourgeoisie." He contends that the nature of the councils, except in some localities such as Leuna, was due to the "destructive and effective influence of the Right-wing leaders of the Social Democracy, which expressed itself among the workers and soldiers particularly in their parliamentary illusions as well as in the lack of a leader of the revolution in the form of a Marxist-Leninist workers' party." The documents used by Kleen prove indeed that the workers' and

3. The November Revolution in Berlin

The revolutionary attitude of the masses in Berlin was the product of the same factors which created the movement elsewhere in Germany. But two further aspects lent additional significance to revolutionary developments there. In the first place, Berlin occupied a unique position as the capital and the seat of the central government of Germany; secondly, each of the socialist parties and groups made a concentrated effort in Berlin to utilize the spontaneous mass movement for the realization of its specific political aim.

The left wing radicals were not able to "make" a revolution in Berlin any more readily than elsewhere. The opponents of the revolution recognized that there was a good chance that the Spartacists, Revolutionary Shop Stewards, and leftist elements of the USPD might succeed in supplying leadership to the rebellious masses and subsequently might be able to drive the revolution further. The forces opposing the revolution were comprised not only of the bourgeois political parties, the military leaders, and the governmental officials, but also of the leaders of the Majority Socialists. The SPD was the only one of the opponents to the revolution which could claim a large following among the masses which had already been seized by the revolutionary fever. The Majority Socialist leaders soon realized that if they openly opposed the demands of the masses or remained neutral, they would most certainly alienate the people. Thus, after some initial hesitation, the leaders of the SPD in Berlin decided to attempt to bring the mass movement under their control in order to prevent the radicals on the left from using it to bring about their avowed aim, the socialist republic. This decision was the outcome of

soldiers' councils of Erfurt and Arnstadt and vicinity were not socialist but considered themselves as temporary authorities with the important task on their hands of keeping peace and order until the still to be elected National Assembly would take over legitimately political control. (Walter Kleen, "Ueber die Rolle der Raete in der Novemberrevolution," *Zeitschrift fuer Geschichtswissenschaft,* 4. Jahrgang, Heft 2 [Berlin, Soviet Sector, 1956], pp. 326-31.)

lengthy deliberations among the leaders of the Executive Committee of the party and of the Reichstag faction; it was considered
the best way out of the dilemma in which the party found itself
as the result of the spontaneous uprising. On the one hand, the
SPD was a party of the coalition cabinet and therefore was expected to defend the political *status quo* which, according to the
sincere conviction of the Majority Socialist leaders, contained all
the possibilities of transforming Germany into a genuine democratic system under a monarch. Furthermore, the party had em-
braced ideological reform concepts which were opposed to the use
of violence and force in domestic politics. On the other hand,
inaction would mean the surrender of the people to the exclusive
influence of the left wing radical elements. Thus, the Majority
Socialists made themselves the spokesmen for the masses, adopt-
ing their demand for the abdication of the Emperor and the Crown
Prince.[42] From this moment on, the history of the German Revolution assumed the character of a tug-of-war among the socialist
parties and groups fighting for control over the masses.

The Majority Socialists realized that it would not be possible
to retain their representatives in the coalition government. They
also knew that their withdrawal from the government of Prince
Max would create a crisis which most likely would end with the
fall of the cabinet. This in turn would create a situation in which
the tasks of government would become a responsibility of the
opposition. This was a development which the SPD did not want,
because its leaders were neither willing nor psychologically prepared to take over the responsibilities of government. An examination of the revolutionary events in Berlin must distinguish between two distinct but interrelated developments: (1) the withdrawal of the Majority Socialists' support from the coalition government, and (2) the revolutionary uprising of November 9 as a

[42] August Winnig states that the decision of the SPD was based on the
recognition that the revolution could
not be prevented any longer. The
party capitulated to the principles it
had fought for years and joined the
revolutionary forces in order to gain
control over them. (Winnig, *op. cit.*,
p. 139.)

joint enterprise of all socialist parties and groups. The effects of the resignation of Gustav Bauer and Philip Scheidemann from the cabinet and of the pressure of the revolutionary activities contributed to the first development. In the end, Prince Max appointed Friedrich Ebert as his successor as Reich Chancellor.[43]

After the Majority Socialists took over the government from Prince Max on November 9, they were uncertain as to the strength of their influence among the masses.[44] They were not sure if the workers' and soldiers' councils — the real power factor in Germany at the moment — would be willing to co-operate with the new government or would consider the cabinet to be in unwarranted competition with their own revolutionary governmental institutions.[45] Shortly after Ebert had assumed the chancellorship, he invited the USPD to participate in a coalition cabinet.

---

[43] The appointment of Ebert by Prince Max involves a legal fiction in contemporaneous German constitutional law. According to this fiction, after the abdication of the Emperor, Prince Max became the only authority vested with the power to appoint a Reich Chancellor. Prince Max acted as a trustee for the monarchy. The importance of this fiction was that it gave a degree of legitimacy to the transfer of power from Prince Max to Ebert. This question of legitimacy was of considerable significance for the numerous civil servants and other officials of the imperial authorities because it permitted them to cooperate with the new men without having to violate their oaths to the Emperor. (Prinz Max, op. cit., p. 642.) For adequate accounts of the events which led to the ultimatum of November 7 requesting the abdication of the Emperor and eventually the withdrawal of the SPD members from the coalition cabinet, see Ibid., pp. 605-29; Bernstein, op. cit., pp. 19-28; Hermann Mueller, op. cit., pp. 41-48. A conservative point of view about the abdication of the Emperor is presented by one who remained faithful to him, Graf Kuno von Westarp, Das

Ende der Monarchie am 9. November 1918 (Berlin: H. Rauschenbusch Verlag, 1952). Ebert's first two proclamations addressed to the German people and civil servants also emphasized the legality of the transfer of political power from Prince Max to the leader of the Majority Socialists. For the text of these two proclamations see Hermann Mueller, op. cit., pp. 51-52.

[44] The interpretation supplied by Friedrich Stampfer for the Majority Socialists' overestimate of the strength of the USPD and of the radical elements which was the reason for seeking their collaboration is as follows: No general elections had taken place for the six preceding years. The few elections for substitutes did not permit conclusions about the political disposition of the people. Furthermore, political attitudes change rapidly during revolutionary periods. (Friedrich Stampfer, Die ersten 14 Jahre der Deutschen Republik [2d ed.; Offenbach a. M.: Bollwerk-Verlag, 1947], p. 60.)

[45] F. W. von Oertzen, Die deutschen Freikorps 1918-1923 (2d ed.; Muenchen: Bruckmann, 1936), pp. 235-36; Stuemke, op. cit., p. 138.

He even expressed willingness to include Karl Liebknecht in the government.[46] However, the USPD was not willing to join the SPD in a coalition government without first arriving at a working agreement with the Majority Socialists concerning political aims and the distribution of offices. Ebert's offer disclosed the division of opinion within the USPD. There was a strong minority of Independent leaders in Berlin, dominated by the Revolutionary Shop Stewards. They sided with the Spartacists and strongly opposed collaboration with men like Ebert and Scheidemann, the revisionist "traitors" to the cause of socialism.[47]

The moderates among the Independents, for example, Haase and Dittmann, wanted to join the SPD in an "all-socialist coalition government," provided the Majority Socialists would agree to transform Germany into a "social" republic, would drop for the time-being their plans for an election of a national assembly, would give their consent to turn over all legislative, administrative, and judicial functions to the councils, and would also agree to keep representatives of the bourgeois parties out of the new government. The SPD replied that it also wanted a social republic, but that only the future national assembly, as the elected instrument of the people, could decide this issue with authority. The Majority Socialists plainly refused to transfer to the councils the functions demanded in the USPD proposal, because, according to the SPD, the councils represented only minority groups. Also the exclusion of bourgeois representatives was not feasible because it would aggravate the very difficult task of feeding the population. The negotiations between the two parties resulted in an uneasy

[46] Rudin, op. cit., p. 375. Meinecke believed that Ebert's offer to include Liebknecht was made for tactical reasons. Ebert intended thereby to neutralize the radical elements. However, Liebknecht's counter-demands excluded any possibility of collaboration. (Meinecke, Die Revolution, p. 113.) See also Willi Muenzenberg et al., Karl Liebknecht (Berlin: Verlag der Jugendinternationale, 1931), pp. 59-60.

[47] Ledebour, Barth, and Richard Mueller were strongly opposed to a coalition government with the SPD. Illustrierte Geschichte, pp. 210-11. In his book, Barth included Haase in the group opposed to working with the SPD. Barth himself advocated that the USPD take over the government by itself. (Barth, op. cit., pp. 58-59.)

compromise. Both parties agreed to form a provisional government on the basis of parity. The USPD showed a conciliatory attitude by dropping its original three day time-limit for the coalition but stubbornly remained pledged to support the council system and to fight the summoning of a constituent assembly until after the gains made by the revolution were consolidated.[48]

A six-man provisional cabinet, the so-called Council of People's Commissars, was formed on November 10. It was composed of Friedrich Ebert, Philip Scheidemann, and Otto Landsberg, all Majority Socialists, and of Hugo Haase, Wilhelm Dittmann, and Emil Barth, all Independents.[49] In addition to the socialists who were members of either the SPD or the USPD, the Centrists and the Liberals also participated in the new government. They headed a number of important ministries, such as the Foreign Office (State Secretary Dr. Solf), War Ministry (State Secretary Scheuch), and Ministry of Interior (Dr. Hugo Preuss.)[50]

The program of the new government was published shortly thereafter. It clearly illustrated that Germany had in its People's Commissars a liberal, democratic government in spite of the occasional use of socialist terminology. The significance of the proc-

[48] Berlau, op. cit., pp. 222-23; Illustrierte Geschichte, pp. 210-11; Hermann Mueller, op. cit., pp. 64-65; Bernstein, op. cit., pp. 34-36, 45-49; Stampfer, op. cit., pp. 60-64. The original conditions of the USPD are quoted in Illustrierte Geschichte, p. 210. For the text of the reply of the SPD, the statement of acceptance by the USPD, and a complete compilation of all offices of the new government occupied by socialists of both parties, see Bernstein, op. cit., pp. 35, 45ff.

[49] Bernstein, op. cit., p. 48. The usage of revolutionary terminology for the newly formed governmental agencies such as the Council of People's Commissars was an indication of the Majority Socialists' intention of compromising with the left wing of the socialist movement and with the masses about whose real aims very little was known. The choice of terms which resembled closely those used in the Russian Revolution was as far as the Majority Socialists were concerned, only part of their over-all tactical effort of bringing the revolution under their control.

[50] Rosenberg, Die Entstehung, p. 256; Bernstein, op. cit., p. 48. Thus, there was a certain amount of truth in the charge of the left wing radicals that the Provisional government failed to destroy the old state machinery and that some of the imperial ministers remained in their positions. According to the left wing radicals, only Dr. Preuss could be considered a democrat while all the others were reactionaries of long standing. (Illustrierte Geschichte, p. 222.)

lamation of November 12, 1918, was that it provided the basis for the work of the coalition government, i.e., for the Majority Socialists and the moderates of the USPD, who considered this program as a realistic approach to the problems facing them at that time.

To the German People!

The government created by the revolution, whose political leadership is purely socialist, has assumed the mission of carrying out the socialist program. Even at this [early] time, the government announces the following to be law:

(1) The state of siege is over.

(2) The right to organize and assemble is not subject to restriction, not excepting civil servants and government employees.

(3) Censorship ceases. Censorship for theaters is suspended.

(4) Freedom of speech and press [is guaranteed].

(5) Freedom of religion is guaranteed. No one can be forced to participate in religious activities.

(6) An amnesty is granted to all political offenders. Trials pending for [political] offenses will be suspended.

(7) The compulsory labor service law is suspended, with the exception of those provisions which deal with the arbitration of controversies.

(8) Regulations dealing with servants and emergency law concerning rural laborers are suspended.

(9) The labor protection laws which were suspended at the beginning of the war are re-instated. Additional social-political ordinances will be forthcoming in the near future. Not later than January 1, 1919, the eight-hour normal working day will be in force. The government will do everything to obtain sufficient employment opportunities. A decree concerning unemployment insurance has been prepared. Its financial burden is being distributed among the Reich, State, and community. In the field of health insurance, compulsory insurance will be extended beyond the present limit of 2,500 Marks. The shortage of living quarters will be relieved by making apartments available. A regulated [system] for food

maintenance for the population will be instituted. The government will keep up orderly production, protect property against infringement by individuals, and will protect personal freedom and safety. All elections for public offices will henceforth be subject to the equal, secret, direct general election law, based on proportional representation, for all men and women above twenty years of age. This election law will also apply to elections of the constituent assembly, about which further information will be forthcoming.[51]

Parallel in time with the formation of the socialist coalition cabinet was a second development, the revolutionary mass actions of the workers and soldiers of Berlin. This followed the established pattern of the German Revolution: general strike, fraternization of workers and soldiers, and formation of workers' and soldiers' councils as the organizational institutions of the revolution.[52] Many of these councils were formed in the Greater Berlin area, and a great number of them were under the strong influence of the Revolutionary Shop Stewards and Spartacists. The council system appeared to the radical elements as better suited to carry the revolution further than the cabinet which was in the process of being organized. Therefore, the revolutionary elements, while trying to influence the program and aim of the cabinet during the

[51] Hermann Mueller, *op. cit.,* pp. 83-84. The following is a comment of one of the leading Majority Socialists, Friedrich Stampfer, about this proclamation:

"The proclamation contains at the beginning an unclear statement referring to the realization of the socialist program. Otherwise it is clear and simple. It does not put into effect the socialist program, but it brings the fulfillment of all the timely demands of the Social Democratic program . . ." (Stampfer, *op. cit.,* pp. 67-68.)

[52] The revolutionary events of November 9, 1918, in Berlin are fully described and analyzed in the following: Hermann Mueller, *op. cit.,* pp. 46-53; Bernstein, *op. cit.,* pp. 29-33; Rosen-berg, *Die Entstehung,* pp. 254-55; Volkmann, *Der Marxismus,* pp. 232-43; *Illustrierte Geschichte,* pp. 204-08. The revolution in Berlin took place when the question concerning the abdication of the Emperor had reached its climax. Thus, the Berlin revolution is usually given more credit than deserved for the proclamation of the German Republic. When Scheidemann announced to the people that Germany had become a republic, "he established a historical *fait accompli.*" (Grzesinski, *op. cit.,* p. 50.) However, he only recognized a situation which had become almost unavoidable at that time. The text of his famous proclamation is quoted in Hermann Mueller, *op. cit.,* p. 53.

period of negotiations between the SPD and USPD, sought to utilize the revolutionary spirit of the councils for their own purposes. Their first tactical aim was to create a central revolutionary government which would base its complete authority on the workers' and soldiers' councils. On November 9, through the initiative of the Revolutionary Shop Stewards, a meeting of the left-oriented workers' and soldiers' delegates of the various councils took place in the Reichstag building. Barth was appointed chairman. The meeting assumed for the assembled delegates, which considered themselves the "Provisional Workers' and Soldiers' Council of Berlin," the authority to call a plenary meeting of the workers' and soldiers' councils of Berlin for the following day to elect a central provisional government for Germany. It was further decided that on the morning of November 10, prior to the plenary meeting, new delegates were to be elected, one deputy for each one thousand workers or soldiers. It was a serious attempt of a determined revolutionary minority to create another central government in competition to Ebert's. The Majority Socialists recognized the danger inherent in these moves and were determined to prevent the formation of another central executive agency.[53]

With the substantial assistance of non-political soldiers' delegates, the SPD succeeded in bringing under its control the announced plenary meeting of about 3,000 deputies at the Circus Busch, a large auditorium located in the eastern part of Berlin. Ebert's announcement that his party and the USPD had come to an agreement and had formed a coalition cabinet found overwhelming approval. This completely destroyed the plans of the Revolutionary Shop Stewards and the Spartacists for the creation of a central revolutionary government. The left wing radicals, recognizing defeat, changed tactics. They proposed an "Executive Council of the Workers' and Soldiers' Council of Berlin"

[53] Stampfer, op. cit., pp. 64-65; Hermann Mueller, op. cit., pp. 58ff; Barth, op. cit., pp. 60-61; Bernstein, op. cit., pp. 36-37, 45; Otto Braun, Von Weimar zu Hitler (2d ed.; New York; Europa Verlag, 1940), pp. 16-17.

composed exclusively of Independents and Spartacists as the controlling body for the Provisional government of Ebert and Haase. Even this attempt failed because, following the example set by the Provisional government, the soldiers' delegates, under SPD leadership, insisted on an Executive Council based on parity among the Majority Socialists and Independents. The soldiers also insisted on having as many delegates as the workers. Six Majority Socialists, six Independents, and twelve soldiers were elected to the new Executive Council. The leaders of the Spartacists, Liebknecht and Rosa Luxemburg, who were nominated as representatives for the Independents, absolutely refused to serve in the same body with Majority Socialists.[54] The Circus Busch meeting then promptly gave its official sanction to the Provisional government which became known as the Council of People's Commissars.[55] Thus, the high hopes with which the revolutionary elements had approached the first assembly of the workers' and soldiers' delegates had come to nothing. Even the unanimous adoption of a lengthy proclamation (prepared in advance

[54] The six Majority Socialists were Bueschel, Heller, Hiob, Juelich, Maynz, and Rusch. The Independents were represented by Barth, Eckert, Ledebour, Richard Mueller, Neuendorf, and Wegmann. Soldiers' representatives were Bartusch, von Beerfelde, Bergmann, Echtmann, Gerhardt, Hase, Hertel, Koehler, Lampert, Brutus Molkenbuhr, Walz, and Wumpel. (Hermann Mueller, op. cit., p. 71.)

[55] Ibid., pp. 71-72. The approval of the coalition cabinet by the Circus Busch meeting provided the basis for the claim that the Council of People's Commissars had received its authority from the workers' and soldiers' delegates of the Berlin councils. See for example Ulbricht, Zur Geschichte, p. 28. The Majority Socialists did not like this interpretation and preferred the fiction of the "legitimate" transfer. For an illustration of this point of view see the following quote from an article by Friedrich Stampfer:

"It is a legend that the first socialist government of Germany had been appointed by the congress of workers' and soldiers' delegates. Ebert had taken over from Prince Max the Reich Chancellorship, appointed his Majority Socialist ministers, and completed his cabinet on the basis of negotiations with the party-leadership of the Independents. The giant meeting of the workers' and soldiers' delegates, which took place during the evening of November 10 in the Circus Busch, confined itself to giving approval to the fait accompli. Nobody at that time thought of this as anything more than a formality."

(Friedrich Stampfer, "Nationalversammlung und Sozialdemokratie," Deutscher Revolutions Almanach fuer das Jahr 1919, ed. Ernst Drahn and Ernst Friedegg [Hamburg, Berlin: Hoffmann & Campe Verlag, 1919], p. 76.)

by Daeumig) in which Germany was referred to as a socialist republic where all political power was vested in the councils and the provisional government, elected by the councils, had as its tasks the realization of peace and the socialization of the means of production, was hollow under the circumstances. Characteristic of the attitude of the left wing elements was the proclamation containing greetings to the Russian workers and soldiers who had shown their German brothers the way of the revolution.[56]

The significance of the revolutionary development in Berlin on November 10 lay in the recognition and formalization of the two parallel governmental structures, the old state apparatus headed by the Provisional government and the new council system. Of equal importance was the creation of a connecting link between the two systems in the form of the Executive Council of the Workers' and Soldiers' Council of Greater Berlin. Theoretically at least, the revolution in Berlin had brought into existence a revolutionary institution (the Workers' and Soldiers' Council of Greater Berlin) which claimed authority and jurisdiction over all workers' and soldiers' councils in the Reich and thereby over all Germany as such. An arbitrary claim lacking legal justification, it was an important development because it elected the Executive Council and allegedly also the Council of People's Commissars which did exercise, with certain limitations, authority throughout Germany.[57]

The Executive Council considered itself the legislative and executive power for the entire Reich and for Prussia during the first few days of the revolution and thereby gave a clear demon-

---

[56] Grotewohl, op. cit., p. 78; Hermann Mueller, op. cit., p. 72. The text of this proclamation is quoted in Ferdinand Runkel, Die deutsche Revolution (Leipzig: Verlag Grunow, 1919), pp. 150-52.

[57] Wilhelm Roemer, Die Entwicklung des Raetegedankens in Deutschland (Berlin: Verlag E. Ebering, 1921), p. 21. It is interesting to note that the Executive Council was not recognized as the superior authority for weeks by workers' and soldiers' councils in other parts of Germany or by the central soldiers' council of the Supreme Command of the Army. However, this lack of recognition did not prevent the Executive Council from acting as a supervisory and controlling agency for the new Provisional government. (Oertzen, op. cit., pp. 236-37.)

stration of its intentions to acquire dictatorial powers.[58] The Executive Council's relation to the Council of People's Commissars was temporarily clarified during the later hours of November 10. The Executive Council became the controlling authority of the Provisional government as originally planned, but because of the predominance of Majority Socialists, it actually became a source of support for the SPD members of the Council of People's Commissars.[59]

Thus, the Majority Socialists were successful in reaching their immediate aims: (1) They succeeded in establishing a coalition cabinet with the Independents who agreed to work on the basis of a moderate liberal program. (2) They prevented the left wing radicals from setting up a competitive central revolutionary government during the most confused and unsettled period of the revolution. (3) They even succeeded in utilizing the great powers originally inherent in the workers' and soldiers' councils to strengthen the authority of the Provisional government throughout the Reich.

4.   The Spartacists and the November Revolution

As has been pointed out before, the numerous but small and almost autonomous groups of Spartacists and Left Radicals were

[58] Roemer, *op. cit.,* p. 21. See the first proclamation of the Executive Council of November 12, 1918, which declared that all municipal, State, Reich, and military governmental agencies will continue their activities, but will issue their ordinances in the name of the Executive Council. The text of this proclamation is quoted in Runkel, *op. cit.,* pp. 152-53.

[59] Runkel, *op. cit.,* pp. 153-54; Stampfer, *Die ersten 14 Jahre,* p. 78. The claim of the Executive Council for executive powers also caused considerable friction with the Council of People's Commissars which considered the exercise of executive functions as its exclusive prerogative. The jurisdictional fight was not settled until De-cember 10 when the official Gazette (*Reichsanzeiger*) announced that the Executive Council had the controlling and supervisory powers and the Council of People's Commissars the executive powers. This announcement was a restatement of a previous proclamation, dated November 23, which transferred all executive powers for the Reich and for Prussia to the Provisional government which, however, was supposed to exercise this authority under the control of the Executive Council. (The text of the November 23 agreement is quoted in Hermann Mueller, *op. cit.,* pp. 130-31.) The next change in the relation of the Provisional government to the revolutionary institutions came as result of the

not able to influence substantially the growing revolutionary ferment prior to the outbreak of the spontaneous mass uprising of November 1918.[60] After the beginning of the revolution, these groups, with a few exceptions, failed to become leading elements in the local workers' and soldiers' councils.[61] Even when Spartacists succeeded in getting elected to the councils, they always were a small minority and therefore could not exercise any real influence on local events. In most cases, they became quickly discouraged and preferred to resign from the councils rather than serve with Majority Socialists or with representatives of bourgeois parties who, according to the Spartacists, did everything in their power to end the revolution before any decisive changes in the political and social conditions could be achieved.[62]

The loose organizational arrangement of the Spartacists prior to the founding of the KPD and the influx of doubtful elements into the organization during the November days facilitated the development of ultra-radical and revolutionary-romantic views among some members. The differences in the political concepts of those ultra-left elements and those held by the old core of

first Congress of Workers' and Soldiers' Councils in the middle of December, 1918. (See below pp. 136-144; and Roemer, *op. cit.*, pp. 21-22.)

[60] See p. 78.

[61] An exception was, for example, the situation in Hamburg where the Left Radicals (who had joined the Spartacists in October) gave the workers' and soldiers' council the character of a genuine revolutionary agency. The Council took over the *Hamburger Echo* and appointed Paul Froelich as its editor-in-chief. From November 8 on he published the newspaper under the name: *Die Rote Fahne, Official Organ of the Hamburg Workers' and Soldiers' Council*. (*Illustrierte Geschichte*, pp. 191-92.) In Bremen the workers' and soldiers' council was also guided by "class conscious workers." All militaristically-minded teachers were dismissed from the schools, all reactionary officials were discharged from the police, and a Red Guard was organized to function as the executive force for the council. In Brunswick, the workers' and soldiers' council aso organized a Red Guard, purged the courts, and confiscated the landed property belonging to the Duke. (Grotewohl, *op. cit.*, p. 78.) A photographic reproduction of a proclamation of the Bremen Workers' and Soldiers' Council, dated November 9, 1918, is presented in *Illustrierte Geschichte*, p. 200. It is one of the few examples of official pronouncements of workers' and soldiers' councils during the November Revolution in which the revolutionary program of the Spartacists can readily be discerned.

[62] See for example the situation in Wuerttemberg as described by Wilhelm Keil, *op. cit.*, pp. 84-122.

Marxist-trained Spartacists became most apparent in questions which had a direct bearing upon the revolutionary tactics of the Spartacist League. For example, the members of the lunatic fringe advocated armed uprisings conducted by minorities and the use of terror as an instrument of the revolution. They also declared that a dictatorship of a minority had become unavoidable because the masses continued to follow the "bureaucrats" and "traitors of the working class."

Thus, they oscillated continuously between the mystical notion of an elite, a contempt for 'the reactionary masses,' and an equally irrational belief in the genuine revolutionary character of the exploited and dependent people.[63]

While these "syndicalist-putschist elements" failed to gain the upper hand in the Spartacist League because of the overwhelming influence of such old leaders as Rosa Luxemburg and Karl Liebknecht, they succeeded at times in causing local "revolutionary actions" which did not receive the approval of the Spartacist leaders.

Thus, most of the activities of the Spartacists during the November Revolution were the product of the influence of the Spartacist leaders, based on the latter's contemporaneous political concepts and evaluation of the revolutionary events. Probably the best source for a study of Spartacist behavior during this period is the various short- and long-range programs of action developed during that time. In fact, most of the available statements and proclamations made by Rosa Luxemburg and Liebknecht demonstrate the interrelation of their political concepts, their evaluation of the revolutionary situation, and their recommendation for specific actions.

The Spartacists were aware that neither their own strength nor their influence among the masses constituted real power factors at the outbreak of the uprising. Therefore during the initial

[63] Flechtheim, *op. cit.,* p. 41.

phase of the revolution, they attempted to bring about a decision of the issue between bourgeois democracy and proletarian dictatorship in favor of the latter by two surprise moves.[64] After the failure of the attempts made by the left wing radical groups in Berlin, Spartacist policies were directed at changing the bourgeois character of the German Revolution into a proletarian revolution like the Bolshevik revolt in Russia. The Spartacists believed that only a proletarian revolution could achieve the political, social, and economic changes required for realizing their ultimate aim, the socialist society. Thus, their revolutionary tactics were strongly influenced by their determination to push the revolution further. Rosa Luxemburg regarded the November Revolution as only the beginning. According to her, all that it had accomplished was the elimination of the monarchy which in itself was meaningless as long as the capitalist class, "the imperialist bourgeoisie," had not been destroyed.

The abolition of the capitalists' rule, the realization of the socialist society: this and nothing less is the historical contents of the present revolution. A tremendous task which cannot be done quickly by means of a few decrees coming from above, but can only be achieved through determined mass action of the working people in town and country. . . .[65]

Karl Liebknecht believed that the November Revolution was nothing more than the destruction of the old autocratic state machinery. The German Revolution could not be considered a successful undertaking as long as the rule of the capitalists and of

[64] See above, pp. 87, 93-96.

[65] Rosa Luxemburg, "Der Anfang," quoted in Luxemburg, *Ausgewaehlte Reden*, II, p. 594. Liebknecht summarized the ultimate aim of the revolution as follows: "Abrogation of class rule, of exploitation, and of suppression, and realization of socialism — that is, the proletariat's aim." (Karl Liebknecht, "Was ist zu tun?" quoted in Liebknecht, *Ausgewaehlte Reden*, p. 490.) "The removal of the capitalist society, that is the only salvation for the proletariat. . . ." (Karl Liebknecht, "Was will der Spartakusbund?" quoted in Liebknecht, *Ausgewaehlte Reden*, p. 507.)

the socialists who had "betrayed" the International in August 1914 continued. However, Liebknecht was convinced that the proletariat would eventually make use of its dormant political power and would end the economic class rule of the bourgeoisie. He referred to this part of the revolution as its social phase, and he confidently announced in an address to the proletarians of all countries (co-signed by Rosa Luxemburg, Mehring, and Zetkin) that "Germany is pregnant with the social revolution. . . ."[66]

Under the impact of the events in Russia, the Spartacists accepted the Bolshevik example of a dictatorship of the council system as the proper organizational form of the proletarian revolution.[67] A leaflet disseminated on November 8, 1918, on the eve of the mass uprising in Berlin, clearly indicated the Spartacists' intention of creating a "German Socialist Soviet Republic."

Workers and Soldiers!

Your hour has arrived. Now you are taking matters into your own hands after long endurance and stagnant days. It is not an exaggeration to say that in these days the world is looking at you and you are holding the fate of the world in your hands.

Workers and soldiers! Since the hour of action has arrived, there must be no return. The same "socialists," who for four years have served as souteneurs for the government and who in the past weeks have promised you every day "government of the people," parliamentarization, and other nonsense, are now doing everything to hinder you in your struggle in order to make the movement fade out.

Workers and soldiers! What your comrades and colleagues in Kiel, Hamburg, Bremen, Luebeck, Rostock, Flensburg, Hanover, Magdeburg, Brunswick, Munich, and Stuttgart could do, you also can do. Because on what you can achieve, on your tenacity and on the outcome of your fight, the victory of your brothers in those places and the success of the proletariat of the entire world depend.

[66] Karl Liebknecht, "An die Proletarier aller Laender," quoted in Liebknecht, *Ausgewaehlte Reden*, p. 480. Karl Liebknecht, "Der neue Burgfrieden," quoted in Liebknecht, *Ausgewaehlte Reden*, pp. 468-471.

[67] Tormin, *op. cit.*, p. 70; Meinecke, *Die Revolution*, p. 113.

Soldiers! Act like your comrades in the navy, unite with your brothers in workers' clothes. Do not permit yourselves to become a tool against your brothers, do not obey the commands of your officers, do not shoot at the fighters for freedom.

Workers and soldiers! The immediate aims of your struggle must be

(1) Liberation of all civilian and military prisoners.

(2) Abolition of all individual states [of the German Federation] and elimination of all dynasties.

(3) Elections of workers' and soldiers' councils, elections of delegates [to the councils] in all factories and military units.

(4) Immediate establishment of relations with other German workers' and soldiers' councils.

(5) Assumption of governmental authority by the commissars of the workers' and soldiers' councils.

(6) Immediate [establishment of] contact with the international proletariat, especially with the Russian Workers' Republic.

Workers and soldiers! Now prove that you are strong; now demonstrate that you have the sense to use your power.

Long live the socialist Republic!

Long live the International!

The Group International (Spartacist League)

Karl Liebknecht Ernst Meyer[68]

Only two days later, on November 10, 1918, a proclamation in the second issue of the Berlin *Rote Fahne* and generally ascribed to Rosa Luxemburg presented a more comprehensive program of the Spartacist League.[69] It contained the following immediate demands:

(1) Disarmament of all policemen and all officers and soldiers who do not accept the new order; arming of the people; all trustworthy soldiers and proletarians who are armed retain their weapons.

[68] Spartakusbund [Karl Liebknecht], *Arbeiter und Soldaten*, quoted in Liebknecht, *Ausgewaehlte Reden*, pp. 466-67.

[69] During the afternoon hours of November 9, 1918, a group of Spartacists occupied the printing plant and the editorial offices of the *Berliner Lo-*

(2)   Transfer of all military and civilian offices and headquarters to representatives of the [Berlin] Workers' and Soldiers' Council.

(3)   Transfer of all weapons and ammunition reserves as well as armament factories to the Workers' and Soldiers' Council.

(4)   Control over all means of transportation by the Workers' and Soldiers' Council.

(5)   Abolition of military justice. Replacement of brute obedience (*Kadavergehorsam*) by voluntary discipline for soldiers controlled by the Workers' and Soldiers' Council.

(6)   Abolition of the Reichstag and of all parliaments as well as of the existing Reich Government; taking over of the government by the Berlin Workers' and Soldiers' Council until a Workers' and Soldiers' Council representing the entire Reich can be formed.

(7)   Nation-wide elections of workers' and soldiers' councils which are the only agencies vested with legislative and administrative authority. The entire rural and urban working population, regardless of sex, is to participate in the elections of the workers' and soldiers' councils.

(8)   Abolition of all dynasties and individual states [of the German Federation]; our watchword is a unitary socialist German republic.

(9)   Immediate establishment of relations with all workers' and soldiers' councils in Germany and with the socialist brother parties abroad.

---

kal-Anzeiger and printed there the first few issues of *Die Rote Fahne*. Rosa Luxemburg was opposed to the forceful occupation of the "bourgeois" paper and its transformation into the Spartacists' organ because she was certain that her group did not have enough strength to defend this seizure against its numerous enemies. As soon as difficulties developed, the Spartacists gave up the plant. Finally on November 18, arrangements were completed with another printing plant and the new *Rote Fahne* was published. Rosa Luxem-burg and Liebknecht signed as responsible editors. However, Rosa Luxemburg was actually managing the newspaper assisted by Paul Levi, August Thalheimer, Paul Lange, and others. (Froelich, *Rosa Luxemburg*, pp. 310-11; *Illustrierte Geschichte*, pp. 205, 211-12.) Hermann Mueller describes the difficulties *Die Rote Fahne* experienced at the Scherl publishing house of the *Berlin Lokal-Anziger* as the refusal of the workers of the printing plant to print the paper. This resulted in the week-long interruption in the publish-

(10) Immediate recall of the Russian embassy to Berlin.[70]

At the end, the proclamation categorically announced that any collaboration with the "socialist traitors" was beyond considera-tion.[71]

In Rosa Luxemburg's first article in the new *Rote Fahne* of November 18, 1918, entitled "The Beginning," she drew up the main points of the Spartacists' program for transforming the "limited revolution" into a genuine proletarian revolution:

The aim of the revolution [i.e., a socialist society] clearly deter-mines its source; the mission [of the revolution] determines its method. *All power in the hands of the working masses, in the hands of the workers' and soldiers' councils; protection of the achievements of the revolution from the lurking enemies*: all this provides the general di-rection for all measures the revolutionary government [is supposed to undertake].

Every step, every action of the government should point in this direction like a compass:

(1) Completion and re-election of local workers' and soldiers' councils. . . .;

(2) permanent session for those bodies representing the masses and transfer of the intrinsic political power from the small committee of the Executive Council to the broader forum represented by the Workers' and Soldiers' Council;

(3) calling the Reich parliament of the workers' and soldiers' councils into session as quickly as possible, in order to make the proletarians of all Germany into one class and one com-pact political power and to rally them behind the work of the revolution as its defensive arm and its assault force;

(4) [undertaking] immediate organization not of the "farmers" but of the rural proletarians and small farmers who as a social class are still outside the revolution;

ing of the Spartacists' organ beginning with November 12. (Hermann Mueller, *op. cit.*, p. 122.)

[70] See above, pp. 65-66.
[71] *Illustrierte Geschichte*, p. 212.

(5) formation of a proletarian Red Guard for the permanent protection of the revolution and conscription of a workers' militia
to prepare the entire proletariat to be on the alert at all times;

(6) removal of the agencies taken over from the absolutist military police state, the administration, judiciary, and army;

(7) immediate confiscation of dynastic property and estates and
landed estates as a temporary first measure to secure the
food supply for the people, because hunger is the most dangerous ally of the counter-revolution;

(8) summoning of the Workers' World Congress to meet immediately in Germany in order to emphasize distinctly and
clearly the international character of the revolution; only
in the International, in the world revolution of the proletariat
is the future of the German Revolution anchored.[72]

In contrast to this program, which Rosa Luxemburg considered only as "the first and most urgent steps" of the revolution,
were the actions and omissions of the "revolutionary government"
of Ebert and Haase. Her attack and criticism of the proposed constitutent national assembly was an important revision of her views
as expressed in *The Russian Revolution,* written as late as the fall
of the same year. The change in her opinion regarding the national assembly was probably the result of the developments of
the first week of the German Revolution. Her criticism ran as
follows:[73]

What is the present revolutionary government doing?

It does not disturb the state administrative machinery from top to
bottom, leaving it quietly in the hands of the past supporters of the
Hohenzollern absolutism and of the future instruments of the counterrevolution;

it calls for the constituent national assembly [and intends] to
create thereby a bourgeois counter-weight to the representative body
of the workers and soldiers; it thereby shifts the revolution onto the

[72] Luxemburg, *Der Anfang,* pp. 595-
96.

[73] See above, p. 57, n. 63; see also
Froelich, *Rosa Luxemburg,* p. 313.

track of a bourgeois revolution and filches the socialist aims of the revolution;

it does nothing to destroy the notorious power of the capitalist class rule;

it does everything to mollify the bourgeoisie, by announcing the sanctity of private property, by assuring the inviolability of the capitalist arrangement;

it permits the very active counterrevolution to operate and fails to bring this to the attention of the masses and fails to warn the people emphatically.

. . . .

The result of the first week of the revolution: nothing fundamental has been changed within the state of the Hohenzollerns, the workers' and soldiers' government is acting as a substitute for the imperial government which has gone bankrupt. . . .

But revolutions do not stand still. . . .[74]

All major aspects of the revolutionary program of the Spartacists were related to the strengthening of the council system which was regarded by the left wing radicals as the only method of bringing about their aim of a unitary German socialist soviet republic. Other points of the program which did not directly refer to the councils — such as the necessity of proletarian control over the means of coercion, precautions to be taken against reactionary assaults on revolutionary achievements, and emphasis on the international character of the proletarian revolution — were conceived only as instrumental to the perpetuation and strengthening of the council system, the organizational manifestation of the proletarian revolution.

The Spartacists strongly advocated the council system in preference to the "bourgeois democracy" not because they believed the former could produce a better representation of public opinion; on the contrary, they recognized that it could be used with great advantage to falsify the popular sentiment, since the fran-

[74] Luxemburg, *Der Anfang,* pp. 596-97.

chise was limited to the workers and soldiers. The council system could actually facilitate the perpetuation of a minority rule and still make it appear as being backed by a sizeable majority. The Russian manipulation of their soviets had clearly demonstrated their utility to the Spartacists.[75] This could be achieved only when the workers' and soldiers' councils were the sole organs of state power and were not subordinate to any other type of governmental agency such as the Provisional government.[76]

Tormin uses a different approach to explain the position of the Spartacists toward the council system. He claims that it was the result of "their concept concerning the nature and aim of the revolution." Since the Spartacists could not hope to reach their aim, "the socialist and extremely democratic state," by democratic means because they were a small minority, they saw in the council dictatorship the best instrument for its realization. Tormin concludes that this was the situation which forced the Spartacists to change from the concept of social democracy to the "dictatorship of the councils."[77]

The council system, regardless of the role it was to play in the revolutionary program of the Spartacists, did appeal to the great masses of German workers and soldiers — as the spontaneous and rapid creation of thousands of such councils demonstrated. The masses which for years had been kept from active political participation saw in the councils a means to exert direct influence, at least in the formulation of local policies.[78]

---

[75] Max Weber, *Gesammelte Politische Schriften* (Munich: Drei Masken Verlag, 1921), p. 346; Berlau, *op. cit.*, p. 218.

[76] Roemer, *op. cit.*, p. 19; in addition to the book by Walter Tormin referred to above, Roemer, *op. cit.*, is also an excellent presentation of the impact of the council system upon revolutionary developments in Germany.

[77] Tormin, *op. cit.*, pp. 86-87.

[78] *Ibid.*, p. 56. Roemer goes one step further in explaining the psychological motivation for the mass participation in the council movement. He claims that in the past the only political right the worker had was to join a party and vote. This ended all his political activity, because policies were not determined by him but by the party leadership. The combination of the political impotence of the old system and the desire for power by the individual worker who had been denied this opportunity in the past might explain his interest in the active, direct participation which the councils

Rosa Luxemburg defined the functions and the operational significance of the councils as follows:

The workers' and soldiers' councils were then the organs of the revolution, pillars of the newly-formed order, executors of the will of the masses in working clothes and soldiers' uniforms. The workers' and soldiers' councils had a tremendous amount of work in front of them. They had the task, first of all, of putting into operation the will of the revolutionary masses of the people and of building up the entire social and political state machinery in the proletarian-socialist meaning [of the term].[79]

It was understandable, therefore, that the Spartacists did their utmost to support the council system against all its opponents and also tried to obtain a majority of sympathetic council delegates in order to utilize the councils "to push the revolution further."[80] However, the councils remained primarily under the influence of the SPD and the trade unions. Even representatives of the bourgeois parties found entrance. In the soldiers' councils, the bourgeois elements often succeeded in obtaining a dominant influence, simply because leaders among the soldiers quite frequently came from the middle classes.[81] Thus, only the

seemed to offer. (Roemer, op. cit., pp. 1-2.)

Not only the workers but also the soldiers and to a lesser degree the farmers wanted to be active in determining their own fate. (Tormin, op. cit., p. 61.) Walter Goerlitz reports that ". . . the millions of German soldiers [created] their own representation in approximately 10,000 soldiers' councils. At the end of November, a central soldiers' council was constituted, a kind of army parliament, such as the history of the German army had never before known." (Walter Goerlitz, Der Deutsche Generalstab [Frankfurt a. M.: Verlag der Frankfurter Hefte, 1950], p. 296.) The farmers' councils played a very insignific-

ant part in the German Revolution. Only in certain parts of the Reich, e.g., Bavaria, Silesia, and Hanover, they appeared but hardly ever transcended their initial stage. They never obtained any real importance although in individual cases they did expropriate landed estates and distributed the land among farmers. (Roemer, op. cit., p. 18; Grotewohl, op. cit., p. 71.)

[79] Rosa Luxemburg, "Um den Vollzugsrat," quoted in Luxemburg, Ausgewaehlte Reden, II, p. 630.

[80] Ulbricht, Der Zusammenbruch, pp. 24-25.

[81] Bernstein, op. cit., p. 174; Flechtheim, op. cit., pp. 38-39; Grotewohl, op. cit., p. 72; Illustrierte Geschichte, pp. 216-18. It is not surprising then

Spartacists and certain circles among the bourgeoisie were ready to see in the councils the beginning of the Bolshevizing of Germany.[82]

On November 12, 1918, when the People's Commissars subtly announced the meeting of a constituent national assembly, they thereby made it known that they intended to place the formulation of the future constitution and governmental structure of Germany in the hands of representatives of all social classes.[83] This move was bound to provoke strong opposition from the Spartacists and other left wing radicals, who, as has been pointed out above, wished to transfer all political, social, and economic powers to the workers' and soldiers' councils. One of the most precise formulations of the Spartacists' point of view in this matter was expressed by Rosa Luxemburg. Her antagonism to the national assembly must be seen within the context of the growing controversy of national assembly versus council system. Her opposition to the national assembly, the "bourgeois counter-weight" to the councils, constituted an important point in her article "The Be-

---

that Max Weber was able to write in a letter the following remarks about the councils:

"One can really be happy about the plain objectivity of the simple people from the trade unions and also of many soldiers, for example in the local workers' and soldiers' council to which I am attached. They have done their work really excellently and have done everything without [a lot of] talk, this I must admit. The nation as such is after all a people of discipline. . . ." (Weber, *op. cit.*, p. 482.)

[82] Meinecke, *Die Revolution*, p. 114.

[83] See the contents of the governmental program of the Provisional government on pp. 92-93 above. Cf. also Tormin who considers this announcement by the People's Commissars as the end of the first phase of the German Revolution and possibly even the end of the entire revolution. (Tormin, *op. cit.*, p. 65.) Barth, the left wing member of the Provisional government, wrote in his book that he requested the deletion of the sentence in the governmental proclamation of November 12 which made a reference to the constituent assembly; he was out-voted five to one. (Barth, *op. cit.*, p. 68.) The utility of a national assembly, based on universal and equal franchise, for establishing a new constitution for Germany was already discussed between Prince Max and the SPD before the outbreak of the November uprising. It was agreed that only a call for a constituent national assembly might prevent the outbreak of a violent revolution. (Prinz Max, *op. cit.*, p. 598.) Nevertheless, after the outbreak of the revolution, Prince Max proposed on November 9 the summoning of a national assembly to serve as the representative agency which should decide on the future German constiution and also on the question of a monarchy. (*Ibid.*, p. 616.)

On November 9 during the nego-

gınning," published on November 18.[84] However, in her attack in *Die Rote Fahne* on November 20 against the Independents, who approved of the national assembly in principle but wanted to postpone its formulation until the revolutionary gains had been consolidated, she seemed to regard this issue as the most decisive one for the future course of the German Revolution.[85] The following are substantial excerpts from Rosa Luxemburg's article "The National Assembly."

From the *Deutschen Tageszeitung,* the *Vossischen,* and the *Vorwaerts* to the Independent [i.e., USPD] *Freiheit,* from von Reventlow, Erzberger, Scheidemann to Haase and Kautsky, a unanimous call is heard for the national assembly with an equally unanimous cry of anguish because of the plan to place the power into the hands of the working-class.

The entire "people," the entire "nation" is supposed to be called on to decide by majority decision the future fate of the revolution.

The solution is a foregone conclusion for the admitted, disguised spokesmen of the ruling classes. [However] we do not discuss things with the guardians of the capitalist money safes either *in* the national assembly or *about* the national assembly.

The leaders of the Independents are also joining the ranks of the protectors of capitalism in this issue.

As pointed out by Hilferding in *Freiheit,* they intend thereby [i.e., by means of the national assembly] to make it unnecessary for the

---

tiations conducted between Prince Max and Ebert which eventually led to the appointment of the latter as Reich chancellor, Prince Max suggested again a constituent national assembly as the means of working out the future constitution. Ebert's answer was in the affirmative, "We can declare our agreement with the principle of this national assembly." (*Ibid.,* p. 636.)

[84] See above, pp. 104-6.

[85] Tormin correctly pointed out that the Independents were divided on this issue. The right wing sided with the SPD and the left wing with the radicals. It is also interesting to note that officially the Independents avoided giving reasons of principle for their proposal for postponing the national assembly. They justified their request with such practical considerations as that prisoners of war had not yet been returned, political parties did not have enough time for their campaigns, and the fate of the occupied territories was still uncertain. (Tormin, *op. cit.,* p. 71 and p. 71, n. 1.) See also Runkel, *op. cit.,* p. 155.

revolution to use force [and to eliminate] the civil war with all its terror. Petit-bourgeois illusions. . . .

These profound Marxists have forgotten the ABC's of socialism.

They have forgotten that the bourgeoisie is not a parliamentary party, but a ruling class which is in possession of economic and social means of coercion.

These Junkers and capitalists will remain peaceful only as long as the revolutionary government is content with pasting little beauty spots on top of the capitalist wage arrangement. . . .

The present idyl, where wolves and sheeps, tigers and lamb graze peacefully side by side as in Noah's Ark, will last only until the very minute when socialism becomes serious.

. . . When the bourgeoisie is hit in its heart — and its heart beats in the cash register — it will put up a life and death struggle to retain its control and will use thousands of open and concealed means of resistance against socialist measures.

. . . The "civil war" which they seek to banish from the revolution with uneasy anxiety, cannot be banished. Civil war is only another name for the class struggle, and the idea that socialism can be introduced without a class struggle and through parliamentary majority decisions is a ridiculous petit-bourgeois illusion. . . .

In the Great French Revolution, the first decisive step was taken in July 1789 when the three separate estates combined in a unified national assembly. This decision determined the entire future course of events; it was the symbol of victory of a new bourgeois society over the medieval feudal estates.

. . . .

[Thus] the national assembly is superannuated inheritance from the bourgeois revolutions, ...

The fight over the national assembly is carried out under the battle cry, democracy or dictatorship! . . .

The question today is not democracy or dictatorship. The problem, placed on the agenda by history, is: *bourgeois* democracy or *socialist* democracy. The dictatorship of the proletariat means democracy in the socialist sense. The dictatorship of the proletariat does not mean bombs, revolts, uproars, and "Anarchy," as the spokesmen of the capitalist profit system willfully falsify, but it connotes the use of all political power to bring about socialism, to expropriate the capitalist class — and because it is based on the will of the revolutionary majority of the proletariat, it is within the spirit of socialist democracy.

Without the conscious intent and action of the majority of the proletariat there can be no socialism. In order to clarify this conviction, to strengthen this will, to organize this action, a class organ is necessary: the Reich parliament of the urban and rural proletarians.

The summoning of this kind of workers' representation in place of the traditional national assembly of the bourgeois revolutions alone constitutes an act of the class struggle, a break with the historic past of the bourgeois society, a powerful means to wake up the proletarian masses of the people, a first frank and blunt declaration of war against capitalism.

. . . Parliamentary cretinism was a weakness yesterday; today it is an ambiguity; tomorrow it will be treason.[86]

This article was significant not only because it contained Rosa Luxemburg's statements on the left wing radicals' determined opposition to the national assembly, but also because it clarified the Spartacists' concepts of "socialist democracy" and "dictatorship of the proletariat." These terms, as defined by Rosa Luxemburg, were not interchangeable but applied to the same situation, the class rule of the proletariat. According to her, the rule of the proletariat was a socialist democracy because the majority decisions of the working class set the over-all policies to be pursued by the revolutionary government and therefore did not constitute a rule by a majority. It was a dictatorship of the proletariat because it excluded all social classes, except the working class, from participating in the political process. The disenfranchised classes were subject to severe political, social, and economic restrictions. Important for examining Spartacist actions during the immediate post-revolutionary period is also the great emphasis placed on the "majority will" of the proletariat because this could mean — and actually did for Rosa Luxemburg and other Spartacist leaders —

[86] Rosa Luxemburg, "Die National-versammlung," quoted in Luxemburg, *Ausgewaehlte Reden,* II, pp. 603-07.

that the Spartacists could not make their claim for power until they had succeeded in gaining the support of the majority of the working class. Thus, the primary objective of their tactics became their concern for gaining the patronage of the masses. Methods used for this purpose included various propaganda media and stressed the revolutionizing effects of mass strikes and street demonstrations.[87]

Any success the Spartacists enjoyed in those endeavors was due not only to their own theories and related or unrelated actions but was influenced to a considerable degree by the prevailing tendencies among the masses. The Spartacists themselves recognized correctly the spontaneous character of the German Revolution and also its primary, limited aim of ending the war. Possibly because of their great confidence in the masses, they overestimated the socialist potentialities of the revolutionary movement. Since they did not realize how weak was socialist sentiment among the people, they also failed to recognize the actual and potential influence of the moderate socialists and of the bourgeois parties with their program of political democracy.[88]

[87] Richard Mueller, *Der Buergerkrieg in Deutschland* (Berlin: Phoebus Verlag, 1925), p. 13. These aggressive activities played an important part in the consolidation process of the German Revolution which was attempted by the SPD and the right wing of the USPD. (Cf. Chapter IV.) It will also be of interest to examine to what extent these principles, formulated by Rosa Luxemburg and later reinforced by the program of the Spartacist League of December 14, 1918, and of the program of the KPD, were followed in practice. (Cf. Chapter V.)

[88] Flechtheim, *op. cit.*, p. 35; for a characterization of the German Revolution by Liebknecht, see Liebknecht, *Reden*, pp. 322-30; Karl Liebknecht, "Das, was ist," quoted in Liebknecht, *Ausgewaehlte Reden*, p. 473; Liebknecht, *Was ist zu tun?* p. 485.

Consolidation Versus Continuation of the Revolution

1. *The "Limited Revolution" of the SPD*

The initial phase of the German Revolution ended when the SPD leaders succeeded in obtaining a strong position within the Provisional government and the Executive Council and began using their power to consolidate the political achievements brought about by the spontaneous mass uprising. The Majority Socialists in the government considered themselves only as trustees of the people until general elections could be held.[1] This point of view was strongly attacked by the other socialist factions.

The next phase of the German Revolution was characterized by the impetuous conflict between two hostile camps. One side, led by the SPD, consisted of the protagonists of the constituent national assembly. The other was composed of the left wing radicals who worked for the continuation of the revolution, expecting that through the workers' and soldiers' councils and the use of propaganda and "revolutionary actions" they would eventually succeed in transforming the "bourgeois" revolution into its proletarian counterpart. The struggle between these two groups, each of which rallied around its respective symbol — national assembly or council system — was the fight between two fundamentally different interpretations of the meaning of the revolution and its ultimate aims.[2]

---

[1] Stampfer, *Nationalversammlung,* p. 76; see also Berlau, *op. cit.,* p. 215.

[2] Berlau interpreted this controversy as follows: "The struggle between the

During this second phase of the revolution, in spite of the fundamental controversy raging within the socialist movement, the Provisional government succeeded in improving considerably the over-all conditions of the working class. Noske's assertion that "the satisfaction of all political democratic desires immediately followed the 9th of November" is an exaggerated version of the situation.[3] However, even Communist appraisals of the work of the Provisional government admit that some long-overdue and significant changes were accomplished during this period.[4]

One of the first steps of the new government was to repeal all laws and ordinances which the imperial authorities had proclaimed during the war. The SPD members of the government seemed to have forgotten, as did some of their colleagues from the USPD, that they had originally given their approval to these restrictive war-time laws.[5] These first legislative acts of the revolutionary government included not only repeals of laws and decrees considered especially oppressive by the people, but also such new and important provisions as the eight-hour work day, the right to unemployment compensation payable from public funds, and the expansion of health insurance. All these measures "decreased considerably the rule of capitalism over the workers and

system of councils and a national constitutional assembly elected on the wildest democratic franchise was therefore not so much an academic struggle over the comparative merits of each system, as it was in the last analysis, a struggle between two contending interpretations of the purposes of the revolution and the mandate bestowed on the revolutionary government by the events of November 9." (Berlau, *op. cit.*, p. 219.)

[3] Noske, *Von Kiel bis Kapp*, p. 60.

[4] Otto Grotewohl, after listing the "social and democratic advances" made during the reign of the Provisional government, claims that these achievements should really have been the outcome of the 1848 Revolution. The November Revolution stopped short when it did not press for such decisive reforms as the expropriation of large estates and the democratization of the governmental administration, school system, and military forces. (Grotewohl, *op. cit.*, p. 81.) Walter Ulbricht also states that the social reform program of the SPD and USPD did not go beyond the framework of the bourgeois-capitalist society. (Ulbricht, *Zur Geschichte*, p. 26.)

[5] See the text of the proclamation of November 12, 1918, quoted above, pp. 92-93.

improved greatly the social position of the workers in relation to [the owners of] property."[6]

Many of the workers expected that the Provisional government would start immediately with the socialization of industry.[7] These demands for socialization created a very difficult problem for the government because they involved a number of factors beyond its control. On the one hand, it was necessary that something be done because of public pressure; on the other, realistic considerations concerning the post-war economic conditions of Germany seemed to indicate that it would be wise not to interfere with industry and the national economy. For example, evidence was available that the industrialists were reluctant to convert their factories to peace-time production primarily for fear of eventual expropriation. The Provisional government, furthermore, questioned its own authority to invade private rights as extensively as would be required for socialization without having the explicit sanction of the national assembly.

The government tried to work its way out of the socialization problem at a meeting of the People's Commissars on November 18, 1918. It was decided that only those branches of industry which were ripe for socialization should be socialized, and a Socialization Commission was appointed to investigate the situation and make recommendations before the government took any action in this matter.[8]

[6] Bernstein, *op. cit.,* p. 176. For a full discussion of the legislative work of the Provisional government see [Social Democratic Party of Germany,] *Nichts getan? Die Arbeit seit dem 9. November 1918* (Berlin: Arbeitsgemeinschaft fuer staatsbuergerliche u. wirtschaftliche Bildung [1919]. An appendix of this pamphlet contains a listing of the most important decrees and laws for the workers promulgated by the government after November 9, 1918. (*Ibid.,* pp. 29-32.)

[7] This is not an assertion based on the claims of left wing radicals or of Communists. For example, Ulbricht

describes this particular issue in his history of the German labor movement. (Ulbricht, *Zur Geschichte,* p. 30.) The demands for socialization, as part of the price of victory in the revolution made by the German workers, were even reported by moderate Social Democrats. For example, see Hermann Mueller, *op. cit.,* p. 200.

[8] Bernstein, *op. cit.,* p. 178; Hermann Mueller, *op. cit.,* pp. 196-99. This commission was comprised of leading socialist economists and theorists such as Karl Kautsky, who was elected as chairman of the commission, Heinrich Cunow, Rudolf Hilferding, Professors

The Socialization Commission met for the first time on December 5, 1918. Five days later, it published the first preliminary report which constituted the platform for its work. The following significant statements were made:

> The Commission is conscious of the fact that the socialization of the means of production can only be accomplished during an organic evolution lasting for some time. The first prerequisite for any economic re-organization is the revival of production. The economic situation of Germany demands, first, the re-establishment of export industry and foreign trade.
>
> The Commission is of the opinion that the present organization of these branches of the economy must be retained. . . .
>
> However, the Commission believes that those branches of the national economy in which capitalist-monopolistic arrangements have developed should be considered first for socialization. . . .[9]

The report of the Socialization Commission made it clear that the government was not supporting indiscriminate nationalization of the means of production and did not intend to socialize every branch of the economy even in the distant future. The program of the Commission restored confidence among business people and thereby contributed to the revival of the national economy.[10]

On January 7, 1919, the Socialization Commission reported its preliminary findings to the government. They added nothing new to the work program of December 1918. The Commission warned of the dangers inherent in a doctrinaire transformation of the economy and advised that the situation of each individual branch of the economy be studied to determine how much socialization would be advisable.[11]

Karl Ballod, E. Franke, E. Lederer, and several others. (*Ibid.,* p. 197.)

[9] Bernstein, *op. cit.,* p. 177.

[10] *Ibid.* The *Nationalzeitung* wrote in a stock market report on December 16, 1918: "The greatest concern of the [stock] exchange, i.e., the danger of Bolshevism and equally the danger of a general socialization of industry, can now be regarded as completely overcome." (Quoted in Ulbricht, *Zur Geschichte,* p. 30.)

[11] Stampfer, *Die ersten 14 Jahre,* pp.

Karl Kautsky in particular tried to convince the workers that socialization was practically impossible because of the condition of Germany's post-war economy.

The economic base on which socialism was supposed to be erected was the immense wealth created by capitalism and which should have made it possible to create a rule of well-being for everybody. This wealth has been almost completely destroyed during nearly five years of war and war-time conditions; thus the economic base of socialism has become extremely reduced.[12]

While socialization was being considered, studied, and postponed, the trade unions and the employers' associations arrived at a general agreement on November 15, 1918, which for the first time made the unions the official and recognized representative agencies of the workers. The employers' associations accepted another agreement which provided that henceforth collective bargaining was the sole means for settling wage questions and for determining working conditions. This so-called November Agreement was celebrated by union and SPD leaders as a great labor victory while the left wing radicals bitterly denounced it as a violation of the principle of the class struggle.[13]

In its effort to establish law and order and to solve urgent domestic and foreign problems the Provisional government believed that it must rely on the cooperation of the well-trained and

77-78, Hermann Mueller, *op. cit.,* pp. 207-08.

[12] Karl Kautsky, "Aussichten der Revolution," ed. by E. Drahn and E. Friedegg, *Deutscher Revolutions-Almanach fuer das Jahr 1919* (Hamburg-Berlin: Hoffmann & Campe Verlag, 1919), p. 28. Otto Grotewohl refers to a publication by Kautsky, *Sozialdemokratische Bemerkungen zur Uebergangswirtschaft,* L e i p z i g, 1918, in which Kautsky declares that during the change from war-time to peace-time economy, the prevailing system or organization of production should not be disturbed. Only after the change has been accomplished is it possible to begin transforming capitalism to socialism. (Grotewohl, *op. cit.,* pp. 61-62.) Also see the discussion concerning the problems of socialization in August Mueller, *op. cit.*

[13] Stampfer, *Die ersten 14 Jahre,* p. 75; Flechtheim, *op. cit.,* pp. 37-38. Flechtheim places the date of the November Agreement at November 11, while Stampfer dates it at November 15.

smoothly-functioning official bureaucracy. Hence the proclamations of November 9 and 12, 1918, in which Ebert called upon all civil servants to support the new "legitimate" government and assured government officials that their previously acquired rights would be fully protected.[14] Most government employees continued in their positions, although in spirit they remained the same old imperial bureaucrats and never became converted, democratically-inclined civil servants. The decision to rely on these officials, who by origin and tradition were reactionary and monarchist-minded, was one of the most significant taken by the Provisional government. It perpetuated the autocratic spirit among the German civil service including the judiciary which at a later date decisively supported elements hostile to the democratic German Republic.[15]

An even more significant step was the conclusion of a working agreement with the Supreme Command of the German Army. It was — and still is — generally believed that the Ebert-Groener Pact, as this arrangement later became known, was one of the most decisive influences in the period immediately following the November uprising. To a large extent, it directed the course of subsequent revolutionary developments and also made it possible for the professional officer corps, symbolized by the representatives of the General Staff, to weather the revolutionary storm and to regain afterwards its influential position in German political life.

Ebert and the Majority Socialists have been severely attacked by the political left as well as by liberal democratic circles for having reached an agreement with the leaders of the former imperial army and for having collaborated with the German General Staff. Communists, as a matter of course, charged that Ebert deliberately made common cause with the reactionary officers in order to destroy the revolutionary workers — in particular the Spartacists — and thereby to prevent developments from exceeding the dimensions of a bourgeois revolution.[16] This agreement

[14] See above, p. 89, n. 43; Grzesinski, *op. cit.,* p. 80.
[15] *Ibid.,* p. 79.

[16] Grotewohl, *op. cit.,* pp. 83-84. Paul Froelich claims that the Ebert-Groener Pact was concluded with the

was also called a "natural" alliance because both Ebert and the Supreme Command were opposed to real changes in Germany.[17] Neither of those assertions can be supported by factual evidence. The real difficulties in which Ebert, as People's Commissar in charge of internal and military affairs, found himself as the result of the Allies' demands for a speedy evacuation and demobilization of German military forces and of his sincere intention to re-establish law and order, were far weightier than all the sinister motives ascribed to him.[18] Ebert could have chosen either the Supreme Command, which was still in control of the field armies, or the soldiers' councils as the instrument for carrying out the evacuation. However, the time limit of 30 days hardly permitted him any other choice than the Supreme Command.[19]

Ebert also needed a reliable armed force to make law and order of the chaotic conditions which followed the breakdown of the old authority during the revolution. There were many armed workers and soldiers in Berlin, but the Provisional government could not depend on them. Many of these armed men were organized in quasi-military "revolutionary" units which fought against each other for supremacy; the regular army units were still far from the capitol. Each political faction aspired to have its own military formation. The Spartacists organized the National Association of Deserters (*Reichsbund der Deserteure*). The Independent Chief of Police, Emil Eichhorn, with the sanc-

immediate aim of suppressing the workers in Berlin. (Froelich, *Rosa Luxemburg,* p. 318.)

[17] William Ebenstein, *The German Record* (New York-Toronto: Rinehart & Co., 1945), pp. 195-96.

[18] This writer agrees with Waite's interpretation of Ebert's actions. Waite claims that Ebert was prompted by the pressure of events when he turned to the Supreme Command for help.

"Ebert's real mistake was not made on the night of November 9. At that time, he made the only decision possible. His mistake — and it proved to be a fatal one — was in continuing to rely on the Army even after it had proved faithless and in failing to try to build an army sympathetic to the Republic until it was much too late." (Robert G. L. Waite, *Vanguard of Nazism* [Cambridge: Harvard University Press, 1952], p. 6.)

[19] *Ibid.,* pp. 3-4. Arthur Rosenberg calls this the first great mistake of the Republic. Military experts tend to believe that the former generals were essential for this complicated undertaking. (*Ibid.;* see also Goerlitz, *op. cit.,* p. 296.)

tion of the Executive Council, formed from the ranks of socialist workers and soldiers a Security Force (*Sicherheitswehr*), which was considered the military force of the USPD. In addition there was the People's Naval Division (*Volksmarine-Division*), consisting of approximately 3,200 sailors primarily from Cuxhaven and Kiel, which occupied and settled down in the Imperial Palace and the Stables (*Marstall*). On November 17 the City Commandant of Berlin, Otto Wels, began to organize a volunteer army, the Republican Soldiers' Army (*Republikanische Soldatenwehr*) which eventually reached a total of 15,000 men. Ebert expected the Supreme Command with its regular units to assist him in making order of this highly explosive situation in Berlin.[20] The situation in which the Provisional government found itself was summarized by Otto Braun, a leading Majority Socialist and later Prussian Premier:

. . . Many who condemn the position taken by the Reich Government during that time overlook completely the serious situation in which it found itself. Without having a dependable instrument of power, it was supposed to control the frantic outbreaks of violence of the misled masses. [Military] formations which were organized to protect the government soon made impossible demands and threatened to use force if they were not met; they even arrested the government for a time. . . . Nothing else could be done but to make use of the remaining organized parts of the regular army which, to be sure, were commanded chiefly by reactionary officers. . . .[21]

[20] Waite, *op. cit.*, pp. 2-3; *Illustrierte Geschichte*, pp. 234-36; Erich Otto Volkmann, *Revolution ueber Deutschland* (Oldenburg: Gerhard Stalling, 1930), p. 119. For details on the Republican Soldiers' Army, see also Oertzen, *op. cit.*, p. 248; Noske, *Erlebtes*, p. 80; Anton Fischer, *Die Revolutions-Kommandantur Berlin* ([Berlin], 1922]), pp. 8-11. Revealing is the admission of Lt. Anton Fischer, who later succeeded Otto Wels as City Commandant and who assisted in the organiza-tion of the *Republikanische Soldatenwehr,* that the so-called volunteers were quite interested in the monetary aspect of their services. Since the funds available at the *Kommandantur* were not sufficient, large amounts of money came from bourgeois circles which were interested in supporting a military force serving the moderate Majority Socialists against the dangers from the radical left. (*Ibid.*)

[21] Braun, *op. cit.*, p. 84.

The motives behind the willingness of the military to collaborate with Ebert and the Majority Socialists during this period of flux were primarily to safeguard the unity and integrity of the Reich against a possible Bolshevik assault and to preserve the authority, prestige, and reputation of the professional German officer corps.[22] The specific demands which the military made in return for their assistance to the Provisional government were: (1) summoning of the national assembly, (2) disarming of the civilian population, and (3) abolition of all workers' and soldiers' councils.[23]

The "Ebert-Groener Deal" did not work out satisfactorily for Ebert. The Supreme Command recognized that while it was still in control of the field army it had strong bargaining power, but that as soon as the troops were in Germany for any length of time they would inevitably disperse. Therefore, Groener and Hindenburg soon pressed Ebert to fulfill their demands, in particular the disarmament of the workers, the abolition of the workers' and soldiers' councils, and the ousting of the Independents from the

[22] Wheeler-Bennett, *op. cit.,* p. 22; Goerlitz, *op. cit.,* p. 297. For detailed information on the establishment of contact between Ebert and Groener over a secret telephone line running from the Reich Chancellery to Army headquarters at Spa and on their conversation and agreement, see Waite, *op. cit.,* pp. 4-9; Volkmann, *Revolution,* pp. 67-68. Also see *Illustrierte Geschichte,* p. 233 for an extract of Groener's statement in the *Munich Dolchstossprozess* in 1925.

General von Luettwitz explained the background of the collaboration of the military leaders with the Provisional government as follows: "The old officer corps gave its support to the People's Commissars not because of its admiration or its political conviction, but because of the pressure of time which categorically demanded the prevention of [duplicating] Russian conditions [in Germany]. The situation during the early part of December, 1918 was such that this could be done only in collaboration with the Ebert government. The time had definitely passed when the troops, independently and on their own, could possibly have nipped the revolt in the bud and could have suppressed it." (Freiherr Walter von Luettwitz, *Im Kampf gegen die November-Revolution* [Berlin: Vorhut Verlag, 1934], p. 17.)

[23] Goerlitz, *op. cit.,* p. 298; Wheeler-Bennett, *op. cit.,* pp. 28-29. Wheeler-Bennett describes the intimate contact between Ebert and Groener as follows: "Each night between eleven and one, the two men in whose hands the destiny of Germany rested talked together without fear of being overheard and, in Groener's words, 'reviewed the situation from day to day according to developments.' Indeed this secret wire became a kind of umbilical cord which bound the infant German Republic to its progenitor and protector, the German Army." (*Ibid.,* p. 28.)

Provisional government — if necessary with the use of armed force which they were ready to supply. Ebert believed that this action might bring about a civil war which he wished to avoid under all circumstances.[24]

When the long-promised front divisions finally arrived in Berlin — the troops which were to empower the Provisional government to deal forcefully with the difficult situation in the capital — they dispersed rapidly, partly because of the effective leftist propaganda and partly because the soldiers wanted to be home for Christmas. Shortly after the first troops arrived on December 11, roughly only 1,400 men of the original nine or ten divisions remained.[25] As early as December 16, the military leaders as well as Ebert realized that the plans based on the returning field army had failed.[26]

In order to provide the government with reliable troops, Major von Schleicher's suggestion was accepted. He had recommended the organization of volunteer corps recruited from among veteran army men and non-commissioned officers and commanded by imperial officers.[27]

[24] *Ibid.*, pp. 28-29. According to Walter Goerlitz, Ebert ". . . was afraid of a civil war with all its horrible consequences, the same civil war which the General Staff regarded as indispensable to the clarification of power relations and to the re-establishment of order." (Goerlitz, *op. cit.*, p. 300.)

[25] *Illustrierte Geschichte*, p. 234. See also Edgar von Schmidt-Pauli, *Geschichte der Freikorps 1918-1924* (Stuttgart: Robert Lutz Nachfolger Otto Schramm, 1936), pp. 178-79; Volkmann, *Revolution,* pp. 125-35; Noske, *Erlebtes,* p. 81; Wheeler-Bennett, *op. cit.,* pp. 30-31.

[26] Volkmann, *Revolution,* pp. 135-36.

[27] This proposal by Schleicher was made December 20, 1918, during a meeting of the General Staff officers in Berlin. It followed the example set by volunteer corps organized for the defense of the eastern border of the Reich and authorized by Hindenburg as early as November 24. (Goerlitz, *op. cit.,* pp. 300-01; Konrad Heiden, *Der Fuehrer* [Boston: Houghton Mifflin Co., 1944], p. 243.) There appears to be some willful distortion of the beginning date of the formation of the notorious Free Corps. Many of their units were organized during the later part of December, 1918. Ebert and Noske, for example, visited the "Free Corps Maercker" on January 4, 1919. (Volkmann, *Revolution,* p. 171.) Therefore, Hermann Mueller is absolutely incorrect when he asserts that the Free Corps were organized after the outbreak on January 4, 1919, of the so-called "January Uprising." Mueller claims that these voluntary formations were supposed to provide the government with the necessary freedom of action in order to carry

Simultaneously with the build-up of a military force by former imperial officers with the sanction of the Majority Socialists, several propaganda organizations financed by reactionary circles operated a vicious campaign against the radical left. For example, the Anti-Bolshevik Liga disseminated hate literature against the Spartacists and in particular against Rosa Luxemberg and Liebknecht. These activities, organized primarily by extremists of the right, were designed to get mob action against the revolutionary workers. The propaganda was also very strongly anti-Semitic.[28]

The attitude of the Western Allies toward Bolshevik Russia and toward the workers' and soldiers' councils in Germany became an issue in the political struggle within Germany for and against the consolidation of the revolution. The pro-consolidation forces asserted that the Western Allies would never permit Germany to follow the Russian example because this would bring Bolshevism too close to their own home territories.[29] Concrete examples of hostile actions by the Allied occupation authorities, especially the French, against the councils were cited. Indigenous opponents of the council system emphasized that the Allies openly refused to deal with representatives of the councils and did not hesitate to show preference for officials of the old bureaucracy.[30]

No information is available on the effectiveness of this anti-council propaganda. However, the Executive Council in Berlin

out preparations for the election of the constituent national assembly. (Hermann Mueller, op. cit., p. 192.) The basis for Mueller's statement is the fact that the first official announcement by the Provisional government concerning the formation of Free Corps is dated January 9, 1919, when the January uprising was well underway. However, numerous units of this type were definitely in existence prior to that date. (Goerlitz, op. cit., p. 301; Stuemke, op. cit., p. 163.) For a very thorough study of the entire Free Corps Movement, see Waite, op. cit.

[28] Hermann Mueller, op. cit., pp. 108-10, 122; Illustrierte Geschichte,

pp. 236-38; Froelich, Rosa Luxemburg, p. 320.

[29] Ebenstein, op. cit., p. 196.

[30] Ernst Fraenkel, Military Occupation and the Rule of Law (London: Oxford University Press, 1944), pp. 25-36. In a speech delivered on November 28, 1918, Liebknecht confirmed the alleged practice of the Allies of dissolving the workers' and soldiers' councils in the territory occupied by their troops. Liebknecht interpreted this as symptomatic of Allied fear that their own troops might become "infected" by the revolutionary spirit. (Liebknecht, Was ist zu tun?, p. 493.)

found it necessary to take steps to counteract its influence. The Executive Council distributed leaflets in which the bourgeois newspapers were accused of printing false allegations concerning the Allied attitude towards the councils. These leaflets asserted that the Allies did not demand the abolition of the workers' and soldiers' councils, and to prove this point, the city of Trier was given as an example: here the American commandant had officially recognized the local council.[31]

2. The Left Wing Radicals' Opposition to Consolidation

The Spartacists and the left wing radicals within the USPD fought with determination against the consolidation efforts of the combined powers of the Majority Socialists, bourgeois politicians, and military leaders. The opposition of the revolutionary radicals to the summoning of a constituent national assembly remained unchanged. They continued to view the assembly as nothing but an instrument for continuing the suppression of the working class. The radicals also did not share the optimism of the SPD which expected a socialist majority in the assembly; on the contrary, they anticipated a victory of the bourgeois political parties.[32]

Rosa Luxemburg's opposition to the national assembly increased steadily after it became known that all political forces of the right, including the Supreme Command, had become supporters of the "new democracy" to be founded by the constituent assembly. In December she identified the national assembly as "a counterrevolutionary fortification against the revolutionary proletariat."[33] In an article in *Die Rote Fahne*, she described the two alternatives faced by the German people:

[31] Vollzugsrat des Arbeiter-u. Soldatenrates, *Die buergerliche Presse arbeitet gegen die Revolution* ([Berlin, leaflet], December 17, 1918).

[32] "The capitalists and Junkers will utilize the war-weariness of the shopkeepers and the speculative spirit of the farmers, they will incite the small property owners against the workers, and it is quite probable that the majority in the national assembly will not favor the class-conscious workers, but will be on the side of the bourgeoisie." (Karl Radek, *Die deutsche Revolution* [Moscow, November, 1918], p. 17.) Karl Liebknecht also shared this opinion. (Liebknecht, *Was will der Spartakusbund?*, p. 508.)

[33] Rosa Luxemburg, "Die Wahlen zur Nationalversammlung," quoted in

Either national assembly or complete power to the workers' and soldiers' councils, either renunciation of socialism or most violent class struggle of the armed proletariat against the bourgeoisie: that is the dilemma.[34]

In spite of the Spartacists' violent opposition to any action directed toward a consolidation of the unfinished revolution, they did not plan, prepare, or organize an armed uprising with the intention of overthrowing the government — regardless of the many allegations of their numerous contemporary enemies. Neither their political utterances and written statements nor their actions can be used to support these claims which were widely disseminated not only by "bourgeois" and military circles but also by the Majority Socialists. In fact, both the political concepts and the actions of the Spartacists at that time followed a very simple and open pattern which does not resemble the deceptive tactics of contemporary Communist parties.

Their short-range revolutionary tactics were based on the following assumptions: (1) the revolution was being betrayed by the Majority Socialists who were supported in their endeavors by the traditional enemies of political, social, and economic progress; (2) most of the workers were unaware of the course which developments took after the mass uprising of November and, therefore, could not understand the "treacherous" actions of the SPD and of the moderate wing of the USPD.[35]

The Spartacists' conviction of the political immaturity of the workers and soldiers did not affect their confidence in the masses. It was merely a statement of fact which called for specific remedies.

Luxemburg, *Ausgewaehlte Reden,* II, pp. 651-52.

[34] Rosa Luxemburg, "Nationalversammlung oder Raeteregierung," quoted in Luxemburg, *Ausgewaehlte Reden,* II, p. 640.

[35] Liebknecht blamed the policies of the Majority Socialists for the confused state of mind of the masses and for a lack of political and social consciousness. (Karl Liebknecht, "Was ist zu tun?," quoted in Liebknecht, *Ausgewaehlte Reden,* p. 486.) The soldiers were especially ignorant about socialism. (Karl Liebknecht, "Der neue Burgfrieden," quoted in Liebknecht, *Ausgewaehlte Reden,* p. 469.)

Revolutionary propaganda and "revolutionary actions" were the means by which the Spartacists intended to educate the masses and gradually win over the majority of the working class. The revolutionary actions referred to were nothing more than street demonstrations and strikes, primarily of a political nature. Because of their political content, leading inevitably to clashes with the "reactionary" forces of the government, they would attract more and more workers and revolutionize growing segments of the masses. It was nothing but an extension of the old "revolutionary gymnastics," as the opponents of the Spartacists called Liebknecht's tactics before and during the November uprising.

While Liebknecht tended more toward action, Rosa Luxemburg believed that the principal mission of the Spartacist League was "to arouse a socialist spirit and consciousness in the workers."[36] However, both apparently agreed that the proletarian revolution was only the beginning of a long and tedious road, and both — but particularly Rosa Luxemburg — warned their followers against rash actions.[37] As late as December 23, 1918, after numerous armed clashes between left wing radicals and various other groups, including military formations — struggles which often were used to illustrate the allegation that the Spartacists wanted to overthrow the government by a putsch — Liebknecht declared in a speech in Berlin:

At present the Spartacists are attacked from all sides. The newspapers of the bourgeoisie and the social patriots, from the *Vorwaerts*

[36] Ruth Fischer, *op. cit.,* p. 74. Ruth Fischer believes that the difference in emphasis in these two tactical approaches between Luxemburg a n d Liebknecht reached the nature of a conflict during the months of November and December, 1918. (*Ibid.*)

[37] When Karl Radek returned to Germany from Russia at the end of December, 1918, Liebknecht allegedly told him without disappointment: "We are only at the beginning; the road will be a long one." Radek further reported that Liebknecht, Rosa Luxemburg, and he agreed that the only way to shorten the distance to the ultimate aim was relentless agitation, propaganda, and action. (Liebknecht, *Reden,* p. 366.)

The Communists attach two different meanings to the terms "agitation" and "propaganda." Lenin adopted the definition originally stated by Plekhanov, who is quoted by him as having made the following distinction: "A propagandist presents many ideas to one or a few persons; an agitator

to the *Kreuzzeitung,* abound with the most fantastic lies, with the most insolent misrepresentations, with distortions, and defamations. There is nothing we are not accused of. We are supposed to advocate terror; we are presumed to intend to start the bloodiest civil war; we are presumed to have equipped ourselves with weapons and ammunition in preparation for the armed revolt.[38]

The Spartacists remained confident throughout the consolidation phase that, as long as the workers could prevent the counterrevolutionary forces from suppressing the revolutionary movement, the masses eventually would follow the political program of the Spartacist League.[39] Their confidence in the masses received new impetus when the huge strike movement was started

presents only one or a few ideas, but he presents them to a mass of people." (Alex Inkeles, *Public Opinion in Soviet Russia* [Cambridge: Harvard University Press, 1950], p. 39.)

[38] Karl Liebknecht, "Was will der Spartakusbund?" quoted in Liebknecht, *Ausgewaehlte Reden,* p. 518. A typical example of a bloody clash occurred in Berlin on December 6, 1918. The tension among the various political factions, especially between the Spartacists and the Majority Socialists, was further aggravated by a number of events which transpired on that day; an attempted arrest of the Executive Council by troops, an occupation of the building of *Die Rote Fahne,* and the appointment of Ebert as the new Reich President by a group of soldiers. On that day also three mass meetings of the Spartacists were held which were followed by the usual demonstration marches. The demonstrators marched toward the heart of the city as rumors were being spread that a counterrevolution had been launched. Troops attached to the office of the SPD City Commandant, Otto Wels, attempted to intercept the demonstrators. The ensuing street fighting resulted in approximately 18 demonstrators killed and 30 wounded. For further details on these events, see *Illustrierte Ge-*

schichte, pp. 242-44; Stampfer, *Die ersten 14 Jahre,* pp. 80-81; Oertzen, *op. cit.,* pp. 249-50; Volkmann, *Revolution,* pp. 122-24.

[39] See Liebknecht's warnings about the counterrevolution in *Die Rote Fahne,* November 21, 1918:

". . . . .

"Let us not deceive ourselves. The political power of the proletariat which was seized on the ninth [of November], is almost gone by now and continues to disappear hour by hour.

"Parallel with this process of the weakening of the proletariat goes a most intensive rallying process of all the deadly enemies of the proletariat. In the country as well as in the cities, the counterrevolution organizes [its forces] w i t h increasing cynicism." (Liebknecht, *Das, was ist,* pp. 474-75.)

In the December 2, 1918, issue, he clearly pointed at the dangers coming from the military commanders of the returning front-line units. The Socialists in particular were threatened by them. Liebknecht reported cases where workers' and soldiers' councils were abolished by military commands. He also described other excesses committed by the military against socialist workers. (Karl Liebknecht, "Ruestung der Revolution," quoted in Liebknecht *Ausgewaehlte Reden,* pp. 499-502.)

at the end of November 1918 by the metal workers in Berlin and the miners in Upper Silesia and the Ruhr area. The strikes spread rapidly to other industries throughout Germany and involved great numbers of workers. The workers originally struck for purely economic reasons but soon political demands came into play. Clashes with counterrevolutionary troops resulted in the death of many workers.[40] The Spartacists interpreted the spontaneous mass strikes as an indication that the workers again were beginning to take matters into their own hands in spite of the efforts of the consolidation forces. Rosa Luxemburg believed that these strikes would grow in size and importance and would become the focal points of the revolution. She also predicted that the revolution would assume an economic character and would become a truly socialist revolution.[41]

In an article in *Die Rote Fahne* she greeted these strikes as the beginning of the most powerful phase of direct mass action:

Instead of waiting for the blessed decrees of the government or for the decisions of the famous national assembly, the masses instinctively reach for the only real means which leads to socialism: *the fight against capital.* Up to now, the government has exerted every effort to castrate the revolution and to establish harmony among classes. . . .

The proletarian masses upset . . . the revolutionary class harmony and wave the dreaded banner of the class struggle.

The growing strike movement is proof that the political revolution invaded the social foundation of society. The revolution recalls its own original cause; it puts aside the paper wing of personnel changes and decrees which did not in the slightest effect changes, in the social relation between capital and labor, and places itself upon the stage of events.

. . . .

The strikes which have just broken out are within [the framework] of the present revolution, and are not controversies of a "trade-union

---

[40] *Illustrierte Geschichte*, p. 247.   [41] Richard Mueller, *Vom Kaiserreich*, II, p. 676.

type" pertaining to trifles, to wage problems. They are the masses' natural answer to the powerful shock which capitalism has experienced as the result of the breakdown of German imperialism and the short political revolution of the workers and soldiers. They are the first beginning of a complete settlement between capital and labor in Germany; they introduce the start of a powerful, direct [form of] class struggle in which the outcome can be nothing other than the removal of the capitalist wage system and the introduction of the socialist economy. They release the active social power of the present revolution: the revolutionary class energy of the proletarian masses. They open up the period of direct activity on the part of the great masses. . . .[42]

This interpretation of the strike movement by Rosa Luxemburg was later strongly criticized by the representatives of the official Communist creed because, according to them, it revealed once more her two greatest weaknesses: over-confidence in the spontaneity of the masses, and a lack of appreciation of the role of a revolutionary class party. By the middle of December 1918, however, there were already specific signs that the need for a proletarian party which could supply leadership to the revolutionary masses was increasingly recognized by many of the Spartacists and other left wing radicals.[43]

It is possible to see in Rosa Luxemburg's program for the Spartacist League — published on December 14, 1918, in *Die Rote Fahne* — a conscious step toward uniting the left wing radicals by providing them with a common platform.[44] Considering that it preceded the founding of the KPD by only two weeks and the so-called "Spartacist Uprising" by about three weeks, this comprehensive statement of the Spartacists' political concepts and

[42] Rosa Luxemburg, "Der Acheron in Bewegung," quoted in Luxemburg, *Ausgewaehlte Reden*, II, pp. 618, 620.

[43] See, for example, Oelssner, *op. cit.*, pp. 133-34. Oelssner also referred to another "misconception" of Rosa Luxemburg: "The weakness of the German Revolution," according to him, was not that the revolution had not included in its earlier phase issues related to "the social foundation of society," but that the political revolution was never concluded and that no real decision had settled the question of political power. (*Ibid.*, p. 133.)

[44] *Illustrierte Geschichte*, pp. 259-63.

policies was important for several reasons. First of all, the program re-emphasized the ideological independence of the Spartacists from major Leninist concepts by specifically rejecting the use of terror as a tactical method and the precept of dictatorship by a minority. Secondly, it clarified the position of the Spartacists *vis-à-vis* the Ebert government and any other "bourgeois" government, as a policy of non-participation and non-interference in governmental affairs until the Spartacist League had the support of the majority of the proletariat. Thirdly, it formulated tactics for the long period of class struggle aimed at securing the confidence and support of the masses. Fourthly, it provided the basis for searching discussions among the left wing radicals during the two weeks which intervened between the announcement of the program and the founding of the KPD.[45]

Rosa Luxemburg's clear formulation of these political concepts left no room for misinterpretations, especially of those issues related to the Spartacists' position toward a *coup d'état*. Her statement concerning the rejection of terror reads as follows:

> The proletarian revolution requires no terror methods [to realize] its objectives; it hates and despises violence and murder. It does not require this means of combat because it does not fight against individuals but against institutions. . . . It is not a desperate attempt of a minority to shape the world by force according to its ideals, but the

---

[45] Ruth Fischer's interpretation of the main points of the program are:

(1) ". . . the Spartakusbund would not participate in any kind of workers' or democratic party alliance. If the present government reached an impasse, the Spartakusbund would neither attempt to support it nor attempt to overthrow it; it would neither share in a caretaker successor government, nor take power alone. In effect, the Spartacist program was equivalent to a critical toleration of the Ebert government, combined with militant propaganda against army and for socialist aims."

(2) ". . . the rejection of revolutionary terror, again a conscious and strong rejection of Bolshevik practice. The Spartakusbund emphatically denied punitive measures against their enemies; . . ."

(3) ". . . a program of non-interference in the policy of the new Republic — of absentionism concerning the formation of the new state; that is, participation in elections to the national assembly but as a mere propaganda instrument." (Ruth Fischer, *op. cit.,* p. 75.)

action of great masses of millions of people who are called up to fulfill a historic mission and to transform historic necessity into reality.[46]

In the conclusions to the program, Rosa Luxemburg summarized the position of the Spartacist League as follows:

The Spartacist League is not a party desirous of obtaining political power over the working masses or through the working masses.

The Spartacist League is only the most conscious part of the proletariat [in terms of] objectives, pointing incessantly to the historic task for the entire broad masses of the working class, representing throughout the individual phases of the revolution the ultimate socialist objective and representing in all national issues the interests of the proletarian world revolution.

The Spartacist League rejects the idea of sharing power with Scheidemann and Ebert, tools of the bourgeoisie, because in this type of collaboration, it sees treason to the fundamentals of socialism, strengthening of the counterrevolution, and paralysis of the revolution.

The Spartacist League will never assume governmental power unless it is supported by the clear, decisive will of the great majority of the proletariat in Germany, and in no other way except with their conscious acceptance of the ideas, objectives, and fighting methods of the Spartacist League.

.   .   .   .

The victory of the Spartacist League stands not at the beginning but at the end of the revolution: it is identical with the victory of the millions of masses of the socialist proletariat.[47]

Not all of the opposition to the consolidation policy came from the Spartacists. The left wing of the USPD, on many issues holding views close to these of the Spartacists, formed a powerful opposition force. The moderate USPD leaders, although on an entirely different level of operation (i.e., in the Provisional government), also frequently disagreed with the policies of the Ma-

---

[46] *Illustrierte Geschichte*, p. 261.   [47] *Ibid.*, p. 263.

jority Socialists and eventually, at the end of December, 1918, officially joined the opposition to the Ebert government.[48]

The USPD's position toward the problem of consolidation versus continuation of the revolution was made more complex by the fact that the USPD had accepted governmental responsibilities within the "legitimate" and council governments of the Reich. In addition, the USPD supported two distinct positions since they were divided among themselves.

The left wing of the Independents occupied the seven seats which the USPD originally had in the Executive Council. The Revolutionary Shop Stewards looked upon the Executive Council as their own domain, especially since one of their leaders, Richard Mueller, was its chairman.[49]

The left wing radicals of the USPD, with their strongholds in the Executive Council and among the Revolutionary Shop Stewards, very vigorously opposed the principle of national assembly and favored, as did the Spartacists, the council system. They intended to make it a permanent feature of the governmental structure.[50] On November 13, 1918, Ernst Daeumig, an exponent of the left wing faction of the USPD and a member of the Executive Council, proposed a resolution against the holding of the national assembly. Three days later the Council discussed the matter. Daeumig announced his preference for a "proletarian democracy," the class rule of the proletariat. His proposal was defeated by a vote of twelve to ten and the Executive Council thereby endorsed the national assembly.[51] It was agreed, however, to call a general meeting of all the delegates of the workers' and soldiers' councils for November 19, 1918, at the Circus Busch to discuss the extremely important issue of consolidation versus continuation of the revolution and to give the Executive Council

[48] See below, pp. 147-49.

[49] Hermann Mueller, *op. cit.*, p. 100; Tormin, *op. cit.*, p. 74. Gradually, the Executive Council increased in membership to 45. See also a very interesting description of the continuously expanding work of the Executive Council, Hermann Mueller, *op. cit.*, pp. 107, 111ff.

[50] Oertzen, *op. cit.*, p. 247.

[51] Hermann Mueller, *op. cit.*, p. 128.

an opportunity to report on its activities. At the meeting Richard Mueller vigorously opposed the national assembly and, like the Spartacists, referred to it as an instrument of the counterrevolution. It was at this meeting that he earned his nickname *"Leichenmueller"* (Corpse-Mueller) because of the following statement in his speech:

We, the workers' and soldiers' councils must defend our power, even by force if it cannot be done otherwise. Whoever advocates the national assembly forces us to fight. I announce openly to you: I have risked my life for the revolution and I shall do it again. The national assembly is the road to political dominance by the bourgeoisie; it is the road which leads to fighting; the road to the national assembly proceeds over my corpse . . .[52]

Haase attempted to pacify the assembled delegates by declaring that it was impossible to lose the revolutionary achievements because the proletariat had the majority. He asserted furthermore that in Germany democracy and socialism belong together. The meeting achieved no positive results although it contributed to increased tension between the Executive Council and the People's Commissars.[53]

The moderates among the USPD were represented in the Provisional government by Haase and Dittmann. (Barth, another Independent People's Commissar, opposed from the beginning anything the Ebert government did, but lacked the influence to do something about it.) They were opposed to the extreme forms of collaboration which the Majority Socialists undertook with the bourgeois and military representatives. However, they also opposed the revolutionary tactics of the Spartacists which were interpreted by some moderate USPD followers as preparations for a *coup d'état*.[54]

[52] *Ibid.*, p. 129.
[53] *Ibid.*, pp. 129-30.
[54] Haase (who was the People's Commissar in charge of foreign affairs and "colonial affairs") was apparently quite dissatisfied with the collaboration between the USPD and the Majority Socialists in the Provisional government. On November 26, 1918, he wrote the following in a letter to his

The moderates among the Independents were in complete disagreement with their leftist faction on the issue of the national assembly. Under pressure from the left, a general meeting of the Berlin USPD organization was held on December 15, 1918, at which Haase was able to achieve an important victory over the left wing radicals. He succeeded in obtaining support for his moderate policies: participation and preparation for the elections for the national assembly. The meeting endorsed the position of the moderates, 485 to 195 votes.[55]

3. The Struggle for Consolidation

During the month of December 1918, the Majority Socialists attained two major political achievements in their fight for the consolidation of the German Revolution. The first was the crushing defeat suffered by the council system at the First Reich Congress of Councils. The second was the establishment of an all-Majority Socialist government, an outgrowth of the fighting between regular troops and revolutionary military units during the Christmas period and the subsequent resignation of the USPD members from the Provisional government.

The workers' and soldiers' councils in Germany did not challenge the Executive Council of the Berlin Workers' and Soldiers' Council, which claimed jurisdiction over the entire country, until

son Ernst: ". . . The *Scheidemaenner* [people like the SPD leader Scheidemann], also kept bourgeois representatives in important political [governmental] positions. We still have not been able to accomplish the discharge of Solf [who had been foreign minister] from the Foreign Office, who without consulting me, publishes decrees in the same old manner. . . . The revolutionary process is still in its beginning phase. How it will continue depends on the work which the government will perform . . ." (Hugo Haase, *Hugo Haase sein Leben und Wirken* [Berlin: E. Laubsche Verlagsbuchhandlung, 1929], p. 173.)

[55] Stuemke, *op. cit.,* pp. 172-73; Hermann Mueller, *op. cit.,* pp. 234-35. Characteristic of the position of the moderates was the answer Haase gave during a meeting of the People's Commissars on December 28, 1918, in regard to his willingness to support any actions against a possible putsch by the Spartacists. Haase declared that he would oppose any violent threat against the government regardless of the quarters from which it came, but he added that he did not believe the Spartacists intended to stage a *coup d'état. (Ibid.,* pp. 235-36.)

the controversy over the future governmental structure — democratic, parliamentary republic through a constituent national assembly, or a council republic based exclusively on the council system — became the most urgent issue of the day. Pressure exerted by the councils to summon a Reich Congress of Councils became increasingly strong, because it appeared to the councils that the Executive Council was in favor of a class dictatorship. Thus, on November 23, 1918, after some delaying tactics, the Executive Council called the First Reich Congress of Councils for December 16, 1918, in Berlin.[56]

The Majority Socialists as well as the left wing radicals placed great expectations in the Reich Congress, each side hoping to get the support of the delegates for their respective concepts of the future Reich constitution. Rosa Luxemburg called upon the Congress to elect a Central Council which would make up for the omissions of the past and would take action against the counterrevolutionary forces which were poised to destroy the revolutionary institutions, the workers' and soldiers' councils. In order to save the revolution, Rosa Luxemburg proposed that the future Central Council undertake immediately after its inception the following four measures:

(1) It must eliminate the center of the counterrevolution, the point where all nerves of the counterrevolutionary conspiracy come together; it must remove the cabinet of Ebert, Scheidemann, and Haase.

(2) It must demand the disarming of all front units which do not unconditionally recognize the political authority of the workers' and soldiers' council and are being converted into a bodyguard for the cabinet of Ebert and Haase.

[56] Richard Mueller, *Vom Kaiserreich*, II, p. 98; Tormin, *op. cit.*, p. 94. Mueller claims that the People's Commissars demanded the Reich Congress because they hoped they would be able to work better with a central council elected by council representatives from all of Germany than with the Executive Council elected by the Workers' and Soldiers' Council of Berlin. (Hermann Mueller, *op. cit.*, p. 211.) Grzesinski presents the erroneous version that the Provisional Government convoked the Congress. (Grzesinski, *op. cit.*, p. 57.)

(3) *It must demand the disarming of all officers [of the military forces] and of the White Guards organized by the government of Ebert and Haase and it must create a Red Guard.

(4) It must reject the national assembly as an attack against the revolution and the workers' and soldiers' councils.[57]

The Russian Bolsheviks also saw the great influence a Reich Congress could exert on the further course of the German Revolution. They wished to assist the left wing radicals with, at the very least, advice and the prestige which the presence of a number of Bolshevik leaders at the Congress would give. On December 5, Lenin appointed a five-man delegation consisting of the expelled Joffe, Radek, Bukharin, Rakovsky, and Ignatov to participate in the Reich Congress at Berlin. But the Provisional government refused to grant permission for this delegation to enter Germany.[58]

In their evaluation of the general political situation, the Spartacists greatly overrated the revolutionary spirit among the masses. As a result, the outcome of the Reich Congress — the rejection of the council system — came as a great disappointment to them. The left wing radicals found in what they called the "outdated" composition of the Congress the explanation for the decisions made by the delegates; thus they did not have to admit the obvious fact that the majority of the German workers remained faithful to traditional Social Democratic concepts and were plainly opposed to a class dictatorship. The left wing radicals stressed the fact that the delegates were not chosen directly by the workers and soldiers but were actually representatives of the local councils which in most cases still had the same composition as when they were organized in the wake of the revolution. Therefore, the radicals claimed, they did not represent the true attitude of the

[57] Rosa Luxemburg, "Auf die Schanzen," quoted in Luxemburg, *Ausgewaehlte Reden*, II, pp. 635-39.

[58] Lionel Kochan, *Russia and the Weimar Republic* (Cambridge, England: Bowes Publishers, 1954), p. 13.

Only Radek, as already mentioned above, managed to reach Berlin disguised as an Austrian prisoner of war. He came too late for the Reich Con-

masts.[59] This assertion of substantial changes in the disposition of the masses toward the objectives of the radicals must be seriously questioned in view of the results of the January elections, in which the Majority Socialists obtained a large majority of the socialist votes.[60] Because of their superior organization throughout Germany, the SPD had a decided advantage during the selection of delegates for the Reich Congress. Nevertheless, the percentage-wise majority of the Majority Socialists among the delegates was not as "outdated" as claimed by the left radicals.[61] The generally unfriendly attitude of the Congress toward the political left was also reflected in its refusal to admit Rosa Luxemburg and Karl Liebknecht to the Congress even in an advisory capacity.[62]

The outcome of the main issue of the Congress — national assembly versus council system — was a foregone conclusion considering the overwhelming number of SPD delegates and soldiers who were under the influence of the Majority Socialists unless the radicals through outside pressure could change substantially the opinions of many of these delegates. The Spartacists wasted no

gress but was there for the founding congress of the Communist Party of Germany. (*Ibid.*, p. 14.)

[59] Froelich, *Rosa Luxemburg,* pp. 323-24; *Illustrierte Geschichte,* p. 249.

[60] The SPD obtained 11,400,000 votes and the USPD 2,300,000 votes. The KPD did not participate in the elections. (*Ibid.*, p. 307.)

[61] In order to prove the "inherent conservative" character of the Congress, the left wing radicals assembled some interesting statistical information. A total of 489 delegates had voting privileges: 405 were workers' councils and 84 soldiers' representatives. The political affiliation of the delegates was reported as follows: 288 Majority Socialists, 80 Independents, 10 Spartacists, 25 Democrats, 11 independent radicals, 25 members of a special soldiers' faction, 50 without party affiliation. (*Ibid.*, pp. 249-50.) Otto Grote-

wohl gave a somewhat different breakdown, but essentially he presents the same picture. (Grotewohl, *op. cit.,* p. 73.)

The professional composition of the Congress was given for most delegates: 195 paid party officials [such as party and union officials, editors, etc.], 164 from the SPD, 31 from the USPD, 179 workers and employees, 71 intellectuals [it is not clear if these 71 are a separate group or if they belong to other categories], 13 active army officers, 3 representatives of agricultural organizations, 1 tenant of a large landed estate. (*Illustrierte Geschichte,* p. 250.) Robert Leinert (SPD), Fritz Seger (USPD), and Gomolka (front-soldiers) were appointed as chairmen of the Congress. (Hermann Mueller, *op. cit.,* pp. 215-16.)

[62] Had Liebknecht really wanted to attend the meetings as a delegate, he

time. On the first day of the meeting, a workers' delegation presented to the Congress in the name of 250,000 Berlin revolutionaries a resolution which contained the following:

(1) Germany is a unitary socialist republic.

(2) All powers are vested in the workers' and soldiers' councils.

(3) The Executive Council elected by the Congress of Councils is the supreme legislative and executive authority and has the power to appoint and discharge People's Commissars and all Reich officials.

(4) Abolition of Ebert's Council of People's Commissars.

(5) Immediate, energetic execution, through the Central Council, of all measures necessary for the protection of the revolution, primarily the disarmament of the counterrevolution, arming of the proletariat, and organization of the Red Guard.

(6) An immediate proclamation by the Central Council addressed to the proletarians of all nations requesting them to form workers' and soldiers' councils for the purpose of fulfilling the common tasks of the socialist world revolution.[63]

The delegates failed to be impressed by the "workers' delegation" even after the effort was repeated two days later. A motion by Max Cohen-Reuss to hold elections for the national assembly as early as January 19, 1919, was accepted by a vote of 400 to 50. Daeumig's proposal to call for a new Congress of Councils which should decide on the future constitution for Germany and to vest the supreme legislative and executive powers in the council system was defeated, 344 to 98.[64]

could have been sent by his "National Association of Deserters" as a representative of the soldiers. It is quite possible that the interpretation by von Oertzen is correct; namely, that Liebknecht could only have made speeches as a delegate. He preferred to make use of the Congress by exerting pressure from the outside. (Oertzen, *op. cit.*, p. 254.)

[63] Quoted in *Illustrierte Geschichte,*

p. 251. The terms "Executive Council" and "Central Council" are apparently used here interchangeably. Usually, "Executive Council" is the name used for the executive committee of the Berlin Workers' and Soldiers' Council, and "Central Council" is applied to the executive committee elected by the Reich Congress of Councils.

[64] For a detailed discussion of the events of the Congress of Councils in

Thus the Congress of Councils had, in the words of Daeumig, committed suicide by voting against the council system and for the early election of a national assembly.

With a second major issue — the elimination of the influence of the old imperial army — the left wing radicals had more success with the delegates of the Congress because ". . . though divided on many points of Socialist doctrine and dogma, the Congress was unanimous and vociferous in its determination to put an end once and for all to the Officer Corps."[65] On this issue the Spartacists also employed pressure from the outside. On the second day of the meeting, December 17, 1918, a delegation of soldiers representing the entire Berlin garrison, including the People's Naval Division, Eichhorn's Security Force, and even Otto Wels' Republican Soldiers' Army, insisted that:

(1) The Supreme Soldiers' Council composed of elected delegates from all soldiers' councils, assumes command of all army troops and of the navy.

(2) All insignia of rank are prohibited. All officers are to be discharged. . . .

(3) The soldiers' councils will be responsible for the reliability and discipline of the troops.[66]

These demands became the basis for the so-called Seven Hamburg Points which the Congress adopted. The adoption of this anti-militaristic proposal placed Ebert in a very difficult position. He defended his military allies as best he could. Hindenburg let his fury be known, declaring that he would not follow the provisions set forth.[67]

relation to the issue of national assembly versus council system, see Bernstein, *op. cit.,* pp. 82-84, 91-95; Hermann Mueller, *op. cit.,* pp. 216-19; Tormin, *op. cit.,* pp. 97-100; Stampfer, *Die ersten 14 Jahre,* pp. 81-83. A motion to postpone the national assembly until March 16, 1919 was also defeated; only 50 votes were cast in its favor. (*Ibid.,* p. 82.)

[65] Wheeler-Bennett, *op. cit.,* p. 32.
[66] Quoted in *Illustrierte Geschichte,* p. 252; see also Hermann Mueller, *op. cit.,* pp. 217-18.
[67] For the text of the Seven Hamburg Points see *Illustrierte Geschichte,* p. 253. The name derives from the fact that it was proposed by the Hamburg delegation. Wheeler-Bennett, *op. cit.,* p. 32; Volkmann, *Revolution,* pp.

On December 20, 1918, the Congress was to elect the new Central Council which was to assume the functions of the Executive Council as the control organ of the People's Commissars until the meeting of the national assembly.[68] Having lost their fight for the perpetuation of the council system, the left wing radicals demanded that the powers of the Central Council be enlarged at the expense of the Council of the People's Commissars. There was a heated discussion on the interpretation of the term "supervision" in the adopted proposal of Luedemann-Kahmann-Severing which, against the votes of the left radicals, had transferred all legislative and executive powers to the Council of People's Commissars for the period before the meeting of the national assembly. The motion defined the functions of the Central Council as "supervision of the German and Prussian cabinet" and "the right to appoint and discharge People's Commissars, and until the final settlement of the governmental structure, also the People's Commissars of Prussia."[69] Haase viewed this arrangement as requiring the People's Commissars to present legislative drafts to the Central Council and to seek its advice in important cases. However, if the Central Council should disagree with the People's Commissars, the latter had the right to make a decision indepen-

---

137-45; Oertzen, *op. cit.*, pp. 255-56; Hermann Mueller, *op. cit.*, pp. 182-86; Waite, *op. cit.*, pp. 8-9. The Seven Hamburg Points became law because they were adopted by the Congress of Councils. However, they were never implemented. On December 20, 1918, a joint meeting of the People's Commissars with the newly-elected Central Council took place. General Groener and Major von Schleicher were invited to attend. The members of the Central Council agreed that they had gone too far in accepting the Hamburg Points. It was decided that this law had no validity for the units of the field army, border troops, and navy. As far as the home army was concerned, i.e., the army administrative units and the units slated for demobilization, special or-

ders implementing the Hamburg Points were to be worked out. (Oertzen, *op. cit.*, pp. 256-57; Volkmann, *Revolution*, pp. 149-51.)

For another version of this meeting, see Barth, *op. cit.*, pp. 93-94.

[68] The official announcement made on December 21, 1918, read as follows: "The Central Council of the German Socialist R e p u b l i c has been formed and has taken over the governmental business for the Reich and Prussia. The Executive Council of the Workers' and Soldiers' Council of Greater Berlin continues its activities for the Greater Berlin area." (Quoted in Roemer, *op. cit.*, pp. 22-23.) Cf. above, pp. 96-97.

[69] Hermann Mueller, *op. cit.*, pp. 218-19.

dently.[70] The left wing radicals insisted that the entire legislative powers remain with the Central Council. A vote of 290 to 115 decided to retain Haase's interpretation of the division of jurisdiction between the two Councils.[71] Against the advice of Haase, Dittmann, and Hilferding, the USPD factions decided not to participate in the election for the Central Council. The USPD left wingers like Ledebour and Richard Mueller, who forced their party to leave the supreme council organ to the Majority Socialists, justified their decision by insisting that they did not wish to participate in the strangulation of the council system.[72]

The twenty-seven persons on the list of the SPD were elected to the Central Council. Among them were Max Cohen-Reuss (who became chairman), Hermann Mueller, Albert Grzesinski, and Robert Leinert.[73]

The First Congress of Councils was a complete victory for the SPD with the one exception of the military issue. (But the Majority Socialists were able to straighten out quickly the tensions which the adoption of the Hamburg Points had created between the Supreme Command and the Provisional government. As has been pointed out above, in practice nothing was done about these Points.) In the first place, the proponents of the councils were turned down by the council delegates themselves; secondly, the

[70] For the text of Haase's statement, see Bernstein, *op. cit.,* p. 93.

[71] *Ibid.,* p. 95.

[72] Hermann Mueller, *op. cit.,* p. 223; Stampfer, *Die ersten 14 Jahre,* p. 83.

[73] For a listing of the members of the Central Council see Bernstein, *op. cit.,* p. 95. Hermann Mueller reports interesting details of the work of the Central Council and its organizational structure. (Hermann Mueller, *op. cit.,* pp. 239-40.) When the national assembly met, the Central Council relinquished the political power it had obtained from the Reich Congress. (Roemer, *op. cit.,* p. 24.) However, it did continue with some functions and only ended its activities in the middle of July 1920. (Grzesinski, *op. cit.,* p. 64.) A second Congress of Councils met in Berlin on April 15, 1919, and changed the Central Council into a kind of workers' interest representation. The notion of political councils had been eliminated by the Majority Socialists in all bodies over which they held control. (Roemer, *op. cit.,* pp. 30-32.) The last item on the agenda of the Reich Congress was the problem of socialization. The Congress directed the People's Commissars to start soon with the socialization of "ripe" industries as recommended by Hilferding in his report to the delegates. (Bernstein, *op. cit.,* pp. 95-99; *Illustrierte Geschichte,* p. 254.)

Congress reaffirmed the SPD aims of the revolution — the democratic, parliamentary republic; and thirdly, the delegates added to the general optimism and confidence with which the public looked upon the coming national assembly.[74] Of paramount importance was the fact that the Central Council was composed exclusively of SPD members, a situation which considerably weakened the position of the Independent People's Commissars.[75]

Shortly after the Majority Socialists had won this major battle in the Reich Congress of Councils, difficulties with the People's Naval Division in Berlin gave them a pretext to impress the left wing radicals with the military strength they thought they could muster against any attempt to seize power. Whether this display of force was a deliberate act on the part of Ebert and the Supreme Command or was the result of a situation thrust upon them is most difficult to determine; the available accounts relating to the People's Naval Division are contradictory. Nationalists and Majority Socialists usually described the sailors as a group of mercenaries and looters; the left wing radicals made them out to be revolutionary idealists.[76] Even more important, the information relating to the incidents which brought out the bloody fighting on December 24, 1918, is also contradictory. The sailors allegedly had agreed to vacate the Imperial Castle and to reduce the strength of their division as of January 1, 1919, to 600 men in return for 80,000 marks.[77] For reasons which are not quite clear Ebert and the City Commandant refused to pay the money in spite of the agreement made with the sailors. The left wing radicals

[74] Tormin, op. cit., p. 101. Hermann Mueller believed that great credit is due to the Congress because its decisions opened the road to the national assembly. (Hermann Mueller, op. cit., p. 224.)

[75] Rosa Luxemburg wrote on December 20, 1918, in Die Rote Fahne about the new Central Council. She claimed that this development finally achieved "the Ebert-'control' over the Ebert-government. Control of the devil by his mother-in-law." (Rosa Luxemburg, "Eberts Mamelucken," quoted in Luxemburg, Ausgewaehlte Reden, II, p. 648.)

[76] Compare, f o r example, Volkmann, Revolution, p. 133 with the account in Illustrierte Geschichte, pp. 254-55.

[77] The agreement, signed by all six People's Commissars, is quoted in Bernstein, op. cit., p. 104. (The Imperial Castle and Stables were used by the sailors as headquarters.)

charged that the violation of the agreement was a willful provocation intended to incite the sailors to rash actions. The sailors reacted to Ebert's decision with the arrest of the People's Commissars, the cutting of all telephone lines from the Reich Chancellery, and the seizure of Wels and two other Majority Socialists as hostages. Ebert used the direct telephone line to the Supreme Command (the sailors did not know of its existence) to ask for immediate help. On the same day, units of the First Guard Cavalry Rifle Division under the command of General von Lequis were sent from Babelsberg, located a few miles from the center of Berlin, with the mission "to finish once and for all the People's Naval Division."[78] There is no doubt that Ebert, without notifying the USPD People's Commissars, gave orders to General von Lequis to liberate Wels and to force the People's Naval Division into unconditional surrender.[79]

The military action of the regular troops of the Supreme Command was a complete fiasco. After initial successes against the outnumbered sailors, fortune changed. Armed workers and units of Eichhorn's Security Force and the Republican Soldiers' Army came to the assistance of the sailors. On the same day, December 24, 1918, Major von Harbou, Chief of Staff of Army Corps Lequis, phoned the Supreme Command and declared that it was impossible to rely on the existing regular troops. The Supreme Command then decided to step up the organization of the Free Corps units in order to have the military force needed to handle the "internal chaos."[80]

The military outcome of the conflict gave the People's Naval Division a victory over the Provisional government. However, negotiations conducted after the cessation of fighting effectively

[78] Oertzen, op. cit., p. 258; Stampfer, Die ersten 14 Jahre, p. 85.

[79] Schmidt-Pauli, op. cit., p. 181; Illustrierte Geschichte, pp. 257-58; Richard Mueller, Der Buergerkrieg, p. 9.

[80] Oertzen, op. cit., pp. 259-60; Richard Mueller, Der Buergerkrieg,

pp. 11-12; Illustrierte Geschichte, pp. 256-57; Schmidt-Pauli, op. cit., p. 181. For very detailed accounts of the Christmas fighting and its background, see Bernstein, op. cit., pp. 100-21; Volkmann, Revolution, pp. 152-64; Hermann Mueller, op. cit., pp. 224-33.

neutralized the unit. The sailors were attached to the Republican Soldiers' Army and thereby came under the jurisdiction of the City Commandant. (Otto Wels was replaced on December 28, 1918, by Lieutenant Anton Fischer.) The division of General Lequis was withdrawn immediately. On the other hand, the sailors obligated themselves to vacate the Castle and in the future never to support an action directed against the government.[81]

The Christmas incident had far-reaching political repercussions which overshadowed the military setback suffered by the SPD and which eventually led to the second major political gain of the Majority Socialists in December. The Independent People's Commissars objected to the decision of Ebert, Scheidemann, and Landsberg giving unlimited authority to the Minister of War to deal with the People's Naval Division. They were even more alarmed since it had been done without consulting the USPD members of the Provisional government. Therefore, on December 27, Haase, Dittmann, and Barth directed eight questions to the Central Council, the alleged supervisory agency of the Council of People's Commissars. They made it clear that their continued support of the government depended upon the Council's answer. The questions were: Does the Central Council approve the action of the Majority Socialist cabinet members during the night of December 23-24, when unlimited authority was conferred on the Minister of War? Does the Council approve the methods employed by the troops of General von Lequis (i.e., a ten-minute ultimatum and artillery fire against the Castle and Stables)? What is the Council prepared to do about the Hamburg Points adopted at the Reich Congress? Does the Council endorse the Supreme

[81] Bernstein, op. cit., p. 118. Richard Mueller stresses the fact that no attempts were made by the left wing radicals to seize power on the evening of December 24, even though it was generally known that the government was without protection. The Spartacists called for mass demonstrations for the following day, December 25, to protest the actions of the Majority Socialist People's Commissars. (Richard Mueller, Der Buergerkrieg, pp. 15-17.) In the course of these demonstrations, the Vorwaerts building was occupied by a group of about 500 men. However, this action was neither planned nor ordered by the Spartacists or by the Revolutionary Shop Stewards. On the following day, the plant was again freed. (Noske, Erlebtes, p. 82.)

Command's defiance of the decisions of the workers' and soldiers' councils? Does the Council approve the transfer of the seat of government from Berlin as recommended by Ebert, Scheidemann, and Landsberg? Does the Council approve the limited demobilization of the army to peace-time strength instead of complete demobilization? How does the Council feel about the socialist republic's reliance for protection on the old imperial generals and units or on a newly-formed democratic people's army? Does the Council endorse immediate socialization of the industries ripe for it?[82]

After three hours of deliberation, the Central Council gave its reply. Because of its complete SPD composition, its answer was hardly a surprise. It was a complete endorsement of the actions of Ebert, Scheidemann, and Landsberg. The Independents thereupon withdraw from the Council of People's Commissars, from almost all other governmental offices of the Reich, and from the Prussian government.[83]

The Central Council, upon recommendation of the remaining People's Commissars, appointed three additional Majority Socialists, Gustav Noske, Rudolf Wissel, and Paul Loebe, as replacements. Loebe, however, declined, and since no substitute was elected to take his place, the Council of People's Commissars from then on was restricted to five members. Noske was assigned to handle military affairs for the Provisional government.[84]

[82] Text of this series of questions is quoted in Bernstein, op. cit., p. 123.

[83] The text of the reply of the Central Council to Haase, Dittmann, and Barth is quoted in ibid., pp. 123-24. The statement delivered by Haase justifying the resignation of the Independents from the government is quoted in ibid., p. 124. Bernstein claimed the withdrawal of the Independents was "an inglorious and unfortunate capitulation" to the principles of the Spartacists.

The withdrawal of the three USPD members from the Council of the People's Commissars was followed by the resignation of almost all Independents from leading positions in the Reich and Prussian governments. Bernstein, Kautsky, and Wurm were the exceptions and they remained in their offices because no immediate replacements were available. (Ibid., pp. 127, 130.)

[84] Stampfer, Die ersten 14 Jahre, pp. 86-87. General Groener allegedly demanded from Ebert the appointment of a strong man to replace a USPD member. Ebert suggested Noske. This choice was quickly endorsed by Groener since he and the other military leaders had great confidence in Noske's

The appointment of Majority Socialists as replacements for the Independents in the cabinet was advantageous to internal agreement. The Central Council and the Council of People's Commissars were composed exclusively of Majority Socialists. Both agencies could work harmoniously for law and order and for the preparation of the national assembly. The SPD enjoyed a monopoly of political authority.[85]

The new government announced its general policies to the people:

It is our intention to protect the Reich from upheavals until the national assembly meets, and then the elections will determine if the majority of the people wishes another government or if it stands behind us. We are convinced that only a government which does not have to overcome internal frictions — that is, a government made of one piece of wood — can accomplish this, and we believe that we are that government.[86]

Although it was a great advantage for the Majority Socialists to have been freed from the troublesome Independents in both the Central Council and the Cabinet, this development had for the over-all socialist movement in Germany some very unfortunate and lasting effects. The resignation of the USPD members from the Provisional government, for example, probably removed the last chance of a reunification of the two socialist parties. The resignation also pushed the Independents into the camp of the revolutionary opposition, and many of their adherents eventually joined the ranks of the Communists.[87]

abilities and attitude. (Waite, *op. cit.,* pp. 13-14; Noske, *Erlebtes,* p. 82.)

[85] Starting on December 29, 1918, the SPD government referred to itself as Reich government or Cabinet instead of the Council of People's Commissars. This change in name was one of the many indications of the efforts made by the Majority Socialists to overcome the "period of the councils." (Tormin, *op. cit.,* p. 101, n. 2.) Ebert was appointed as chairman of the Cabinet. All laws and decrees were henceforth signed in the name of the Reich government. (Hermann Mueller, *op. cit.,* pp. 241-42.)

[86] Quoted in Stampfer, *Die ersten 14 Jahre,* p. 87. For other governmental proclamations pertaining to the policies of the new all SPD government, see Bernstein, *op. cit.,* pp. 129-31.

[87] Hermann Mueller, *op. cit.,* p. 238; Volkmann, *Revolution,* p. 168; Ri-

The great demonstrations which took place in Berlin on December 29, 1918, gave evidence of the deepened cleavage within the German socialist movement. That day was almost like a general mobilization of forces prior to the commencement of open warfare. The USPD, the Revolutionary Shop Stewards, and the Spartacists had called upon the workers to attend the funerals of the victims who perished in the fighting on December 24, and to demonstrate against the "blood-stained government of Ebert" and against the entire counterrevolution. The SPD had also called for a demonstration on the same day under the slogan "against the bloody dictatorship of the Spartacist League" and the fight against "the terror of a minority." Both sides drew large crowds, and the demonstrating masses moved through the streets of Berlin until the late evening hours.[88]

4. *The Founding of the Communist Party of Germany*

During the month of December 1918, a growing number of Spartacists came to believe that any organizational connection with the USPD was out of the question, because of the policies and actions of the party's leadership and especially of the Independent People's Commissars. The moderate USPD leaders had endorsed the principle of the constitutional national assembly and, according to the Spartacists, had thereby placed themselves solidly on the side of the "counterrevolution." Karl Liebknecht explained the position of the Spartacists as follows:

The reactionary decisions of the [Reich] *Congress of Councils* were achieved with the cooperation of the USP-cabinet members. The large majority of the USP leaders made propaganda for the *national assembly* and fought against the *council system*. This act of treason committed against the revolution was completed at the Congress of Councils. The demand for a party congress, to make it possible for the masses of party comrades to make the decisions, was refused. . . . The leaders of the USP have helped to create the *prerequisites* for the

chard Mueller, *Der Buergerkrieg,* p. 13. Mueller, *Der Buergerkrieg,* pp. 20-24;
  [88] Stuemke, *op. cit.,* p. 186; Richard *Illustrierte Geschichte,* pp. 269-70.

rapid development of the counterrevolutionary forces, which are at the base of the events of December 6 and 24. . . .[89]

The Spartacists, in forcefully demanding the summoning of a party conference, also wanted to take advantage of the increasing opposition within the USPD toward its right wing leaders.

We wanted to provoke the condemnation, by the USP members, of the compromised leaders. The request of the Revolutionary Shop Stewards as well as our ultimatum of December 22 demanding a party congress were refused.[90]

Simultaneous with their challenge of the right-wing leaders of the USPD, the Spartacist League called the delegates of its groups to Berlin for a national conference to begin on December 30. The urgency on the part of the Spartacists to found their own party was not primarily the result of their realization of the USPD's policies. It was due to at least two other major developments. One was the growing conviction, as the result of the huge strike movement which spread throughout Germany, that only a proletarian class party could provide the essential unified leadership for the "spontaneous revolutionary masses."[91] The other was the pressure being exerted by the Bremen Left Radicals for the founding of an independent party.[92]

[89] Karl Liebknecht, "Die Krise in der USP," quoted in Liebknecht, Ausgewaehlte Reden, p. 523.

[90] Ibid. Richard Mueller interpreted the short-term ultimatum, requesting that the USPD congress be held before the end of December, and the type of arguments used in the demand as proof that the Spartacist leaders intended to found their own political party. (Richard Mueller, Der Buergerkrieg, p. 88.)

[91] For the Spartacists' interpretation of the strike movement, see above, pp. 129-31.

[92] On December 24, the Bremen Left Radicals held a conference in Berlin with representatives of their groups from Northern Germany, Saxony, Bavaria, and the Rhineland. The main issue was to decide whether to remain independent and form their own party or to join the Spartacist League. Karl Radek, the only member of the ill-fated Soviet delegation to the Reich Congress of Councils who managed to get through to Berlin, attended this conference and convinced the Left Radicals and the representatives of the Spartacists, Leo Jogiches, that they should join forces in order to "strengthen the revolution." The Reich Conference of the Left Radicals decided to unite with the Spartacists, provided that the latter would leave the USPD. On the issue of participation in the election of

The Reich Conference of the Spartacist League actually started on December 29, 1918, with a closed meeting in which the decision was made to separate from the USPD and to form a new party. Only three votes were cast against this motion.[93] From December 30, 1918, to January 1, 1919, the Spartacists and the Left Radicals held the Founding Congress of the new party in the Banquet Hall of the Prussian House of Representatives. On the first day of the congress, Karl Liebknecht declared the following in his speech about "the crisis in the USPD":

> Solidarity with Haase, Barth, and Dittmann is no longer possible. . . . Today, it has become necessary publicly to draw the dividing line and to constitute ourselves as a *new independent party*. . . . Our program and our fundamental principles have been in use for some time; all we have to do is to make them official. It is not necessary to make something new of ourselves. The masses already know what we are and what we represent. . . .[94]

A motion made by Fritz Heckert (Chemnitz) to call the new party Communist Party of Germany (Spartacist League) was accepted by an overwhelming majority.[95]

the national assembly, about half the delegates were for it and half against. In order not to decide this important question on the basis of a close vote, the conference adjourned until the delegates could consult with the members in their respective localities. When the conference reconvened on December 30, only one delegate still advocated participating in the elections. (*Illustrierte Geschichte*, p. 264.)

The leaders of the Spartacists had also been preoccupied with the founding of a party during December. They met on several occasions with the leaders of the Revolution Shop Stewards to find ways and means to improve the collaboration of the two revolutionary factions and to establish a stronger organizational union. Richard Mueller reported that during these meetings the question of a possible withdrawal from the USPD and the founding of a new political party had been discussed. The Revolutionary Shop Stewards expressed their preference for remaining within the USPD in order to enable them to enlarge their influence among the masses of the members who still followed the right-wing leaders. The Spartacists were strongly in favor of founding a new party. (Richard Mueller, *Der Buergerkrieg*, p. 86.)

[93] Kommunistische Partei Deutschlands (Spartakusbund), *Bericht ueber den Gruendungsparteitag der Kommunistischen Partei Deutschlands (Spartakusbund)* (Berlin, 1919), p. 3 (hereafter cited as KPD, *Gruendungsparteitag*).

[94] Liebknecht, *Die Krise in der USP*, p. 524.

[95] KPD, *Gruendungsparteitag*, p. 6.

The 87 delegates and 16 guests at the congress represented 46 different localities. It was a highly heterogeneous group. Very few of the delegates were genuine revolutionary Marxists. Most of them were fanatical and radical utopians who seriously believed that their immediate aim, the rule of the councils, would be realized very soon. They refused to see or to understand the various tactical problems which the actual situation entailed. The influence of these vague political notions, held by a majority of the delegates, was much in evidence during the discussions and found reflection in some of the decisions taken at the congress.[96]

The question of participation in the elections for the national assembly was the first major issue faced by the congress. (The opposition to the national assembly as "an instrument of the counterrevolution" was unanimous and, therefore, did not require discussion.) It was an important problem because it involved the position which the Communists were to take toward "bourgeois parliamentarianism." Paul Levi spoke for the Spartacist leaders, who demanded participation in the elections in order to work against the national assembly from within. He emphasized that the elections would take place regardless of how vigorously the revolutionary forces opposed it. Even the use of violence against the assembly would have no lasting effect because the real power of the bourgeoisie would not suffer seriously from a minority attack. The use of force was opportune only when it could be combined with assumption of political power, and this could be done only with the support of the majority of the working class. Levi also reminded the delegates that the national assembly would undoubtedly control the political life of Germany for months to

[96] Tormin, op. cit., p. 111. At a later date, the KPD determined that the majority of the participants at the founding congress of the party were people who were not Communists and had never even read the Spartacists' program. (Ibid., p. 111, n. 3.) Richard Mueller states that the majority of the delegates were anarchists, syndicalists, and putschist elements. (Richard Mueller, Der Buergerkrieg, p. 88.) The "very insufficient political experience and lack of theoretical knowledge" of many of the delegates was also explained by the fact that many new elements had joined the League; they distinguished themselves primarily by their "revolutionary enthusiasm and readiness for action." (Illustrierte Geschichte, p. 265.)

come, and it was important, therefore, for the revolutionary forces to be represented in the assembly in order to utilize it as a propaganda forum. Most of the speakers in the discussion which followed Levi's presentation were opposed to participation in the elections. Otto Ruehle declared that it would be equivalent to an endorsement of the national assembly. Rosi Wolfstein advocated political mass strikes against the assembly. The majority of the delegates were opposed to participation and neither Rosa Luxemburg nor Liebknecht were able to change their determination to boycott the elections. A vote of 62 to 23 ruled against participation.[97]

The contents of Levi's speech was significant not only because it revealed what most of the Communist leaders understood as participation in the elections and in the national assembly, but also because it was a strong re-statement of a fundamental Spartacist principle — here related to an actual political situation — that an overthrow of the government can be achieved only with the support of the majority of the working class. The original internal democracy of the party was convincingly illustrated when the leadership was out-voted by the rank and file. The newly-founded KPD had not yet learned the meaning of Lenin's "democratic centralism."[98]

The Founding Congress also revealed the widespread confusion which prevailed among the delegates concerning the position the Communists should take in regard to the trade unions. Paul Lange in his report on economic conflicts asserted that the unions were against the socialization of the economy, and that they were doomed as a result. The economic agencies which

[97] KPD, *Gruendungsparteitag*, pp. 9-13; Oelssner, *Rosa Luxemburg*, pp. 138-39; Ruth Fischer, *op. cit.*, pp. 77-78.
[98] The lack of understanding and failure to apply Lenin's concept of "democratic centralism" is one of the points which Otto Grotewohl criticizes about the first congress. (Grotewohl, *op. cit.*, p. 57.) Leo Jogiches was great-

ly disappointed with what he called the "lack of enlightment among the members of the Spartacist League." He arrived at the conclusion that the founding congress was held too soon. (*Illustrierte Geschichte*, p. 266.) Ruth Fischer reports a conversation she had with a "Mr. G. F.," who attended the congress. He had told her "that during the session Jogiches asked him

should handle the interests of the workers were the factory councils:

> The organizations necessary to bring about socialism are the factory councils, which in collaboration with the workers' councils direct the internal affairs of the individual factories, regulate the working conditions, control the production, and eventually will have to take over the entire direction of the factory. . . .[99]

In the discussion following Lange's report, demands were made for immediate withdrawal from the trade unions. Rosa Luxemburg's intervention prevented this matter from being given a "premature vote."[100]

The delegates adopted the Spartacist program of December 14, 1918, as the party platform. This event indicated that the organizational change from the Spartacist League to the KPD involved no basic changes in political thought or in fundamental tactical concepts. In her speech, "Our Program and the Political Situation," Rosa Luxemburg gave a detailed account of the developments of the German Revolution and of the lessons learned from them by the revolutionary Marxists. Possibly for the benefit of the new, impatient elements among the ranks, she discussed the revolutionary tactics which the Spartacists would have to pursue in order to support the proletarian revolution:

> . . . what is the general tactical guiding principle applicable for the situation which shall confront us in the immediate future? The next thing you may be hoping for is the fall of the Ebert-Scheidemann government and its replacement by a pronounced socialist-proletarian-revolutionary government. However, I would like to draw your attention to what is happening at the lowest political level. We must not have [the same] illusion we held during the first phase of the revolution on the ninth of November, that all that is necessary for a socialist revolution is to overthrow a capitalist government and replace it by

---

whether or not he should blow up the whole affair." (Ruth Fischer, *op. cit.*, p. 79, n. 31.)

[99] KPD, *Gruendungsparteitag*, p. 15.
[100] Tormin, *op. cit.*, p. 111; *Illustrierte Geschichte*, p. 266.

another one. The victory of the proletarian revolution can be achieved only when one goes about it in the opposite way; the Ebert-Scheidemann government must be undermined through social and revolutionary mass actions of the proletariat step by step. . . .

. . . history does not make it as simple for us as it was in the case of the bourgeois revolutions when it was sufficient to overthrow the central authority and replace it by a few or a few dozen men. We must work from the bottom up; this is necessary because of the mass character of our revolution which is pointed at the very core of society; it is one of the requirements of the present proletarian revolution that we must seize political power not from the top but from the bottom. . . . On the bottom where the individual employer faces his wage slaves, down there, where all executive organs of political class rule are standing face to face with the objects of this rule — the masses — there we must little by little tear away from the oppressors their powers and seize them for our purposes. . . .[101]

Rosa Luxemburg knew well that many of the revolutionaries were greatly concerned about the length of time it would take before the revolution could be built from the bottom up. Therefore, she made the following statement:

. . . The revolution is capable of accomplishing its achievements with tremendous *speed*. I cannot predict how much time this process requires. Who among us counts and who cares, if our lives last long enough to see it happen![102]

The future organization of the party was another concern of the congress. Hugo Eberlein proposed that the revolutionary program and tactics of the KPD should be the decisive factors in forming the organization.

We are faced with the question of whether we should establish an election club or a political combat organization. The organizations of the old Social Democrat Party were, except during election times, dull and empty. . . . We must build our organization along entirely dif-

[101] Rosa Luxemburg, *Rede zum Programm*, quoted in Luxemburg, *Ausge-* *waehlte Reden*, II, pp. 683-84, 687-88.
[102] *Ibid.*, p. 688.

ferent lines if we wish to maintain our readiness for action. . . . We demand that all political power be taken over by the workers' and soldiers' councils. The factory councils are at the base of the power [of the workers' and soldiers' councils]. We must adapt our organization to this situation. Therefore, it probably will be best to set up Communist groups in the factories. The shop stewards of the factories will form the conference of the functionaries of the community which in turn appoints the party office for the community (*Ortsleitung*). In addition, meetings with the unemployed, etc. must be arranged. In the rural and industrially poor areas other solutions must be found. This type of organization has the advantage of increasing readiness for combat. This organizational form, however, must not be made schematic but must be adapted to local conditions. Individual localities must retain complete freedom in the selection of their own organization. It is not permissible to dictate from above. Individual organizations must have complete autonomy. They must not wait for direction from the top of the organization, but must work on their own initiative. The task of the central office is primarily to sum up external developments and assume political and ideological leadership. . . .[103]

No discussion took place, and the proposals were turned over to the program and organization commission for further study. However, the significance of the proposals was the strong emphasis placed on local autonomy and on the factory groups as the basic units for party organization. The general conviction was that here was the source of all political and economic powers.

The congress elected a Central Committee composed of Hermann Duncker, Kaete Duncker, Hugo Eberlein, Paul Froelich (as representative of the Bremen Group), Paul Lange, Leo Jogiches, Paul Levi, Karl Liebknecht, Rosa Luxemburg, Ernst Meyer, Wilhelm Pieck and August Thalheimer.[104]

On the last day of the congress, Liebknecht and Pieck reported the failure of the negotiations conducted with the Revolutionary Shop Stewards who had been invited to join the new

[103] KPD, *Gruendungsparteitag*, pp. 43-44.

[104] *Illustrierte Geschichte*, p. 267.

party. The Revolutionary Shop Stewards made their acceptance of the offer contingent upon the adoption of five points by the party congress: (1) repeal of the anti-parliamentary decision concerning non-participation in the elections for the national assembly; (2) complete parity of the KPD and Revolutionary Shop Stewards in party leadership and in party committees; (3) precise definition of street demonstration tactics and agreement that no actions were to be taken without prior approval by the Revolutionary Shop Stewards; (4) joint editing of the party newspaper and of all propaganda literature; (5) deletion of the designation "Spartacist League" from the party's new name. Liebknecht found these demands unacceptable; he was especially incensed about point three which was directed against the alleged putsch tactics of the Spartacists.[105]

The failure of these unification efforts deprived the new party of a substantial number of members and also of the opportunity to win over, through the Revolutionary Shop Stewards, the radical elements among the workers. The KPD had only a few thousand members throughout Germany. In Berlin there were barely fifty members. It was an elite party or the framework for a mass party which remained isolated from the socialist masses for a considerable time.[106]

The events at the Founding Congress demonstrated that the Russian Bolshevik had nothing directly to do with the creation of the KPD or with its program and tactics. Karl Radek attended the congress as the official representative of the Bolsheviks. However, he could do no more than underline the formal solidarity which existed between German and Russian revolutionaries.

---

[105] Richard Mueller, *Der Buergerkrieg*, pp. 88-89; *Illustrierte Geschichte*, p. 267. Tormin states that the demands of the Revolutionary Shop Stewards were primarily intended to keep utopian radicalism under control. (Tormin, *op. cit.*, p. 112.) Richard Mueller, who attended the negotiations between the two revolutionary groups, gave this intention as the real reason for the actions of his organization. (Richard Mueller, *Der Buergerkrieg*, p. 88.)

[106] Flechtheim, *op. cit.*, p. 47; *Illustrierte Geschichte*, p. 267. Richard Mueller speaks of scarcely one thousand Spartacists. (Richard Mueller, *Der Buerkerkrieg*, p. 85.)

The congress also gave evidence that the left wing radical leadership had insufficient authority over the rank and file and that it was unable to control effectively its members. The lack of control was partly caused by the internal party democracy. Thus it was possible that in spite of Rosa Luxemburg's violent opposition to adventurous and putschist policies, so-called "revolutionary actions" could get out of hand. Possibly Leo Jogiches was correct when he noted that the Spartacist members were not yet ready to form a political party.[107]

---

[107] Richard Mueller expressed the same opinion. He called the founding of the party a serious mistake. He believed that the Spartacists should have remained within the USPD where they could have exerted beneficial influence on that party's policies. (Richard Mueller, *Der Buergerkrieg,* p. 90.)

The Spartacists and the January Uprising

Part
3

"The Spartacist Uprising"— Civil War in Berlin

Chapter 5

1. *The Test of Strength*

The hostile encounters between the Majority Socialists and the left opposition during December 1918 had deepened the cleavage within the German socialist movement. Mutual animosity had grown in intensity. The rival demonstrations on December 29, 1918, at the occasion of the funeral for the victims of the Christmas incident, had illustrated the great antagonism existing between the "government" socialists and their opposition on the left. The attitude of the SPD leadership toward the left wing radicals was expressed in a candid article in *Vorwaerts*:

The despicable actions of Liebknecht and Rosa Luxemburg soil the revolution and endanger all of its achievements. The masses must not sit by quietly for one minute longer while these brutal beasts and their followers paralyze the activities of the republican governmental offices, incite the people more and more to a civil war, and strangle with their dirty fists the right of free expression.

They want to demolish and destroy with lies, slander, and violence everything which dares oppose them. They pose with boundless insolence as the masters of Berlin, in spite of the fact that at least nine-tenths of the population hate and despise their actions from the bottom of their souls. . . .[1]

[1] Extracts of this *Vorwaerts* article are quoted in *Illustrierte Geschichte*, p. 269. The accusation that the radical left "strangles free expression" is a reference to the occupation of the

161

Middle class circles joined the Majority Socialists in their attacks against the left wing radicals. At the end of December 1918, the so-called "Berlin Citizens' Council" distributed a leaflet which, in the manner of the SPD, blamed primarily the Spartacists for the unrest and violence.

Workers, Soldiers! The Christmas blows of the Spartacist group lead directly into the abyss. None of us wishes to spill blood. However, it is easier to cure a mad dog with biblical phrases than [to change] the Spartacists with gentle persuasion. The brutal **force** of these criminals can be countered only with force. If they intend to strike us down, we shall defend our skins. The hypocritical outcry of the Spartacists about the "blood bath" does not divert us from their intention to pit workers against workers and soldiers against soldiers.

Do you want peace? Then every man must see to it that the Spartacists' rule of violence comes to an end!

Do you want bread? Then see to it that all wheels are turning!

Do you want freedom? Then eliminate Liebknecht's armed sluggards!

When you are united, then the entire pack will run away.

Do you want to be hungry? Then listen to Liebknecht!

Do you want to become slaves of the Entente? Liebknecht can arrange this.

Long live law and order!

Down with the dictatorship of the anarchists![2]

In their propaganda warfare against the left wing radicals, the Majority Socialists and their allied forces blamed *Spartakus* for all violence and unrest. This practice appears to have been a deliberate attempt by those who favored the consolidation of the revolution or opposed the revolution altogether. Therefore *Spartakus* was used as the catch-all term even though the Spartacists were very few in number.[3]

Vorwaerts building immediately following the Christmas fighting.

[2] Quoted in *Illustrierte Geschichte*, pp. 269-70.

[3] For a discussion of the Spartacists' strength, see above, p. 157, 157n.

There are several reasons for this practice of making the Spartacists the focal point of public hatred: (1) It is conceivable that the SPD and other opponents of the left radicals acted according to their convictions, actually believing that the Spartacists were the most dangerous elements among the revolutionaries and were retarding the process of consolidation. The fate of the Russian Kerensky government, liquidated by a determined Bolshevik minority, could have served as a warning. (2) The public censure may have been an intentional over-simplification of a complicated situation — a device frequently used in political propaganda warfare. The selection of the weakest among a multitude of opponents and the use of it as a symbol of the entire opposition is convenient because it helps raise the morale of the censuring side. In addition, a defeat of the weakest component of the opposition can be developed, propaganda-wise, into a major and decisive event. (3) This practice could have been an attempt to drive a wedge between the various radical groups on the left. Making the Spartacists the root of all political evil could have been interpreted by the Revolutionary Shop Stewards and the left wing of the USPD as evidence of a more conciliatory SPD attitude toward them. (4) It also could have been a means of discrediting all the oppositional forces by identifying them with the "blood-thirsty" Spartacists. This would have been an especially desirable objective for the period preceding the elections to the national assembly and could have been designed to reduce the influence of the USPD upon the masses.

Whatever the reason, or combination of reasons, using the Spartacists as a symbol of political evil indicated that the Majority Socialists were concerned almost exclusively with the danger from the left. They apparently were not afraid that their military dependence on the imperial officers would eventually lead them into a political subjugation by the alleged reactionary forces. This attitude can possibly be explained by the blind confidence of the SPD leaders in the security provided by democratic elections.

At the end of December, 1918, in spite of their improved political position, Ebert and his government felt insecure because of the lack of military forces to defend themselves against the *coup d'état,* presumably being prepared by the radical left.[4] The Majority Socialists regarded the armed workers, the various "revolutionary" military units which had failed to come to the support of the government during the Christmas incident, and the unreliable troops of the Berlin garrison as the forces which the left wing radicals would try to bring under their control in order to overthrow the government and to create a council dictatorship, following the Bolshevik example. On the other hand, the Spartacists, the Revolutionary Shop Stewards, and large parts of the Berlin organization of the USPD suspected that the SPD government, in alliance with the volunteer units commanded by the former imperial officers and the reactionary political forces, were planning to suppress the revolutionary workers by force.

In the opinion of this writer, neither side intended to start a civil war at the beginning of January. Even if the Ebert government had wanted to suppress the revolutionary danger of the left and disarm the civilian population in order to assure peaceful elections for the national assembly, the troops needed for this operation were not then available. On the opposite side, the newly-formed KPD had adopted as one of its planks the principle of obtaining mass support before attempting to seize political power.[5]

---

[4] Many bourgeois circles and SPD leaders seriously believed in the coming *coup.* For example, Meinecke wrote ". . . the most dangerous zero point was around the end of the old and beginning of the new year 1918/19 when one was physically defenseless against the Bolsheviks, . . ." (Meinecke, *op. cit.,* p. 118.)

There is also the report of a telephone call from Ebert to General Groener at the end of December, asking impatiently when he could count on the promised volunteer units, the Free Corps. He pleaded urgently that the insurrection was imminent and that he had no military forces at his disposal to s u p p r e s s the uprising. (Volkmann, *Revolution,* p. 170; *Illustrierte Geschichte,* pp. 272-73.)

[5] The unruly and noisy elements of the KPD who urged an immediate "proletarian revolution" lacked influence within the party and among the workers. It should be noted, however, that this situation was not generally known outside the party; this fact may have contributed to the fears of a *coup,* then widespread in government circles.

The Revolutionary Shop Stewards and the left wing of the USPD were also against a *coup d'état*. The negotiations conducted by the Spartacists with the Shop Stewards during the Founding Congress of the KPD had given evidence of the latter's strong antiputsch views.

Mutual suspicion caused the period at the end of December and the beginning of January to be marked by high tension. Any move in either camp which could be interpreted as an attempt to challenge or change the precarious power balance was almost certain to set off a test of strength, a civil war. The so-called "Eichhorn Incident" was the fuse that ignited the week of fighting which entered history under the misnomer of "Spartacist Uprising." Rudolf Hilferding, one of the USPD leaders, called it appropriately "the revolution's battle of the Marne."[6]

2. *The Eichhorn Incident — The Immediate Cause of the Uprising*

Emil Eichhorn, a left wing USPD Reichstag deputy, became the Berlin Chief of Police in the wake of the November Revolution. His imperial predecessor, von Oppen, sent a message to USPD party headquarters on November 9 requesting that a representative be designated to negotiate the surrender of the police. Eichhorn was appointed by the USPD to head the police force for the time being. On the next day, the Berlin Workers' and Soldiers' Council formally approved Eichhorn for this position.[7]

The sequence of the Eichhorn incident was as follows: Eichhorn's dismissal from office as Chief of Police by the Prussian

---

[6] Hermann Mueller, *op. cit.*, p. 246.

[7] For a detailed account of Eichhorn's appointment and early activities as chief of the Berlin police, see Emil Eichhorn, *Eichhorn ueber die Januar-Ereignisse* (Berlin: Verlagsgenossenschaft Freiheit, 1919), pp. 7-28. Noske's version that Eichhorn took over the office on his own responsibility and made an unidentified workers' and soldiers' council appoint him to this position prior to the time when any government was formed and then proceeded to create a so-called new police, is an example of the highly distorted reports on the January events. (Noske, *Erlebtes*, p. 80.) Most of the accounts examined in the preparation of this study were found to be influenced markedly by the political views of the respective authors.

government; his refusal to comply with this order; immediate support from the left wing radical organizations in Berlin in his attempt to defy the Prussian government.

The Majority Socialists had a simple explanation for the discharge of Eichhorn by the Prussian Minister of Interior, Paul Hirsch. They claimed they were justified in dismissing the USPD Chief of Police, who refused to withdraw from the key position in Berlin, in spite of the fact that the Independent members of the Prussian government had resigned, following the example set by Haase, Dittmann, and Barth. The SPD had become increasingly alarmed by Eichhorn's activities. His open favoritism toward the left wing radicals was a thorn in their side. He was accused of giving agents of the Revolutionary Shop Stewards leading positions in his Security Force, of having indirectly helped the mutinous sailors during the Christmas incident by keeping his police neutral, of having armed 1,500 workers who then assisted the rebellious People's Naval Division, and finally of having publicly declared his opposition to the coming constituent national assembly. The SPD newspapers opened a concerted campaign against Eichhorn, demanding his immediate dismissal from office. On January 3, 1919, Eichhorn appeared before the Prussian Minister of Interior as requested, even though he had earlier announced that he recognized only the Executive Council as his superior authority. Confronted with the charges, Eichhorn promised to answer them in writing. The Prussian SPD government claimed to be convinced more than ever that it could no longer tolerate the situation created by a hostile Chief of Police, and on the following day it officially dismissed Eichhorn. Eugen Ernst, the Prussian Minister of Police, was appointed as his successor. Majority Socialists' accounts of the incident stress that the left wing opposition used this completely legal and justifiable dismissal as a welcome pretext for beginning their long-planned fight against the government.[8]

[8] Bernstein, *op. cit.,* pp. 131-34. The text of Hirsch's letter of dismissal to Eichhorn is quoted in *ibid.,* p. 133. See also Hermann Mueller, *op. cit.,* pp.

Quite naturally, the left wing radicals viewed the discharge of Eichhorn in an entirely different light. They believed it was a premeditated action by the SPD, intended not so much as a seizure of an important executive office but primarily as a provocation to the revolutionary workers of Berlin. The leftist opposition insisted that the SPD leaders knew the workers could not afford to give up the position of the Chief of Police without a struggle.[9] In order to prove their accusations against the Majority Socialists, the left wing radicals charged that the attack by the Social Democratic and bourgeois newspapers against Eichhorn was intended to prepare public opinion for his discharge. This censure had started before January 3, the withdrawal date of the Independents from the Prussian government. Furthermore, the preparatory attack was not accidental, but allegedly was a well-coordinated affair managed by the Political-Parliamentary-News-Service, a semi-official mouthpiece of the Ebert government.[10] The left wing opposition also circulated a statement ascribed to the successor to Eichhorn — Eugen Ernst — who, on the day after the suppression of the January Uprising, supposedly revealed to a correspondent of the *Manchester Guardian* that

a success of the Spartacists was *a priori* impossible; we (the Majority Socialists) forced them to resort to force prematurely because

246-50; Grzesinski, *op. cit.*, pp. 61-62; Noske, *Von Kiel bis Kapp*, p. 48; and Volkmann, *Revolution*, p. 173. Volkmann's report of the incident is similar to other SPD accounts. According to Hermann Mueller, who is obviously mistaken, Eichhorn refused to appear before the Prussian Minister of Interior.

[9] Richard Mueller, *Der Buergerkrieg*, p. 28. Walter Ulbricht asserts that the attack was also d i r e c t e d against the Executive Council which originally appointed Eichhorn. This assertion is hardly justified since the Executive Council was by then completely under the dominance of the SPD, a situation which was clearly demonstrated when the council readily endorsed Eichhorn's dismissal order on January 6, 1919. (Ulbricht, *Zur Geschichte*, p. 37; Hermann Mueller, *op. cit.*, p. 248.)

[10] Eichhorn, *op. cit.*, p. 58. Richard Mueller reported that on January 1 this news service circulated the following item: "Each day Mr. Eichhorn remains in his office as Chief of Police means added danger for the public safety." According to Mueller, this newspaper release carried the additional assertions that Eichhorn was in the pay of the Russian government and that he was preparing a civil war. (Richard Mueller, *Der Buergerkrieg*, p. 26.) See also *Illustrierte Geschichte*, p. 270.

of our preparations. They had to fight before they were ready and therefore we were in a position to challenge them successfully.[11]

The interpretation by the left wing radicals of the over-all situation was as follows:

The government people who decreed the dismissal of Eichhorn knew that they thereby most severely provoked the Berlin workers. The government wanted this controversy; they wanted it in order to fight, defeat, and disarm the working class. If this provocation had failed and Eichhorn had submitted to the order, then they would at least have gained the chance to change completely the police system in Berlin, to drive away the organized workers with whom Eichhorn had built up the Security Force and replace them with mercenaries. . . .[12]

When Eichhorn received his dismissal order, he reported to the party offices of the Berlin organization of the USPD. On the evening of the same day — January 4, 1919 — a joint meeting of the Central Committee of the Berlin organization of the USPD and the Revolutionary Shop Stewards had been scheduled to deal with routine matters. After learning about Eichhorn's discharge, the discussion switched to the steps that should be taken to prevent the government from carrying out its intention. Against the vote of a few Independents, it was decided to call the workers and soldiers to a protest demonstration the next day, Sunday, January 5. No further details were worked out except the text of a joint proclamation. The Central Committee of the KPD was notified of the action which the USPD and the Revolutionary Shop Stewards had agreed upon. The Communists decided to join the other two organizations and to insist that the counter-measures to the

---

[11] *Illustrierte Geschichte*, p. 271. Richard Mueller believed that the charges against Eichhorn were nothing but falsehoods and were made public only to influence public opinion for the planned attack against Eichhorn and the revolutionary workers of Berlin. (Richard Mueller, *Der Buergerkrieg*, pp. 26-29.) For Eichhorn's own defense against the charges, see Eichhorn, *op. cit.*, pp. 50-51, 60-61.

[12] *Illustrierte Geschichte*, pp. 270-71.

government's provocation be kept within the framework of power-ful protest demonstrations. The Central Committee then felt that a violent overthrow of the government would lead nowhere, since a proletarian government could not remain in power in isolated Berlin for longer than a few days.[13]

The text of the joint proclamation was immediately dissemi-nated in leaflet form and was published the next morning in *Die Rote Fahne* and *Freiheit*. It read as follows:

Attention! Workers! Party Comrades!

The Ebert-Scheidemann government has heightened its counter-revolutionary activities with a new *contemptible conspiracy* directed against the revolutionary workers of Greater Berlin: it tried *malici-ously to oust Chief of Police Eichhorn from his office*. It wished to replace Eichhorn with its willing tool, the present Prussian minister of Police, Ernst.

By this action, the Ebert-Scheidemann government wishes not only to remove the last trusted man of the revolutionary Berlin workers, but primarily it intends to *establish in Berlin a despotic rule antagonistic to the revolutionary workers*.

[13] *Ibid.*, p. 273. Eichhorn, *op. cit.*, pp. 67-69. Richard Mueller, *Der Buer-gerkrieg*, p. 30. Richard Mueller quotes from a Communist leaflet dis-tributed shortly before the January fighting which reflected the lack of in-tention on the part of the KPD to seize political power at that time: "If the Berlin workers would forcefully disperse the national assembly today and would throw the Scheidemann and Ebert people into jail, while the work-ers in the Ruhr, in Upper Silesia, and the agricultural laborers of the area east of the Elbe remain inactive, the capitalists would be able to subjugate Berlin tomorrow by starving it out." (Richard Mueller, *Der Buergerkrieg,* p. 30.)

According to a Communist report, published at a later date, the Central Committee of the KPD took the fol-lowing position toward the Eichhorn incident: "The members of the Cen-tral Committee agreed that all de-mands which would necessarily result in the fall of the Ebert government must be avoided. Our demands were specified as follows: rescinding the dis-missal of Eichhorn, disarming the counterrevolutionary troops (S u p p e unit, etc.), and arming the proletariat. None of these demands involved in any form the fall of the government, not even the demand for arming the pro-letariat, because at that time, the gov-ernment still had a large following among the proletariat. We also agreed then, that this constituted a minimum program which must be carried out with a maximum of energy. It was supposed to be the impressive result of a powerful revolutionary action. . . . It was in this sense that we issued the slogans for the demonstrations." (Quoted in *ibid.*)

Workers! Party Comrades! The person of Eichhorn is not the main issue; you yourselves will lose the last remnants of your revolutionary achievements through this major blow.

The Ebert government with its accomplices in the Prussan Ministry intends to support its power through bayonettes and *to secure* for itself the *grace of the capitalist bourgeoisie,* whose disguised representative it was from the very beginning.

By this blow directed against the Berlin police headquarters, the entire German proletariat, the entire German Revolution is to be struck.

Workers! Party Comrades! *This you cannot and must not permit!* Therefore, turn out for powerful *mass demonstrations.* Prove your power to the autocrats of today; prove that the revolutionary spirit of the November days has not been extinguished.

Come today, Sunday, at 2 p.m. to the impressive mass demonstrations in the Siegesallee!

Come in masses! Your freedom, your future, the fate of the Revolution is at stake! Down with the despotism of Ebert, Scheidemann, Hirsch, and Ernst! Long live revolutionary, international socialism! Berlin, January 5, 1919.

> The Revolutionary Shop Stewards and Confidence Men of the large factories of Greater Berlin.
>
> The Central Committee of Greater Berlin Social Democratic Election Association of the Independent Social Democratic Party.
>
> The Central Committee of the Communist Party of Germany (Spartacist League).[14]

The Majority Socialists as well as the leftist opposition had interpreted the events related to Eichhorn's dismissal from a purely political point of view. Both sides of the conflict failed to recognize that a strong personal element was also involved: the intrigues of Lieutenant Anton Fischer, the city commandant and successor to Otto Wels. Because of jurisdictional disputes and their political alignments, an intense enmity had developed dur-

[14] Quoted in Bernstein, *op. cit.,* p. 134.

ing November and December of 1918 between Eichhorn's Security Force and Wels' Republican Soldiers' Army.[15] Fischer anticipated an ultimate clash between the two militant organizations. In order to strengthen his position, he succeeded as early as December in bribing a number of Security Force leaders to make common cause with him against their Chief of Police. When the concerted campaign of the Majority Socialists against Eichhorn began, Fischer thought the time had come for him to take a more prominent part in the final assault against his personal and political antagonist.[16] On January 4, 1919, supported by two members of the Executive Council, Molkenbuhr and Frank, Fischer convinced the Prussian Minister of Interior that he could unseat Eichhorn once a dismissal order was issued.[17] It is probable that Fischer's intervention aggravated considerably the prevailing tense situation and thereby directly contributed to the events which followed the Eichhorn incident.

3. The Major Events of "Spartakus Week"

On Sunday, January 5, 1919, in response to the joint proclamation of the leftist opposition, huge throngs of workers surged into the streets and marched through the main arteries of Berlin shouting defiance at the "counterrevolutionary" Ebert government. The number of participants in the demonstrations surpassed even the most optimistic expectations of the left wing radicals.[18] Great masses of people formed into marching columns, their revolutionary spirit further kindled by fiery speeches from

---

[15] For details on the tensions, jurisdictional disputes, and mutual accusations of the two forces, see Eichhorn, op. cit., pp. 28-35, 42-46; Anton Fischer, op. cit., pp. 52-53.

[16] Oertzen, op. cit., p. 269. Volkmann, Revolution, pp. 173-74. Fischer admitted that he had "bought" members of the Security Force. (Anton Fischer, op. cit., pp. 55f.)

[17] Anton Fischer, op. cit., p. 54; see also Richard Mueller, Der Buerger-

krieg, p. 41; Oertzen, op. cit., p. 269.

[18] Bernstein believed that the overwhelming mass response of the people was due to the cleverly written proclamation which succeeded in convincing the masses that the government was committing a counterrevolutionary, despotic act by dismissing the "proletarian and revolutionary Chief of Police." (Bernstein, op. cit., p. 133.)

Liebknecht and other leaders, and moved to police headquarters at Alexanderplatz to bring their ovations to Eichhorn and to those who supported him in his struggle against the government. It was indeed a most inopportune time for Anton Fischer and Eugen Ernst to appear in the police building and demand Eichhorn's ouster. Caught in the spirit of the demonstrating masses, even those of the Security Force leaders who had accepted bribes from Fischer declared their loyalty to the Chief of Police and asked him to remain in office. Fischer, greatly disappointed by the betrayal of "his" men among the Security Force, recognized that neither threats nor pleading would change Eichhorn's mind. It would require force.[19]

A number of functionaries of the Revolutionary Shop Stewards and a few members of the Central Committee of the Berlin USPD and of the KPD had come to police headquarters to confer on the next move, in view of the successful response to their joint summons for mass demonstrations. They were not able to arrive at any decision and therefore postponed the conference for the evening of the same day. In the meantime Eichhorn, Ledebour, Daeumig, Liebknecht, and others addressed the huge crowds from the balcony of the police building. All of them severely attacked the Ebert government for its alleged counterrevolutionary activities, although none of the speakers called for violent actions. The demonstrators waited patiently until the evening hours for further instructions; when nothing developed, the mob gradually dispersed.[20]

Later in the evening, about seventy Revolutionary Shop Stewards, the Central Committee of the Berlin USPD, and Liebknecht and Pieck from the Central Committee of the KPD gathered in police headquarters to resume their discussion on further action. It was at this meeting that the decision was taken to overthrow the government.

[19] Anton Fischer, *op. cit.*, pp. 55-59; Eichhorn, *op. cit.*, pp. 69-70; Richard Mueller, *Der Buergerkrieg*, p. 31; and Oertzen, *op. cit.*, pp. 269-70.

[20] Richard Mueller, *Der Buergerkrieg*, p. 32; Eichhorn, *op. cit.*, p. 70.

The impact of the huge mass demonstrations upon the assembled functionaries was so great that they believed sincerely that the masses were ready to overthrow the Ebert cabinet and support a new revolutionary government of the left wing radicals. Reports of spontaneous mass actions, the occupation of the *Vorwaerts* and of other bourgeois newspapers and press services in the area of the Belle-Alliance-Platz convinced the oppositional leaders that the revolutionary workers of Berlin were again taking matters into their own hands. Dorrenbach, the leader of the People's Naval Division, described the high revolutionary spirit of his own unit and of the other troops of the Berlin garrison. According to him, all these units, including troops in Spandau and in other parts of the Reich, were ready to overthrow forcefully the Ebert government. Against the votes of six persons, among whom were Ernst Daeumig and Richard Mueller, the conferees decided to take up the fight against the government with the aim of replacing it with a revolutionary government. It was also decided to maintain the occupation of the newspaper plants and to proclaim a general strike for Berlin. A provisional Revolutionary Committee, comprised of fifty-three persons with three co-chairmen, Ledebour, Liebknecht, and Paul Scholze, was elected. This Committee was charged with the preparation, direction, and coordination of the struggle for power. After the fall of the Ebert government it was temporarily to take over governmental affairs.[21]

The so-called "spontaneous occupation" of the newspaper plants on January 5, followed by the seizure of several public

---

[21] See Richard Mueller, *Der Buergerkrieg,* pp. 32-35 for a detailed description of this revolutionary evening meeting on January 5. Mueller relates the position taken by most of the prominent leaders among the organizations represented at the meeting. He also describes the arguments of the six functionaries, including his own, who were opposed to the decision of overthrowing the government by violence. The other four who shared his and Daeumig's views were Paul Eckert, Heinrich Mahlzahn, Neuendorf, and Oskar Rusch.

See also *Illustrierte Geschichte,* pp. 274-75. A long quote of Ledebour's statement at his trial for treason on the occurrences at this meeting is given in *ibid.* Another account of a participant is Eichhorn, *op. cit.,* pp. 70-72. See also Bernstein, *op. cit.,* pp.

buildings, became one of the most controversial and significant issues of the January incidents. The left wing radicals as well as the Majority Socialists used their respective interpretations of these seizures as proof that the other side had planned this action as a fight to the finish. The opposition of the left insisted that it had neither planned nor ordered the seizure of the buildings; it regarded the occupation of the *Vorwaerts* and of the other newspaper buildings as a spontaneous mass protest action against the continued dissemination of vicious propaganda by these papers against Eichhorn and the revolutionary workers of Berlin. After the conclusion of the January fighting, the leftist forces changed their story into a declaration that they had been deceived by the SPD. They asserted that absolute proof had been obtained that the seizures were the work of *agents provocateurs* who were members of an intelligence organization built up by Anton Fischer during his days as Berlin City Commandant. The left claimed that the occupation of these buildings was designed to lure them into the fight, to tie down their forces in unimportant and isolated locations, and to give the SPD an excuse to use its newly-organized military units for the destruction of the left wing opposition.[22]

On their part the Majority Socialists pointed to the same events as proof that the left wing extremists had been waiting for an opportune moment to start their long-prepared insurrections.[23]

135-36, and Herman Mueller, *op. cit.*, pp. 252-54. Different figures have been given for the number of persons o n t h e Revolutionary Committee. Richard Mueller, Hermann Mueller, and Stampfer set the number at fifty-three. Bernstein claims it had only thirty-three, while Eichhorn speaks of some thirty men.

[22] For details of the personalities and actions of these *agents provocateurs*, see Richard Mueller, *Der Buergerkrieg*, pp. 41-46, 74-75; *Illustrierte Geschichte*, pp. 280-81. R i c h a r d Mueller also describes the wild seizures of the days after January 5, for example, the occupation of the Gov-

ernment Printing Office on January 6 and of the Railroad stations and Main Railroad office building during the night of January 7-8 as actions of small groups of bona fide revolutionaries incited by *agents provocateurs*. While Anton Fischer does not verify this accusation from the left, he confirmed the existence of a "small and unimportant intelligence unit" under the direction of a certain Suckow and Lichtenstein. The unit had about forty men. (Anton Fischer, *op. cit.*, pp. 66-68.)

[23] Hermann Mueller declares that "with the occupation of the newspaper section [of the city], the German Revo-

During its short life the Revolutionary Committee distinguished itself by incredible incompetence and lack of initiative. The only accomplishments of the committee were the creation of a number of commissions which never became operative, the issuance of a few proclamations, and the ordering of an unsuccessful attempt to seize the War Ministry.[24]

The following is the first proclamation which summoned the workers and soldiers to leave their factories and barracks and to demonstrate again in the Siegesallee. Once more thousands of people marched through the streets in protest against the Ebert government and again waited in vain for further instructions from the Revolutionary Committee.

Workers! Soldiers! Comrades!

On Sunday you demonstrated with overwhelming force your intention to destroy the latest malicious assault by the blood-stained Ebert-government.

Now there are more important things in the offing! It is necessary to stop all counterrevolutionary intrigues!

lution entered the decisive week which was to determine everything. In the event of a *Spartakus* victory, the world would have become enriched only by the new Soviet Republic Berlin. The rest of the Reich would not have followed the capital. This time the People's Commissars were determined not to avoid the fight." (Hermann Mueller, *op. cit.,* p. 251.) Bernstein, who in the early part of 1919 returned to the fold of the SPD, did not believe the assertion of Ledebour, Eichhorn, and others that the seizure of the newspapers was the product of revolutionary mass action without direction from the revolutionary leadership. Bernstein stated that the occupations of the v a r i o u s buildings showed too much coordination in time for spontaneous mass actions. He also maintained that the seizure of newspapers was not as a c c i d e n t a l as claimed, but was intended to silence "inconvenient criticism." (Bernstein,

op. cit., pp. 139-40.) Oertzen blames the occupation on groups of armed Spartacists who acted without orders from the leadership. (Oertzen, *op. cit.,* pp. 270-71.) The *Vorwaerts* appeared on January 6, 1919, as the "organ of the revolutionary workers of Greater Berlin." A long proclamation of the first morning edition is quoted in Runkel, *op. cit.,* pp. 205-07.

[24] *Illustrierte Geschichte,* p. 276. Eichhorn emphasizes that there was absolutely no central leadership for any military action. Operations of a military type which did occur during the January fighting were carried out by individual groups without coordination with each other. The reason for this situation was that "the organizations participating [in the uprising] really had no intention of undertaking any military operations" against the government. (Eichhorn, *op. cit.,* p. 52.)

Therefore, come out of your factories! Appear in masses this morning at 11 a.m. in the Siegesallee!

Our task is to strengthen the revolution and bring it to fulfillment! Forward to the fight for socialism. Forward to the fight for the power of the revolutionary proletariat!

Down with the Ebert-Scheidemann government!

Berlin, January 6, 1919.

> The Revolutionary Shop Stewards and Confidence Men of the large factories of Greater Berlin.
>
> The Central Committee of the Greater Berlin Social Democratic Election Association of the Independent Social Democratic Party.
>
> The Central Committee of the Communist Party of Germany (Spartacist League).[25]

The second proclamation was prepared for release after the seizure of power:

Comrades! Workers!

The Ebert-Scheidemann government has compromised itself. It is herewith declared deposed by the undersigned Revolutionary Committee, the representatives of the revolutionary socialist workers and soldiers (Independent Social Democratic Party and Communist Party).

The undersigned Revolutionary Committee has temporarily taken over governmental affairs.

Comrades! Workers!

Join the actions of the Revolutionary Committee.

Berlin, January 6, 1919.

The Revolutionary Committee.

Ledebour   Liebknecht   Scholze[26]

[Liebknecht signed for the absent Ledebour]

---

[25] Quoted in Bernstein, *op. cit.,* p. 138.

[26] *Illustrierte Geschichte,* p. 272. The Revolutionary Committee moved during the night of January 5-6 from the police headquarters to the Imperial Stables, where it was not welcomed by the sailors who intended to remain neutral in the forthcoming fight. So on January 6, it returned to its original location in the police building. (Bernstein, *op. cit.,* p. 150; Anton Fischer, *op. cit.,* p. 63.) The attempted seizure of the War Ministry, ordered by the Revolutionary Committee, was a tragic-comical incident which illustrated the total incompetence of that committee. A sailor was placed in

One of the best descriptions of the situation during these fateful days in January is a sarcastic article printed one year later in *Die Rote Fahne* in reply to Ledebour's claim that he had started the January revolution.

What happened on Monday in Berlin was perhaps the greatest proletarian mass action in history. We do believe that not even in Russia were there mass demonstrations of this size. From Roland to Viktoria, proletarians were standing shoulder to shoulder. Deep into the Tiergarten they were standing. They had brought along their weapons, they had their red flags. They were ready to do anything, to give everything, even their lives. There was an army of 200,000 such as no Ludendorff had ever seen.

Then the inconceivable happened. The masses were standing from 9 in the morning in the cold and fog. Somewhere their leaders were sitting and conferring. The fog lifted and the masses were still standing. Their leaders conferred. Noon came and in addition to the cold, hunger came. And the leaders conferred. The masses were feverish with excitement: they wanted one deed, even one word to calm their excitement. But nobody knew what to say. Because the leaders were conferring. The fog came again and with it the dusk. The masses went home sad. They wanted great things, but they had done nothing. Because their leaders conferred. They conferred in the Imperial Stables, then they went to the police headquarters and continued to confer. Outside the proletarians were standing in the empty [sic] Alexanderplatz, rifles in hand, with light and heavy machine guns. And inside the leaders conferred. In the police headquarters guns were ready for action; sailors were posted at every corner in the corridors; in the anti-chamber was a milling throng of soldiers, sailors, and proletarians. Inside the leaders sat and conferred. They sat the entire evening and the entire night and conferred; they sat during the next morning. When dawn came, they either were still conferring or were conferring again. And again the grey masses marched into the *Siegesallee,* and still their leaders sat and conferred. They conferred, conferred, conferred.

No! These masses were not ready to take over political power, otherwise they would have acted on their own and placed men at the head whose first revolutionary deed would have been to make the leaders in the police headquarters stop conferring.[27]

The end of the Revolutionary Committee was as undistinguished as its brief life. On January 8, after it had become certain that the government was ready to take aggressive military action against the insurgents, the Committee issued as its last deed a leaflet ending with the empty injunctions: "Show those scoundrels your power! Take up arms! Use these weapons against your deadly enemies, Ebert and Scheidemann. Forward to the fight!" On January 9, the Committee is reported to have held its last of a series of useless meetings.[28]

The "declaration of war" by the left wing radicals put the government in a very difficult position. With the announcement of an all-out campaign dedicated to its forceful overthrow, the SPD government found itself with practically no military protection.[29] It turned for help to its followers among the workers. During the night of January 5-6, a leaflet was printed calling on the workers to come to Wilhelmstrasse, the seat of the Reich government, and protect the Republic against the assaults from the "armed bandits of the Spartacist League."

charge of three hundred men and ordered to occupy the War Ministry. Upon their arrival at the Ministry, the sailor handed an official the written order from the Revolutionary Committee demanding the surrender of the building. The official replied that he was willing to comply, provided that the sailor present him a legal document signed by the representatives of the new revolutionary government who had failed to sign the paper before the sailor went on his mission. Thereupon, the sailor left his three hundred men waiting in front of the Ministry while he went back to the Imperial Stables, then the seat of the Revolutionary Committee, to obtain the signatures. Liebknecht and S c h o l z e signed the document for him. On the way out of the Imperial Stables, he overheard members of the People's

Naval Division asking revolutionary workers to leave the building. He also learned that the sailors had decided not to participate in the conflict. Making the policy of the People's Naval Division his own, he put the freshly signed document in his pocket, forgot about his three hundred men, and went home; he stayed away from his unit for eight days, reporting sick. (Richard Mueller, *Der Buergerkrieg*, pp. 37-38; *Illustrierte Geschichte*, p. 276.)

[27] Quoted in Noske, *Von Kiel bis Kapp*, pp. 69-70. ("Roland" is a monument standing in front of the Berlin city hall; "Viktoria" is another designation for the *Siegessaeule* or Victory Column.)

[28] Oertzen, *op. cit.*, p. 275; Richard Mueller, *Der Buergerkrieg*, p. 75.

[29] Bernstein, *op. cit.*, p. 142; Ri-

Workers! Citizens! Soldiers! Comrades!

The armed bandits of the Spartacist League have forcefully occupied the *Vorwaerts* for the second time. The leaders of these bands publicly announced again today their intention to overthrow the government. Murder and bloody civil war and the establishment of the *Spartakus* dictatorship [are their aims]. Mortal dangers are threatening the German people, especially the workers. Anarchy and hunger will be the sequel to the Spartacist rule.

Our patience is now at an end!

We do not intend any longer to be terrorized by lunatics and criminals. Order must finally be established in Berlin, and the peaceful reconstruction of the new revolutionary Germany must be secured. We are asking you, as a sign of protest to the outrage of the Spartacist bands, to stop working and to come immediately with your [political] leaders to the building of the Reich government, Wilhelmstrasse 77.

Workers! Citizens! Comrades! Soldiers!

Appear in masses! Show that you are strong enough to protect your freedom, your rights, and your party property.[30]

Tens of thousands of workers followed the appeal of the Majority Socialists and assembled in front of the Reich Chancellery ready to protect their government. Scheidemann addressed the crowd and promised them arms.[31]

During the morning of January 6, the cabinet met with important members of the Central Council and the Minister of War, Colonel Reinhardt. Ebert declared that his patience with the leftist opposition had come to an end and that the events of January 5 must be countered by the most stringent military measures if the government wished to retain any authority. Additional troops would be needed for the suppression of the uprising. Colonel Reinhardt proposed the employment of the Guard-Cavalry-Rifle-Division stationed in the vicinity of Berlin under the command of General Hofmann. The government believed

chard Mueller, *Der Buergerkrieg,* pp. 46-57.

[30] Quoted in Hermann Mueller, *op. cit.,* pp. 254-55.

[31] Bernstein, *op. cit.,* p. 138; Hermann Mueller, *op. cit.,* pp. 254-55; Oertzen, *op. cit.,* p. 271.

it would be a tactical error to assign to a general the task of suppressing the uprising, because the workers would resent this. Someone else had to be found. Noske was easily persuaded to accept the assignment.[32] He immediately set out to organize the government's military counteraction against the left wing insurgents.[33]

When the government recognized the Revolutionary Committee's failure to take decisive action, it gained courage and began vigorously to improve its over-all position which had looked so hopeless on the morning of January 6. On the afternoon of that day, the Berlin Executive Council — the agency which Eichhorn recognized as his superior office — approved, twelve votes to two, the dismissal of Eichhorn by the Prussian government, thus adding insult to injury. (Daeuming and Richard Mueller were the only Independent Executive Council members present. They cast the two dissenting votes.)[34]

[32] Hermann Mueller, *op. cit.*, p. 256; Bernstein, *op. cit.*, p. 143. The famous discussion leading to Noske's appointment was reported by him as follows: "We were standing around in Ebert's Office quite excited because time was pressing and our followers in the street clamored for arms. I demanded that a decision be made. Somebody suggested: 'Then you take over this job!' I responded to this without hesitation: 'It's all right with me! Someone has to become the blood hound ["hired ruffian" or "Myrmidon"]. I will not s h r i n k from this responsibility.'" (Noske, *Von Kiel bis Kapp,* p. 68.)

[33] Noske was convinced that the only reliable new troops were the sincere patriots, professional soldiers, non-commissioned officers, officers, and reservists who had not yet found suitable civilian occupations. The so-called revolutionary military forces such as the Republican Soldiers' Army w e r e useless. (Noske, *Erlebtes,* p. 114.) On January 6, Noske left Berlin to assemble enough troops to guarantee successful military operations against the insurgents. He moved into the Luisenstift at Dahlem which

for the next few days became the center for the activation of volunteer units. Noske reported that Dahlem looked like a "war camp" within three days. (Noske, *Von Kiel bis Kapp,* pp. 71-72; Noske, *Erlebtes,* p. 84.) Noske worked closely with General Luettwitz who had been appointed on December 25, 1918, as successor to General Lequis as Supreme Commander of all troops stationed in and near Berlin. For detailed information concerning the variety of troops assembled under the command of *"Abteilung Luettwitz,"* l a t e r renamed "Army Corps Luettwitz" (*Generalkommando*), see Luettwitz, *op. cit.*, pp. 22-25; Oertzen, *op. cit.*, pp. 272-73, 290; and Waite, *op. cit.*, pp. 33-39.

(The German Military term, *Abteilung*, usually refers to a military unit of battalion strength. This was obviously not the case here; the unit in question was far larger than a battalion. It was the designation used for the over-all command of the new troops, and its purpose was to conceal its actual strength.)

[34] Richard Mueller, *Der Buergerkrieg,* pp. 52-53. The text of the

The military situation of the government improved with every hour. A Social Democratic Auxiliary Service (*Sozialdemokratischer Helferdienst*) was organized and took over the protection of the Reichstag building and the area around the Brandenburger Tor.[35] A few troop leaders of the Berlin garrison arrived at the seat of government and offered the services of their units. One of them, the leader of the Potsdam troops, Klawunde, was appointed as the new City Commandant, replacing Anton Fischer. The others formed a newly-established garrison council (*Kommandanturrat*). Anton Fischer became Noske's deputy for Berlin.[36] As early as January 6, 1919, the mold was cast for the subsequent events of Spartakus Week which ended in the complete defeat of the scattered, leaderless groups of left wing radicals.

Moderate USPD leaders of the Reich organization and some *ad hoc* workers' committees offered their good offices to the government and to the left wing USPD and Revolutionary Shop Stewards in an attempt to settle the conflict through negotiation. Their efforts were in vain; the preliminary discussions broke down because neither side was willing to make significant concessions. The radicals of the left accused the government of accepting the offer of negotiations only to gain time for its military preparations. The very fact that the left wing opposition would agree to negotiate with the government it intended to overthrow by force was an indication of its weakness or even utter helplessness.[37]

On January 8, the government began its offensive. A proclamation announced its determination to fight force with force. The insurgents were warned that "the hour of reckoning" was near.

Executive Council's approval is quoted in *ibid*.

[35] Oertzen, *op. cit.*, p. 273; Richard Mueller, *Der Buergerkrieg*, pp. 54, 73-74. On January 19, 1919, the Social Democratic Auxiliary Service became a bona fide Free Corps which bore the name "Regiment Reichstag" because of the location of its headquarters. (Luettwitz, *op. cit.*, pp. 25-26.)

[36] Richard Mueller, *Der Buergerkrieg*, p. 54; Anton Fischer, *op. cit.*, p. 65.

[37] For details on the negotiation efforts as seen from the SPD point of view, consult Bernstein, *op. cit.*, pp. 140, 145-53. The position of the left opposition is presented in Richard Mueller, *Der Buergerkrieg*, pp. 48-60 and *Illustrierte Geschichte*, pp. 284-85.

Fellow-Citizens!

Spartakus is now fighting for complete power. The government, which within ten days wants to permit the people to decide freely about their own fate, is to be overthrown by force. *The people are not permitted to speak; their voices are to be suppressed.* You have seen the result! *Where Spartakus rules, all personal freedom and security is suspended.* The newspapers are suppressed; traffic is paralyzed. Sections of Berlin are scenes of bloody fighting. Others are already without water and light. Food depots are stormed. *The food supply for the soldiers and civilian population is interrupted.*

The government is taking all measures necessary to destroy this rule of terror and to prevent its recurrence once and for all. Decisive action will be forthcoming soon. However, it is necessary to do the work thoroughly and this requires preparation. Have patience for a little while longer. Be confident, as we are, and resolutely take your place with those who will bring you freedom and order! Force can be fought only with force. The organized power of the people will end oppression and anarchy. Individual successes of the enemies of freedom, which are magnified by them in a ridiculous fashion, are of only temporary significance.

The hour of reckoning is near!
Berlin, January 8, 1919.

The Reich Government!
Ebert, Scheidemann, Landsberg, Noske, Wissel.[38]

On the same day, units of the Berlin garrison stormed a number of occupied buildings and succeeded in re-capturing the Government Printing Office, the Main Railroad Office and a railroad station, and most of the newspaper printing plants.[39]

The *Vorwaerts* building was attacked by the Potsdam Regiment during the night of January 10-11. Approximately three hundred defenders surrendered after artillery fire had caused a

Noske was greatly opposed to negotiations and to a compromise solution with the insurgents because he was convinced that an ultimate fight was inevitable. (Noske, *Erlebtes,* p. 84; Noske, *Von Kiel bis Kapp,* p. 73.)

[38] A photostat of the above proclamation is contained in *Illustrierte Geschichte,* p. 277.

[39] Anton Fischer, *op. cit.,* pp. 75-76; Bernstein, *op. cit.,* pp. 151-54; *Illustrierte Geschichte,* p. 285.

number of casualties. The police headquarters, the last of the strongholds of the insurgents, fell during the night of January 11-12. Most of Eichhorn's Security Force had gone over to the government side, and less than two hundred men defended the building against the attack by the Maikaefer Regiment.[40]

When Noske, leading approximately 3,000 men, marched demonstratively into Berlin on January 11, 1919, the uprising was all but suppressed. There still was fighting at police headquarters and other isolated places. With the few reliable troops of the Berlin garrison and some of their own units, such as the Social Democratic Auxiliary Service, the government had succeeded in overwhelming most of the leftist strongholds before Noske's Free Corps arrived.[41]

A few days after the first volunteer units, which Noske personally led into the city, had duly impressed the people of Berlin, the final occupation of the capital was completed by the units of Army Corps Luettwitz according to a detailed and carefully prepared plan.[42]

On January 13, Spartakus Week ended in a great fiasco for the left wing opposition. Any further resistance was useless. The

[40] Descriptions of the military events are contained in Schmidt-Pauli, op. cit., pp. 185-87; Runkel, op. cit., p. 213; Oertzen, op. cit., p. 277; Bernstein, op. cit., pp. 157-64. Details of the fightings described from the left wing radicals' point of view are contained in Illustrierte Geschichte, pp. 285-92. The latter report emphasizes the brutal treatment accorded the surrendered defenders and the shooting of parliamentarians by the troops. Major Stephani, the commander of the troops which attacked the Vorwaerts, claimed that he had orders from the City Commandant to shoot any captives carrying arms. Stephani asserted that this order was confirmed over the phone from the Reich Chancellery. (Ibid., p. 290.)
[41] "The soldier decides [sic] the game. Not General Luettwitz's Free Corps, but the bands of undisciplined soldiers of the Berlin and Potsdam barracks and a few republican fighting units assembled hastily during the last few days [suppressed the left wing radicals]." (Volkmann, Revolution, p. 185. See also Richard Mueller, Der Buergerkrieg, p. 92.)
[42] Noske, Von Kiel bis Kapp, pp. 74-75; Noske, Erlebtes, p. 84. The deployment order for Army Corps Luettwitz was Noske's Secret Order I A No. 10 of January 13, 1919. It is quoted in full in Oertzen, op. cit., pp. 278-80. Anton Fischer soon became disgusted with Noske's troops because of their hostility toward the Republican Soldiers' Army. (Anton Fischer, op. cit., pp. 77-78.) A good illustration of Noske's attitude is given in a leaflet which he had distributed the day he entered Berlin, January 11. A photo-

Revolutionary Shop Stewards and the Berlin organization of the USPD asked their followers to return to work.[43] The government had succeeded in establishing its superiority — at least for the period immediately following the bloody January events. Since the fighting potential of the opposition of the left was crushed, the elections to the national assembly could take place without major disturbances and interference.

A factual evaluation of the January events supports the assertion that the "Spartacist Uprising" was not a premeditated undertaking but was an outgrowth of the policy meeting of January 5 held by the left wing factions because of the overwhelming mass response to the Eichhorn incident. The estimate of the revolutionary situation arrived at by the over-optimistic radical leaders — especially concerning the attitude of the soldiers — was incorrect and misleading. However, there is general agreement among contemporaneous observers that a determined leadership could have seized political power in Berlin either on January 5 or 6. How long the revolutionaries could have retained power is another question; it appears that, since the rest of Germany would not have followed the example set in the capital, it would have been only a short "council dictatorship." Because the Revolutionary Committee was divided internally concerning its own objectives, it was incapable of giving directives to the masses which waited patiently for two days. The Revolutionary Committee decided to maintain the occupation of strategically and tactically unimportant buildings instead of seizing the traditional seats of political power, such as the Chancellery and the Ministry of War. In this context it really did not matter if those buildings were originally occupied by spontaneous mass actions or through the agitation of *agents provocateurs*.[44]

An examination of the events leading to the January fighting does not support the assertion that the SPD government provoked

graphic copy is in *Illustrierte Ges-chichte*, p. 276.

[43] Hermann Mueller, *op. cit.*, p. 270.

[44] For various views concerning the short-range possibilities of the revolutionary forces, see Cyril L. R. James, *World Revolutions 1917-1936* (London: Secker & Warburg, 1937), p. 101;

the action of the left wing radicals in order to create a situation in which the government would be justified in suppressing by force. It was not the beginning of a contemplated all-out offensive by the government against the opposition forces. However, once the position of power began to change in favor of the government, the determination to settle the basic issue with the revolutionary trouble-makers won the upper hand.[45]

The number of persons killed during the January uprising remains unknown. Even reliable estimates are not available.[46]

4. *The Spartacists and the January Uprising*

The attitude of the Communists toward the uprising was not uniform. Their views toward an expansion of the mass protest demonstration on behalf of Eichhorn into a full-scale fight for the seizure of political power were divided as follows: (1) Karl Liebknecht and Wilhelm Pieck, the two Central Committee members who participated in the January 5 meeting of the functionaries of the Revolutionary Shop Stewards and of the Berlin USPD, strongly endorsed the uprising. (2) Rosa Luxemburg, Leo Jogiches, and the rest of the Central Committee of the KPD were opposed but believed that, regardless of their views, the new KPD had the moral obligation to support the revolutionary workers in their life and death struggle. (3) Karl Radek was strictly opposed

Volkmann, *Revolution,* pp. 184-85; Meinecke, *Die Revolution,* p. 117; Bernstein, *op. cit.,* pp. 137, 142; Noske, *Von Kiel bis Kapp,* p. 69; Ulbricht, *Zur Geschichte,* pp. 38-39. Richard Mueller blames the lack of initiative displayed by the Revolutionary Committee on the fact that it did not recognize the weakness of the government. (Richard Mueller, *Der Buergerkrieg,* p. 40.)

[45] It is possible that Noske for one was pleased with the opportunity created by the January events. They accelerated the creation of the military instrument which he thought was necessary to establish law and order first in Berlin and then in the rest of the Reich. See his statement in Noske, *Erlebtes,* p. 83.

[46] Bernstein claims that the exact figure was never determined. (Bernstein, *op. cit.,* pp. 156-57.) Halperin claims over one thousand casualties for "Spartakus Week" in Berlin, but fails to indicate on what sources he bases his figure. (Halperin, *op. cit.,* p. 122.) Stampfer stated that one hundred fifty-six persons were killed in addition to Rosa Luxemburg and Liebknecht. (Stampfer, *Die ersten 14 Jahre,* p. 92.) Official reports assert that approximately two hundred people were killed. (*Illustrierte Geschichte,* p. 292.)

to the uprising and urgently advocated discontinuing the hopeless fight before the revolutionary organizations suffered severe defeats which would affect their work for a long time to come.

Liebknecht and Pieck, in siding with the advocates of the uprising, had acted without the knowledge and approval of the Central Committee of the KPD. Liebknecht was severely criticized by Rosa Luxemburg for his unilateral action. How many of the rank and file members of the Spartacists concurred with Liebknecht's endorsement of the all-out struggle for power is not known. During the days of the uprising, Liebknecht spent his time either in conferences with the Revolutionary Committee or with the dispersed groups of entrenched insurgents. He maintained little contact with the party leadership. On January 10, the Central Committee finally ordered Liebknecht and Pieck not to continue their participation in the Revolutionary Committee. This directive was meaningless by then since the committee had already suspended its meetings and had scattered in all directions.[47]

The attitude of most of the KPD leaders, including Rosa Luxemburg and Leo Jogiches, toward the uprising was determined by their conviction that political developments in Germany had not reached the point where an attempt to assume power should be made.[48] The decision of the January 5 meeting in favor of the all-out fight created a difficult problem for the Communist leaders. Should the KPD support the fight of the revolutionary workers in spite of the fact that the Central Committee did not endorse the uprising and was certain from the beginning that the insurrection had no real chance of realizing its objectives? Rosa Luxemburg's views (which doubtlessly reflected the Party's position on this controversial issue) were related by Clara Zetkin on the basis

[47] Froelich, *Rosa Luxemburg*, pp. 339, 342; *Illustrierte Geschichte*, p. 283; Hermann Mueller, *op. cit.*, pp. 253, 270. Liebknecht's actions were certainly no indication of the policies of the KPD during the January Uprising. Runkel, for example, fails to recognize this. (Runkel, *op. cit.*, p. 207.)

[48] Oelssner, *op. cit.*, p. 148. Cf. above, p. 169.

of a letter she had received from Leo Jogiches, who probably was Rosa Luxemburg's closest collaborator during the January days.

Rosa Luxemburg saw the events — as significant and as hopeful as they were — not from the viewpoint of the assault against the Berlin City Hall. She related these events to the prevailing situation and especially to the degree of political maturity of the broad population of all Germany. On that basis, the overthrow of the Ebert government could be, for the time-being, only a propagandistic over-all slogan of the revolutionary proletarians, and not the immediate objective of revolutionary struggles. Under the prevailing circumstances related primarily to Berlin, in the most favorable case they [the revolutionary fighters] could have led to a Berlin "Commune," . . . The aim of the fight could only be a strong defense against the attack of the counter-revolution. Thus the reinstatement of Eichhorn, the withdrawal of the troops which were to subjugate the revolutionary proletariat of Berlin in a violent manner, the arming of the workers, and the transfer of the military command power to the revolutionary political representatives of the proletarians — these were the demands which required action, not negotiations.

Because of this situation, the young Communist Party led by Rosa Luxemburg had a difficult mission, full of conflicts. It could not accept the objective of the mass action — the overthrow of the government; it had to reject this aim, but at the same time it was not permitted to detach itself from the masses which had taken up the fight. In spite of this contradiction, the Party had to remain with the masses; it had to remain among the masses to strengthen the fighters in their struggle against the counter-revolution and to expedite the process of their revolutionary maturation during the operations by making them aware of the purpose of their struggle. Toward this end, the Communist Party had to reveal its own aims and make known its precise estimate of the situation without injuring the revolutionary solidarity it owed to the fighters. . . .[49]

[49] Quoted in Froelich, *Rosa Luxemburg,* pp. 340-41. There is very little information available about the formulation of KPD policies during the uprising and none about the actual participation of the Party or its leaders in the operational phase, except a vague notion of Liebknecht's and

Thus the Communists joined the insurgents not because they believed that the uprising was a politically and tactically well-founded operation, but because of the obligation the Party thought it owed to the revolutionary fighters. "Under the circumstances there was only one decision possible for the Communist Party: to remain with the fighters, to strengthen their power of resistance and their courage, to be ready not only to share in their victories but also in their defeats."[50] The KPD also intended to aid the revolutionary mass action by clarifying and limiting objectives. The aims set by the Communists for the uprising were disarmament of the counterrevolution, arming of the proletariat, merger of all revolutionary troops into a Red Guard, and new elections for the workers' and soldiers' councils in order to bring their composition into harmony with the changes which had occurred since November, 1918. The overthrow of the Ebert government, the main purpose of the uprising as determined by the Revolutionary Committee, became the slogan and general directive for the entire coming phase of the revolution.[51]

The articles of Rosa Luxemburg, "What Are the Leaders Doing?" and "Neglected Duties," in *Die Rote Fahne* present a candid view of the KPD about the revolutionary implications of the January Uprising. They also furnish an insight into Communist attempts to formulate limited and reasonable objectives and to compel the revolutionary leaders of the insurrection to fulfill their obligations.

Those who saw yesterday's [January 6, 1919] mass demonstrations in the Siegesallee, who felt this adamant revolutionary conviction, this magnificent attitude, this energy flowing from the masses, must have reached the [following] conclusions: the proletarians have grown enormously in a political sense through the experience of the last weeks.

Pieck's activities. Froelich asserts that a direct party influence and participation in the fighting existed, although he admits the lack of specific information on the subject. (*Ibid.*, p. 342.) The sources of information for the Party's policy formulation are restricted to the letter of Jogiches mentioned above and a few articles in *Die Rote Fahne*.

[50] *Illustrierte Geschichte*, p. 283.
[51] *Ibid.*

They have realized their strength and lack nothing but to use their power.

However, have their leaders, the executive organs of their will, progressed with them? Have the Revolutionary Shop Stewards and Confidence Men of the large factories, have the radical elements of the USP acquired more energy and more determination in the meantime? Has their capacity for action kept abreast of the growing energy of the masses?

. . . The masses followed the call of their leaders with impetuosity. . . . They are waiting for further directives and actions from their leaders.

What have the leaders done in the meantime, what have they decided? What measures have they taken to secure the victory of the revolution in this tense situation during which the fate of the revolution will be decided at least for the next phase? We see and hear nothing! It may be true that the representatives of the working class are thoroughly and abundantly *conferring*. However, now is the time to *act*.

No time must be wasted. Thorough measures must be taken immediately. Clear and urgent directives must be given to the masses and to the soldiers who remained faithful to the cause of the revolution; . . .

Act! Act! Courageously, decisively, and constantly — that is the . . . duty and obligation of the Revolutionary Shop Stewards and of the honest socialist party leaders. Disarm the counterrevolution, arm the masses, and occupy all positions of power. Act quickly! . . .[52]

. . . the weakness and immaturity of the revolution manifest themselves in the questions: *How* does one conduct the fight to remove the Ebert government? *How* does one convert this increased internal maturity into practical use? Nothing like the last three days have shown so strongly these weaknesses and deficiencies.

The elimination of the Ebert-Scheidemann government does not mean storming into the palace of the Reich Chancellery and chasing away or arresting a few people: it means first of all to seize all real power positions and *hold on* to them and *make use* of them.

[52] Rosa Luxemburg, "Was machen die Fuehrer?" quoted in Luxemburg, *Ausgewaehlte Reden*, II, pp. 689-92.

The experience of the last three days speaks eloquently to the leaders of the working class: Do not talk! Do not confer forever! Do not negotiate! *Act*.[53]

Karl Radek's opposition to the January uprising and to the participation of the KPD in the futile attempt to seize political power cannot be accepted as an indication of the official Soviet attitude toward the events. It is highly doubtful that Radek had any contact with his party during this period. His views are of great interest because they can be cited as proof that the Bolsheviks did not incite the German revolutionary leaders to the uprising contrary to the assertions of Edward Bernstein.[54] On the basis of the information available to this writer, at the beginning of January, Radek was the only official representative of the Bolsheviks in Berlin. As has been said, he shared the belief of Rosa Luxemburg and her associates that the time for the all-out struggle for power had not yet come. He added authority to this conviction because of his reputation among the Communists as an experienced revolutionary tactician. On January 6, he declared his opposition to the decision of the January 5 meeting. On the 9th, he addressed a letter to the Central Committee of the KPD in which he requested that the Party use its influence upon the Revolutionary Committee and the proletarian masses to cease the insurrection immediately. He offered the following reasons for his request:

In your program pamphlet, "What Does the Spartacist League Want?", you explain that you intend to take over the government only when you have the majority of the working class behind you. This absolutely correct stand finds its justification in the simple fact that a government of the workers is unthinkable without an existing proletarian mass organization. At present, the only mass organizations to be considered, the workers' and soldiers' councils, are of only nominal strength. . . . In this situation, one cannot even consider the proletariat's

[53] Rosa Luxemburg, "Versaeumte Pflichten," quoted in Luxemburg, *Ausgewaehlte Reden*, II, pp. 693-97.

[54] Bernstein, *op. cit.*, pp. 139-40.

taking over political power. If the government should fall into your hands as the result of a *coup d'etat,* within a few days it would be cut off from the rest of the country and would be strangled.

In this situation, the action taken by the Revolutionary Shop Stewards in response to the attack of the social-patriotic government against the police headquarters, should have been only a protest action. The advance guard of the proletariat — provoked by government policy and misled by the Revolutionary Shop Stewards, who as the result of their political inexperience are not capable of understanding the power relation throughout the entire Reich — has in its enthusiasm transformed the protest demonstration into a struggle for political power. This enables Ebert and Scheidemann to strike a blow against the Berlin movement which can weaken the entire movement for months. The only force which can prevent this disaster is you, the Communist Party. You have sufficient insight to know that the fight is hopeless; . . . Nothing can prevent a weaker [power] from retreating before a superior force.[55]

Shortly after the last skirmishes ended, Rosa Luxemburg evaluated the events of Spartakus Week. In her article "Order Rules in Berlin" (*Die Ordnung herrscht in Berlin*), she explained that a victory of the proletarians — the overthrow of the Ebert government and the establishment of a socialist dictatorship — could not be expected because of the political immaturity of the German Revolution. The fact that the soldiers, most of whom were from rural areas which were hardly affected by the revolution, could be used for suppressing the revolutionary workers was for Rosa Luxemburg one of the significant symptoms of the general political immaturity of Germany. Under these circumstances a victory of the working class was impossible.

[55] Quoted in *Illustrierte Geschichte,* p. 282. See also Radek's letter written from prison after the January uprising to Alfons Paquet, the well-known German writer and newspaper correspondent of the *Frankfurter Zeitung* who was stationed in Moscow during 1918. Radek strongly emphasized in this letter his opposition to the uprising. He also explained that the KPD was not an effective party and had no control over the masses — a situation different from that of the Bolsheviks in Russia. Therefore, the KPD could neither prevent nor stop the bloody fighting as, for example,

. . . A final and lasting victory in this moment could not be expected. Was, therefore, the fight of the last week a "mistake"? Yes, if it had been an intentional "assault," a so-called "putsch." However, what was the cause of the fighting of the past week? As in all previous instances . . . it was a brutal provocation of the government! . . . The revolutionary working class was *forced* to take up arms. It was a *matter of revolutionary honor* to repel immediately the assault [of the counterrevolution] . . . .[56]

Rosa Luxemburg emphasized that the suppression of the January Uprising was only a defeat in one single engagement, and she predicted that the next day the revolution would proclaim: "I was, I am, I shall be!"[57]

Liebknecht was of the same mind. The uprising was defeated because "the time was not ripe" for it. This could not be helped because the workers had not chosen to start the fight. "The fight was forced on the proletariat by the Ebert-gang."[58]

Indeed, it was a strange twist of history which gave the January Uprising the name of that left wing opposition group within the German socialist movement which officially had nothing to do with starting the insurrection and which became connected with it only to maintain "proletarian solidarity." If the January Uprising must be identified at all with a left-wing faction, then the Revolutionary Shop Stewards, whose functionaries voted unanimously for it, should be first in line for this "honor."[59]

5. *The Aftermath*

The uprising in Berlin did not remain a completely isolated event. Radical groups of the left in several German cities followed the example set in the capital. Newspaper plants were occupied by "revolutionary workers" in Brunswick, Dortmund, Duessel-

the Bolsheviks were able to do during a hopeless uprising in Petrograd in July of 1917. (Alfons Paquet, *Der Geist der russischen Revolution* [Leipzig: Wolf Verlag, 1919], pp. viii-ix.)

[56] Rosa Luxemburg, "Die Ordnung herrscht in Berlin," quoted in Luxem-

burg, *Ausgewaehlte Reden,* II, pp. 709-11.

[57] *Ibid.,* pp. 712-14.

[58] Karl Liebknecht, "Trotz alledem!" quoted in Liebknecht, *Ausgewaehlte Reden,* pp. 526-30.

[59] Professor Bergstraesser regards

dorf, Nuremberg, Hamburg, and Wolfenbuettel (Lower Saxony). In Duesseldorf, the workers' and soldiers' council seized power. A Soviet republic was proclaimed in Bremen. Armed revolutionaries seized the city hall and the banks in Delmenhorst (Lower Saxony). A general strike broke out in the Ruhr. Violent skirmishes occurred in many other places throughout the Reich. But none of these proved to be serious challenges for the authorities. Local security forces, such as police detachments or small military units, suppressed the individual revolts before they were able to advance very far.[60]

After the arrival of Noske's Free Corps in Berlin, a clean-up operation began. Its objectives were to crush the organizations of the left wing radicals and to disarm the civilian population by confiscating all unauthorized weapons. The brutal methods used by the volunteer units during the days following the January Uprising gave Germany a preview of the coming Noske campaign of re-establishing "law and order" throughout the country.[61]

The violent Anti-Spartakus offensive did not decrease in intensity even after the end of hostilities. The revolutionary leaders, especially Rosa Luxemburg, Karl Liebknecht, and Karl Radek, became major targets.[62] Georg Ledebour and Ernst Meyer had

the January Uprising as a putsch instigated by the Revolutionary Shop Stewards of the large Berlin factories and joined by the Communists in spite of their better judgment. (Bergstraesser, *op. cit.,* p. 207.)

[60] *Illustrierte Geschichte,* pp. 281-82. See, for example, the description by Keil of the planned revolt in Stuttgart and its suppression by the security forces of the local provisional government. (Keil, *op. cit.,* pp. 136-37.)

[61] Hugo Haase, the leader of the USPD, described the general situation in Berlin in a letter as follows: ". . . You cannot imagine the conditions in Berlin. White terror rages exactly as it did under the tzarist regime. Even under the Anti-Socialist Law, at least an attempt was made to make it appear that the law was followed. At

present, however, brutal force rules in the open. Disregarding any legal restrictions, soldiers — government troops — with loaded rifles break into apartments at night, make arrests without warrants, and search the apartments without court orders. In the apartment of Oskar Cohn [a leading member of the USPD] a house search was made the day before yesterday. He escaped being arrested only because he was out of town. His property was confiscated. Landsberg, Ebert, and Scheidemann, who try to pose as the guardians of the law, let the hordes of brutal soldiers (*Soldateska*) do as they like. . . ." (Haase, *op. cit.,* pp. 173-74; letter dated January 16, 1919, addressed to "Else.")

[62] On January 13, 1919, the *Vorwaerts* printed the following poem

been arrested as early as January 9 in the latter's apartment. Leo Jogiches and Hugo Eberlein were apprehended when troops, following the re-capture of the *Vorwaerts* building, sacked the offices of the KPD in Friedrichsstrasse. Emil Eichhorn was in hiding for several days and then managed to escape by car into Brunswick.[63]

On January 15, 1919, Rosa Luxemburg, Karl Liebknecht, and Wilhelm Pieck were captured in the apartment of friends living in Wilmersdorf, a residential section of Berlin, by members of the local "Citizen Guard." They were turned over to the Guard-Cavalry-Rifle-Division which had its headquarters at the Hotel Eden. On that same day, Liebknecht and Rosa Luxemburg were brutally murdered by the members of this division. Both were clubbed and shot to death and Rosa Luxemburg's body was thrown into a canal running through Berlin. Her body was

written by Artur Zickler:

Many hundred dead are lying in
a row —
Proletarians!
Iron, powder, and lead do not ask
if a person belong to the right, to
the left, or to Spartakus,
Proletarians!
Who has brought violence into
the streets,
Proletarians?
Who first took up arms
and relied on their results?
S p a r t a k u s!
Many hundred dead are lying in
a row —
Proletarians!
Karl, Radek, Rosa and
companions —
none of them is there, none of
them is there!
Proletarians!

(Quoted in *Illustrierte Geschichte*, p. 293.)

A reward of 10,000 Marks was offered by the "Association for Combatting Bolshevism" for information leading to the arrest of Radek. A photograph of a wall poster announcing this reward is contained in *ibid.*, p.

265. The *Volkswehr*, organ of the Berlin Volunteer Corps, printed the following announcement on January 14, 1919:

"Berlin, January 13. The fear has been expressed that the government would relax its persecution of the Spartacists. We have been assured by influential circles that the achievements made so far are not considered as satisfactory and that all energy will be used to proceed against the Spartacists and the leaders of the movement. The people of Berlin need not believe that the leaders, who for the time being have evaded arrest, will be able to enjoy life elsewhere. The next days will show that the situation has become critical for them." (Quoted in *ibid.*, p. 296.)

[63] For details of the arrest of Ledebour and Meyer, see Bernstein, *op. cit.*, p. 164; Richard Mueller, *Der Buergerkrieg*, p. 71; *Illustrierte Geschichte*, pp. 286-87. For Jogiches' and Eberlein's arrest, see Froelich, *Rosa Luxemburg*, p. 345. Jogiches was released but re-arrested again and murdered in the police prison on March 10 by a plain-clothes man named Tam-

not found until the end of May. Pieck's escape without being harmed by the troops has caused considerable speculation.[64]

schick; the same man also shot the former leader of the People's Naval Division, Dorrenbach, when he "attempted to escape." (*Ibid.*, p. 351-52. Also see Anton Fischer, *op. cit.*, p. 62.) Eichhorn's escape is mentioned in Bernstein, *op. cit.*, p. 164. Radek eventually was arrested by government troops on February 17, 1919, when he attended a meeting of the "Red Soldiers' League." (Stuemke, *op. cit.*, p. 206.)

[64] The Communists c l a i m that Pieck convinced Captain Pabst of the Guard-Cavalry-Rifle-Division that he was really somebody else. He allegedly was transferred to a jail from which he managed to escape. (*Illustrierte Geschichte*, p. 298; see also Fritz Erpenbeck, *Wilhelm Pieck* [B e r l i n : Dietz Verlag, 1952], pp. 99-101.) Since Wilhelm Pieck is a prominent contemporary political figure in the Communist world — he is President of the "German Democratic Republic" — Erich Wollenberg's report of this incident is interesting. A G e r m a n Communist leader, Hans Kippenberger, who was in charge of the "Underground Military Apparatus" of the KPD from 1928 to 1935, was ordered in 1930 by the leader of the KPD, Ernst Thaelmann, to investigate the Pieck incident of January, 1919. Pieck allegedly was a l r e a d y standing up against a wall to be shot when he requested to see an officer alone. This request was granted and subsequently Pieck was permitted to leave the Eden Hotel with a letter of protection signed by the intelligence officer of the Guard-Cavalry-Rifle Division. A l l this occurred prior to the murder of Liebknecht and Rosa Luxemburg. The results of Kippenberger's investigation were never published or made known. After the arrest of Thaelmann in March, 1933, Jonny Scheer took over the leadership of the Party, and after Scheer was taken into custody by the

Gestapo, Walter Ulbricht — the present Secretary General of the Socialist Unity Party of Eastern Germany — ascended to the Party's leadership. He ordered the headquarters of the "Underground Military Apparatus" to be moved abroad. Its central office was o r g a n i z e d in Paris. Kippenberger moved to Paris in 1934.

Great differences developed between Ulbricht and Kippenberger. Ulbricht ordered that Trotskyites and other oppositional Communists be denounced to the Gestapo in order to put them out of the way. When Kippenberger refused to relay this order, Ulbricht relieved him of his functions and sent him to Moscow to report. There, Kippenberger was arrested in 1936 by the Russian Secret Police and upon the request of Wilhelm Pieck, who from 1934 on had been the representative of the KPD leadership with the Communist International, was liquidated by a shot in the neck. The elimination of Kippenberger was a welcome development for Pieck who thereby eliminated a person who knew too much about him. (Wollenberg, *op. cit.*, pp. 576-78.)

The text of the official government announcement about Liebknecht's and Luxemburg's murders is quoted in Runkel, *op. cit.*, pp. 217-20. According to this announcement, Liebknecht was shot when he tried to escape and Luxemburg was lynched by the angry masses in front of the Eden Hotel. On January 17, the USPD organ *Freiheit* challenged this version. (See *ibid.*, pp. 220-22.) Later, the USPD published a pamphlet containing the facts of the investigation about the murder as well as the trial held against the murderers. (Freiheit, *Der Mord an Karl Liebknecht und Rosa Luxemburg* [Berlin: Verlagsgenossenschaft "F r e i h e i t," 1920].) For example, the Majority Socialist version is presented in Hermann Mueller, *op. cit.*, pp. 271-79 and

When the news of the murder of the two leading Communists became known, the leaders of the USPD and the Central Committee of the KPD called the workers to a general strike in Berlin. The response to this summons for a protest demonstration was very poor. It came too close on the heels of the January defeat which had temporarily diminished the fighting strength of Berlin's workers.[65]

The death of these two outstanding Communist leaders was of great significance not only for the immediate future of the KPD but was of even greater importance for its long-run development. Karl Liebknecht and Rosa Luxemburg might have been able to prevent the Russian Bolsheviks from becoming the controlling power of the German Communist movement.[66]

In the middle of January, the Majority Socialist government appeared outwardly as the unquestionable victor of the fight with the left wing radicals. In truth, the January events made "the Ebert government even more dependent on the Army than before, and when the National Assembly met at Weimar on February 6, 1919, it was under the protection of Maercker's bayonets."[67] It has been repeatedly asserted, therefore, that the real victors were the political reactionary forces, represented by the confessedly anti-republican Free Corps and the remnants of regular units, upon which the SPD leaders had primarily relied in suppressing the revolutionary left wing opposition. The pattern set in Berlin was soon followed in many other parts of Germany.[68]

Bernstein, op. cit., pp. 165-71. Representative Communist accounts can be found in Oelssner, op. cit., pp. 150-55 and Illustrierte Geschichte, pp. 292-307. Oertzen's version of the incident is based on his own investigation. He completely exonerates the officers of the Guard-Cavalry-Rifle-Division; otherwise his version comes very close to that of the leftist opposition. (Oertzen, op. cit., pp. 284-89.)

[65] Richard Mueller, Der Buergerkrieg, p. 83.

[66] Bergstraesser, op. cit., p. 205, and James, op. cit., p. 102.

[67] Wheeler-Bennett, op. cit., p. 37. Wheeler-Bennett means here under "Army" not the regular army units, but the newly founded Free Corps which were commanded by nationalistic former imperial officers.

[68] Waite claims that the Free Corps were strongly supported by industry and landed interests. The political and financial independence of the Free Corps was convincingly demonstrated

when many of these volunteer units refused to join the Provisional Reichswehr (Germany Army), which was formed on March 6, 1919. Most of the Free Corps preferred to maintain their independence. One year later, in March, 1920, these forces staged the ill-fated Kapp-Luettwitz Putsch which attempted to overthrow the Weimar Constitution and government and put a military dictatorship in its place. (Waite, *op. cit.*, pp. 78, 137, 140-67, 189-90.) Waite presents in the appendix of his book (pp. 285-96) a long roster of Free Corps leaders who played significant parts in both the Free Corps Movement and in the future Nazi Party or its military organizations, the SA and SS. (See also Ebenstein, *op. cit.*, p. 196.)

The Revolution in Retrospect

Throughout the inter-war period, the November Revolution and the January Uprising remained highly controversial issues between the German socialists and Communists, since both sides considered these events as having determined to a very large degree the further development of the German labor movement and the nature of the Weimar Republic. The Communists continued to accuse the SPD leaders of having consciously betrayed the revolution and of having cooperated closely with the reactionary forces in willfully suppressing the revolutionary workers. The SPD leaders insisted that the Communists' putschist activities had forced them to defend their own revolutionary concepts.

The Communists considered the actions of the Majority Socialists as the primary cause for the failure of the German Revolution. The actions and concepts of the Spartacists also became the targets of Communist criticism. The Spartacists were accused of having neglected organizational work among the workers in spite of the fact that Lenin himself had urged Rosa Luxemburg to break with the reformists of the socialist movement.[1]

---

[1] Lenin allegedly pressed the Spartacists to break with the USPD, but Rosa Luxemburg refused to do so. Then the Communists accused Rosa Luxemburg of failing to understand the necessity of creating an organization with clearly defined principles and aims, which could have served as a collecting point for revolutionary workers who were discontented with the Social Democratic Parties. (James, op. cit., p. 96. See also Ulbricht, Der Zusammenbruch, p. 6.) The Communists' claim that Lenin had advocated the split of the Second International and of the European Social

The Communists asserted that this fateful omission was the reason why the German revolutionary workers were left without the leadership of a genuinely Marxist-Leninist party. The self-criticism, practiced by the Communists, also served to convince the KPD members of the absolute superiority of Bolshevik concepts upon which the successful Russian Revolution was based over the ideological misconceptions introduced by Rosa Luxemburg into the German party. The Communists claimed that not until 1925, when Ernst Thaelmann ascended to the leadership of the KPD, was the Party finally able to acquire a genuine Marxist-Leninist character.[2]

After World War II, the German Communists, primarily in the Soviet Zone of Occupation, undertook a new analysis of the November Revolution of 1918. Otto Grotewohl, one of the leading functionaries of the Socialist Unity Party of Germany

Democratic parties before 1914 is repudiated by Paul Froelich, who reported that the Russian Party historian Sluzki found that Lenin did nothing of the kind. Lenin allegedly did not support the fight of the German radical left against the SPD Center of Kautsky whom he regarded then as the leading socialist theorist. Sluzki claimed that it was Stalin's idea to use Lenin as the authority for the concept of splitting the European labor movements. Sluzki was liquidated in the Great Purge of 1936 to 1938. (Paul Froelich, "Wie die SED Rosa Luxemburg ehrt," *Der Kochel-Brief* [Oberbayern: January-February, 1953], p. 7.)

[2] Matern, *op. cit.*, p. 13. Thaelmann was credited with eliminating the remnants of "Luxemburgism" in the KPD, the name given to the heresy of the followers of Rosa Luxemburg, Oelssner considers "Luxemburgism" as a variation of S o c i a l Democratism. (Oelssner, *op. cit.*, pp. 212-13.) Luxemburg's mistakes were summarized by Thaelmann in 1932 as follows: "We must frankly state that in all questions in which Rosa Luxemburg held an opinion different from that of Lenin, her opinion was wrong; therefore, the entire group of German left wing radicals in the period before and during the war remained, in clarity and revolutionary steadfastness, considerably behind that of the Bolsheviks.

"Only this knowledge gives us an understanding of why the split between revolutionary M a r x i s m and petit-bourgeois opportunism or its Centrist accomplices within the labor movement came so late in Germany. Rosa Luxemburg's invalid concepts of the theory of accumulation [of capital], the agrarian question, the nationality issue, the questions concerning problems of the revolution, the question of the proletarian dictatorship, the question concerning organization, the problems related to the role of the party, respectively to the spontaneity of the masses — all resulted in a series of blunders, which prevented Rosa Luxemburg from reaching the clarity Lenin did." (This is a quote from Ernst Thaelmann, *Der revolutionaere*

(SED),[3] explained the "compelling reasons" for a study of the revolution of 1918:

A thorough examination of the German November Revolution of 1918, its causes, its objectives, and its effects is of urgent necessity for the German working class. [The analysis of the revolution] not only satisfies historical interest but is of the greatest current political significance because it provides doctrines for the further struggle.

The German labor movement — and thereby the entire German people — today faces tasks similar to those facing it in 1918. . . .[4]

A resolution of the Executive Committee of the SED, issued on the occasion of the 30th anniversary of the 1918-19 Revolution on September 16, 1948, formulated the purpose of the study of the November Revolution as follows:

The historical development after 1918 and the horrible catastrophe of 1945 which stood at the end of this development, demands that we occupy ourselves with the causes, objectives, and effects of the November Revolution in order to draw lessons from these experiences for our further struggle and to protect the German working class from once more following the same incorrect and therefore disastrous road.

It is necessary to understand completely the background, the course, and the effects of the November Revolution in order to draw from it the essential lessons. A thorough study of these issues will assist us to train the Party within the spirit of Marxism and Leninism. Therefore, the Party's Executive Committee assigns the entire Party

Ausweg und die KPD [Berlin, 1932], pp. 71-72, quoted in Oelssner, *op. cit.,* p. 214.)

[3] The German term for the Socialist Unity Party of Germany is *Sozialistische Einheitspartei Deutschlands.* Its abbreviation SED will be used hereafter. The SED came into existence at a joint congress of the SPD and KPD of the Soviet Zone. The formal announcement of the merger of the two parties and of the formation of the SED was made on April 21, 1946. (Sozialistische Einheitspartei Deutsch-

lands, *Dokumente der Sozialistischen Einheitspartei Deutschlands* [Berlin: Deitz Verlag, 1952], I, pp. 5-10, [hereafter cited as SED, *Dokumente*].) Otto Grotewohl, referred to above, was one of the left wing SPD protagonists of the merger. He was the chairman of the SPD of the Soviet Zone before the merger. Afterwards, he became the second secretary of the SED. Since 1949 he has been Prime Minister of the German Democratic Republic.

[4] Grotewohl, *op. cit.,* p. 9.

the task of studying the lessons of the November Revolution at conferences, in meetings, and in educational courses, on the basis of these directives. A correct knowledge of the lessons of the November Revolution of 1918 and of the Weimar Republic is a prerequisite for the creation of a party of the new type.[5]

Thus, the analysis of the revolution, allegedly serving the purpose of discovering the major causes for its failure, enabled the SED to claim in its propaganda that the new party was basing its contemporary program on these "scientific" findings. Many of the premises upon which this analysis was based were arbitrary assumptions ascribed by the Communists to the post-World War I situation whether they corresponded to the actual conditions or not. For example, the SED reported the demands of the Spartacist League as being those made by the German soldiers and workers and created thereby the false impression that the "broad masses" expected the following fundamental changes:

(a) Immediate establishment of a close alliance with the [Russian] Soviet Republic in order to provide the German Revolution with a broad international basis and to create a counter-weight to the imperialism of the Entente;

(b) immediate cessation of hostilities on all fronts and punishment of persons responsible for having brought about the war and of war criminals;

(c) destruction of the Junker-bourgeois state apparatus, and establishment of the rule of the workers' and soldiers' councils;

(d) completion of the middle-class revolution by confiscating large landed estates and by transforming it into a socialist revolution [as part of] the struggle for the political rule of the working class;

(e) assumption of control by the people of the large factories, banks and loan-banks, concerns, trusts, and mines as a prerequisite for the socialist revolution.

None of these demands was realized in the 1918 revolution in spite of the fact that the broad masses clamored for these measures

[5] SED, *Dokumente*, II, p. 107.

and the vanguard of the working class conducted heroic fights for their realization.[6]

The SED practice of building on false premises was most likely little more than a convenient tool in their conscious attempt to falsify the facts to make them fit preconceived propaganda patterns. It is also possible, however, that the Communist leaders were deceiving themselves and had become captives of their own system of re-interpreting history. Regardless of the motivation, the end product of the SED's evaluation of the revolutionary events of 1918-19 is of extreme interest because it provides an insight into a number of current problems, e.g., the problem of the unity of the working class, the present role of the SPD, and the "dangers" which "U.S. imperialism" holds for the revolutionary proletariat.

According to the Communists, the most important lesson learned from their investigation of the German Revolution was that to be victorious the working class must be united and must be led by a revolutionary Marxist-Leninist party. Contemporary Communist leaders stress that the German Revolution confirmed that the left wing radicals should have broken with the "opportunists and reformists" of the SPD before World War I. Walter Ulbricht expressed this view as follows:

The class struggle which increased in intensity from the beginning of the imperialist period called for an organization which was capable of leading the working class to victory under these new conditions. *The creation of a revolutionary party of the working class was the order of the day in Germany as in all capitalist countries.*[7]

---

[6] *Ibid.*, p. 115.

[7] Ulbricht, *Der Zusammenbruch,* p. 7. Oelssner, one of the leading SED theorists, considers the failure of the German left wing to sever relations with the "opportunists" and its failure to found a revolutionary party as its "greatest historic guilt." These errors left the masses to the continued influence of t h e "opportunist" leaders. (Oelssner, *op. cit.,* p. 84.) Otto Grotewohl emphasizes that approval of the war appropriations by the SPD leaders on August 4, 1914, should have made it obvious to the radical socialists that the German workers lacked a revolutionary Marxist party to guide them in their future struggle. (Grotewohl, *op. cit.,* p. 53.)

In the opinion of the Communists, there was a definite and direct correlation between the failure of the German Revolution of 1918-19 and the lack of a revolutionary Marxist party.[8]

Another aspect of the organizational problem of the German labor movement which was greatly influenced by the November Revolution — the complex problem of the unification of the divided working class — can be treated here only in a cursory manner.

As has been pointed out before, the bloody fighting during and after the November Revolution resulted in a deep cleavage within the German labor movement.[9] The Communists believed that the German workers were dissatisfied with a divided labor movement, which resulted in a considerable weakening of their position in relation to other social classes and political forces. The KPD proposed to capitalize on this alleged discontent by posing as the protagonists of a re-united labor movement, and thus theoretically increase its influence among the working class.

Throughout the period of the Weimar Republic, the Communists shifted their tactics directed at the unification of the German working class. At times, the Party pursued the policy of forming a united front from above by attempting to reach an agreement with the leadership of the SPD on the basis of a specific action program. At other times, they appealed directly to the Social Democratic workers, inviting them to join a united front, in spite of their leaders' refusal to make common cause with the KPD against the growing dangers of German Fascism. This policy was referred to among the Communists as the united

[8] SED, *Dokumente,* II, p. 117; Matern, *op. cit.,* p. 13; Ulbricht, *Zur Geschichte,* pp. 39-40, 48; Karl Radek, *Die Entwicklung der Weltrevolution* (Moscow: Westeuropaeisches Sekretariat der Kommunistischen Internationale, 1920), p. 21. See also the book *Der Einfluss der russischen Februarrevolution und der Grossen Sozialistischen Oktoberrevolution auf die deutsche Arbeiterklasse,* by the research assistant of the Marx-Engels-Lenin-Stalin Institutes in East Berlin, Klaus Mammach, which was published late in 1955.

[9] During the period of the Weimar Republic, the two major socialist parties were the SPD and the KPD. The USPD, which had played an important part during the Revolution and shortly thereafter, split in October of 1920. Its leaders and members eventually

front from below.[10] Both the united front from above and below (such as the Communist sponsored Anti-Fascist Front) failed to attain their avowed objective of bringing the workers of both parties closer together. This was due, in part at least, to the fact that the KPD appeared to have been primarily interested in utilizing the "nonpartisan socialist combat organization" as a means of alienating the Social Democratic workers from their leaders, whom the Communists referred to as Social Fascists.

That the divided German socialist movement facilitated the growth of Nazi Fascism is generally accepted as valid. The Communists blame the split of the labor movement entirely on the SPD. A post-World War II Communist view indicates that same hatred:

The victory of Fascism in Germany was not inevitable. The imperialist finance capital was able to bring the Fascist war party into power because of the Social Democracy's policy of division [of the German labor movement]. The lessening of the split of the working class and the creation of a unity among the workers on a revolutionary basis were prerequisites for the prevention of a Fascist victory. Under the leadership of Ernst Thaelmann, the KPD fought ceaselessly for this aim. The Social Democracy prepared the road for Fascism and is therefore responsible for the defeat of the German working class.[11]

Not even the Hitler period put an end to the antagonism between the two rival workers' parties, which were then forced un-

joined either the SPD or the KPD. (Flechtheim, *op. cit.*, p. 70; Matern, *op. cit.*, pp. 12-13.)

[10] The first KPD attempt to form a united front from above was made as early as January, 1921. The SPD leaders refused the offer possibly because they either recognized the real intentions of the Communists or they believed that the KPD was then too small and insignificant to deal with. However, not all Communist offers in the following years were rejected. For example, in 1922 the KPD succeeded in forming a united front with the SPD for a short time. (Flechtheim, *op. cit.*, pp. 72, 83.) For information about the discussion within the KPD about their different united front tactics, see *ibid.*, pp. 85-87. A third method of re-uniting the German labor movement would have been organizational unity, the merger of both parties. However, this could not be accomplished on a voluntary basis as long as the members of the two workers' parties remained loyal to their respective organizations.

[11] Matern, *op. cit.*, p. 7.

derground. They continued to accuse each other of having brought on the catastrophe which had befallen the German people, especially the workers. Among the émigrés the old hostilities continued with unrelenting vigor.[12] However, many of the rank-and-file members of both illegal parties, who were persecuted by the Gestapo and frequently suffered side by side in the Nazi concentration camps, came to believe that a united working-class party would be to the advantage of the workers.

When a Socialist Unity Party was founded in the Soviet Zone of Occupation after the war, under the sponsorship of the KPD and the Soviet Military Administration, this party was primarily the product of Communist pressure exerted by the KPD and the Soviet authorities. However, there were a number of left wing SPD leaders and many Social Democratic workers in the Eastern Zone who welcomed a unified socialist party because they saw in the merger an important and desirable strengthening of the German labor movement. Otto Grotewohl's views on this subject are as follows:

After the destruction of Hitler Fascism in 1945, virtually no one believed it possible or desirable to return to the era of fratricide in the German labor movement. On the contrary, among the masses of workers and employees, the conviction of the need for both workers' parties to act in harmony was widespread. From this conviction, the will developed [to move] from common action to common organization. The desire for unity was at first a natural reflex of the German working class from the dreadful and inhuman twelve-year Hitler period, and it corresponded to the pure class feeling of the German worker. The task of the present Socialist Unity Party of Germany, which united both workers' parties in the Soviet Zone of Occupation, consists in transforming the natural class *feeling* into a Marxist class *consciousness*.[13]

---

[12] It is reported that Communist functionaries resorted to such incredible moves in their fight to eliminate Social Democratic influence among the workers as to denounce SPD underground leaders to the G e r m a n Secret Police. Cf. above, p. 195, n. 64, referring to the same practice, but directed against Communist elements.

[13] Grotewohl, *op. cit.*, pp. 134-35.

The SED resolution referred to above summarizes the experiences of the November Revolution as they relate to the issue of the unity of the working class:

The experiences of the November Revolution of 1918 and of the Weimar Republic teach that only the working class is capable of leading the masses in the struggle for a democratic system and for socialism. The renunciation of this important role by the working class leads without fail to the destruction of democracy and to the rule of imperialistic reaction. . . .

In the East Zone, the class-conscious Social Democrats and Communists kept the oath which, under the Hitler regime, they took in prisons, in concentration camps, and in the illegal resistance movement: to end once and for all the division of the labor movement. The working class has become considerably stronger by overcoming the split and has thereby gained for itself decisive influence for its further development. The present task is to establish the unity of the working class ideologically, politically, and organizationally. Ideological compromises are not permissible. Only in this manner can the working class realize its leading role.

The experience of the November Revolution of 1918 and of the Weimar Republic teaches that the working class cannot be victorious without a party which understands the necessity of mobilizing and organizing the class and masses for the revolutionary struggle and of leading them in this fight to victory. It must be a party which unites

The same developments also took place in the satellite countries. In Poland and the Balkan countries, the Soviet authorities "promoted" the merger of the Socialist and Communist parties following "liberation" by the Red Army. A short time after the fusion, the Social Democratic components lost their entire influence and for all practical purposes, the new parties were continuations of the former Communist parties under different names. Also in these instances, a number of the left wing Social Democratic leaders actively supported the Communist endeavor of creating "unity parties." Whether these Social Democrats acted under pressure, or were fearful that the Social Democratic movement would be stamped out, or were opportunists, or were genuinely ideologically convinced cannot be determined on the basis of the material available. Among the leading Social Democrats who advocated the fusion of the Socialist and Communist parties were Zdenek Fierlinger of Czechoslovakia, Arpad Szakasits of Hungary, and Dimitri Neikov of Bulgaria. (Andrew Gyorgy, *Governments of Danubian Europe* [New York: Rinehart & Co., 1949], pp. 43-44.)

the best elements of the working class, which stands on the revolutionary theories of Marxism and Leninism, and which insists on strict
discipline based on the conviction of all members. It must be a party
which is built on the principle of democratic centralism; in which,
through the use of criticism and self-criticism, all hostile and harmful
elements are eliminated; and which, through its own example, gains the
sympathy of the broad masses of the working people and understands
how to win the majority of both the working class and toilers. The
absence of such a party in 1918 was the decisive reason for the defeat
of the revolutionary working class.

Therefore the most important lesson learned from the November
Revolution of 1918 is to make our Socialist Unity Party into a revolutionary fighting party based on Marxism and Leninism.[14]

The merger of the two German labor parties was, as far as the
Communists were concerned, an extremely important achievement of the period following the defeat of the Nazis. It assured
them control of the labor movement and thereby greatly facilitated the establishment of an indigenous administration completely subservient to the Soviet government.

SED propaganda efforts to discredit the SPD have also made
considerable use of the lessons learned from the analysis of the
November Revolution. According to the SED resolution, the
SPD leaders refused to learn from the grim experiences of the
past and continued to pursue the very policies which brought
disaster to the German working class.[15]

. . . In West and South Germany, with the active assistance of
the Western occupation powers, the same disastrous policy, like that
of 1918, is being followed again. Under the leadership of Schumacher
and Ollenhauer, the SPD has adopted anew the same fatal policies of
the leaders of 1918. The right wing SPD leaders in West Germany

---

[14] SED, *Dokumente*, II, pp. 122-24.
[15] The SED resolution repeats the
traditional Communist accusations
against the SPD, beginning with the
assertion that the SPD leaders had
caused the fateful split of the German
labor movement by their actions of
supporting the imperialist war and the
Imperial German government. (*Ibid.*,
pp. 112, 115, 117.)

and in Berlin are full of the same blind hate against the Soviet Union as were the leaders of 1918. They continue with the greatest zeal the Nazis' lie campaign against the Soviet Union — an infallible sign of the reactionary forces — and thereby work in the interest of monopoly capitalism and reactionary elements. Through their acceptance of the Marshall Plan, the right wing SPD leaders submit the German people to Dollar imperialism and thereby betray their national sovereignty. The revival of imperialist reaction in these parts of Germany and the danger of a new world war are the inevitable consequences of this policy.

. . . While keeping up the division of the labor movement, the SPD continues its coalition policy which made the party nothing but an appendage to the reactionary bourgeois parties.[16]

---

[16] *Ibid.,* pp. 120-22. M. D. Zebenko went one step further in his condemnation of the Social Democratic parties in Western Europe. In his publication, *Die reaktionaere Ideologie der Rechtssozialisten im Dienste des amerikanischen Imperialismus* (Berlin: Dietz Verlag, 1953), p. 3., he "proved" that the Social Democratic p a r t i e s operated in the European countries for many years as the "agencies of the imperialists within the labor movement."

Present Communist propaganda attempts to utilize every opportunity to discredit the United States. In 1951, a Soviet historian, A. E. Kunina, in her book dealing with "American plans to conquer the world" during the years from 1917 to 1920, presented the material which Oelssner and other Communist authors needed to link "United States imperialism" with the failure of the German Revolution of 1918-19. A. E. Kunina, *Proval amarikanskikh ulanov gavoevaniia mirovege gospodstva v 1917-1920 gg* [The collapse of American Plans of World Conquest in the Years 1917-1920] (Moskva: Gosudarstvennoe izdatel'stvo politicheskoi literatury, 1951). In the introduction to the second edition of his book about Rosa Luxemburg, Oelssner pays the highest tribute to the contribution of Kunina: "In this book, with the use of American documents, it is proved that the bloody defeat of the revolutionary movement in Germany in the years from 1918 to 1920 and the murders of the leaders of the revolutionary proletariat was not alone the deed of the G e r m a n counterrevolution but that the agents of American imperialism were actively engaged in it as instigators and helpers." (Oelssner, *op. cit.,* p. 5.) For more details on Oelssner's utilization of Kunina's material, see *ibid.,* pp. 145-47. Karl Obermann, Professor of Contemporary History in Eastern Germany, in his book *Die Beziehungen des amerikanischen Imperialismus zum deutschen Imperialismus in der Zeit der Weimarer Republik (1918-1925)* (Berlin: Ruetten & Loening, 1952) undertakes to investigate the first contacts of United States imperialism with German imperialism to determine to what extent the political developments in the Weimar Republic were caused by the cooperation of German and American capitalists. (*Ibid.,* pp. 7-8.) Obermann also makes considerable use of Kunina's "contributions."

Conclusions

THIS STUDY has been concerned with the crisis of the German socialist movement which commenced during World War I and came to a climax in January of 1919 in Berlin with the bloody fighting between the Majority Socialists — supported by regular army units and by the notorious Free Corps — and the left wing radicals. Interpretations dealing with the Spartacist Uprising usually contain one of the following two assertions: (1) The uprising was a deliberately planned and organized attempt by the German Communists and their allied revolutionary organizations to overthrow the provisional Majority Socialist government and to create a Soviet-type proletarian dictatorship. (2) The insurrection was a defensive action of the Berlin proletariat which was deliberately provoked by the government into open rebellion in order to furnish the government forces with a pretext to crush the revolutionary workers and their organizations prior to the elections for the national assembly on January 19, 1919.

The first of these interpretations is found in the writings of Social Democratic authors like Bernstein, Hermann Mueller, and Noske, and in the accounts of exponents of the political right such as Volkmann, Oertzen, and Runkel. The second interpretation is that of the left wing radicals, for example, Richard Mueller, Barth, and Eichhorn, and, of course, of the Communists. An interesting position is maintained by former KPD members who were in the Party during its early period. Representatives of this group, such as Ruth Fischer and Paul Froelich (who are undoubtedly most sincere in their opposition to contemporary Moscow-directed parties), go out of their way to report events which

211

occurred during the time they belonged to the Communist movement in a manner which makes their own contemporaneous actions appear consistent with their present altered views. For example, Ruth Fischer's account, which factually is highly inaccur-
ate, lends itself to strengthening her argument favoring the Communist interpretation of events as far as the guilt of the Majority
Socialists is concerned. Her evaluation, along with that of Paul
Froelich, concerning the philosophy and program of Rosa Luxemburg are, however, at great variance with those of the Communists, who place much of the blame for the failure of the German socialist revolution on the ideological and tactical mistakes
of the early party leaders.[1]

Several "scholarly" interpretations of the Spartacist Uprising
are marked by the fact that they are based on incorrect facts and

---

[1] Compare, for example, the following account of Ruth Fischer with
the events as they can be discerned
from documentary sources generally
available and reported in this study:
". . . Deliberately to provoke the Shop
Stewards, on January 4 Ebert ordered
Eichhorn to leave the police presidium
and appointed as his successor Social
Democrat Eugen Ernst. On January
5, Noske ordered the attack on the
police presidium and on the newspaper
building. The Executive Committee
of the Shop Stewards, recognizing the
importance of this test, decided to
fight to retain Eichhorn. The Spartacist [sic] Central Committee, meeting on the same day, passed a motion
denying support to Eichhorn because
this might lead to the fall of the Ebert
government. When they later reversed
their position, they stated explicitly
that they were still opposed to overthrowing the cabinet.

"Thus, the first and most important
group of German resistance to the
restoration of *Kaiserlich* (Imperial)
imperialism, the Shop Stewards, had
to act alone, estranged from all party
leadership and organization. T h e y
gave the Ebert cabinet an ultimatum,

demanding that Eichhorn be maintained and the army be disarmed and
disbanded immediately (together with
the usual host of social demands).
The Shop Stewards, however, did not
call for the resignation of the Ebert
cabinet; (and of course they did not
know of the agreement between Ebert
and the army) that Comrade Ebert
was really their enemy. [sic] They expected him to yield to their pressure
ultimately and accept a compromise."
(Ruth Fischer, *op. cit.,* pp. 83-84.)

Equally interesting is Ruth Fischer's
evaluation of the possible effects of
an overthrow of the Ebert government
upon the general political development
in Germany. She bases her conjec-
tures on an over-estimate of the potentialities of the "revolutionary situation," just as the left radicals did during the January crisis.

"The rapid overthrow of the Ebert
cabinet, the establishment of a workers' government in Berlin would have
acted like a bellows to the smoldering
fires in Germany. Once the industrial
centers were set in motion, the de-
moralized military would have been
unable to regroup enough cadres. They
would have lost their chance to march

consequently lead to erroneous conceptions about the event.[2] German historians, sociologists, and political scientists of the post-World War I and post-World War II periods fail to deal adequately with what Professor Werner Conze calls "the second revolutionary wave" which commenced after the USPD left the cabinet.[3] Generally, there is a peculiar lack of German works which attempt to provide accurate background information and careful interpretation of the revolutionary events of 1918-19 and of the Weimar Republic. This is true in spite of the fact that it is generally recognized that these evaluations are essential for an analysis of the Third Reich and the most recent political developments in Germany.[4] It is hoped that the analysis of the January Uprising

on Berlin. Just this was their *cauchemar* [nightmare]. In 1919, in spite of all their shortcomings, the Shop Stewards could have crushed the counter-revolution with a minimum of effort and sacrifice. In the continuing duel between the Berlin workers and the General Staff, the officer corps was at its most disadvantageous point since the foundation of the Reich." (*Ibid.*, p. 83.) See also E. H. Carr's remarks on Ruth Fischer in his *Studies in Revolution* (London: MacMillan & Co., Ltd., 1950), pp. 187-89.

[2] For example, A. J. P. Taylor states: "Berlin . . ., turned mainly to the Spartacists, who were radical German nationalists; the rest of Germany, indignant at the failure of the Reich to which everything had been sacrificed, turned mainly to the Independents."

"Rosa Luxemburg . . ., intended to make her peace with the Independent Socialists — a development w h i c h would have ruined the plans of Ebert and Groener. Therefore, in December, 1918, the Provisional government broke the stalemate which had lasted since November, and took the offensive against the Spartacists in Berlin. The High Command by a refinement of political strategy took no part in the operation beyond dispatching its bless-

ing. The 'bloodhound' of order was a Social Democrat, Noske, and his instrument the 'Free Corps,' organizations of out-of-work officers, who would fight against anyone — at first the Spartacists and Independents, later against any democratic government, true condottieri, without any principle or belief other than that of the bullet in the back. . . . The Spartacists were broken; but broken too was the life of the German republic, for it could not exist without a united Socialist movement, and now the blood of Liebknecht and Rosa Luxemburg ran forever between the associates of Ebert and the men of the Left." (A. J. P. Taylor, *The Course of German History* [London: Hamish Hamilton, 1951], pp. 182-83.)

[3] Werner Conze, "Die Weimarer Republik 1918-1933," *Deutsche Geschichte im Ueberblick*, ed. by Peter Rassow (Stuttgart: J. B. Metzlersche Verlagsbuchhandlung, 1 9 5 2 - 5 3), p. 618. However, Professor Conze himself only superficially treats the events connected with this "second revolutionary wave." (See *ibid.*, pp. 618-20.)

[4] Karl Dietrich Brachner, "Zum Verstaendnis der Weimarer Republik," *Politische Literatur*, No. 2 and 3 (Frankfurt a.M., 1952), pp. 69-70.

contained in this study will serve to correct some of the misconceptions concerning the background, nature, and significance for the over-all course of the German Revolution.

Contrary to the widespread assumption that the January Uprising was the product of a deliberate plan (formulated either by the Majority Socialists or by the left wing radicals), this study indicates that it was an outgrowth of the tensions which existed between the highly antagonistic camps within the socialist movement. In the opinion of this writer, the showdown of forces in January was planned neither by the Majority Socialists nor by the left wing radicals. It was a violent outburst of the sharp hostility which then existed between the socialist factions. The immediate cause was an incident which probably in a different situation would have failed to produce such a serious political crisis.

In order to bring the January insurrection into proper relationship with the over-all crisis of the German socialist movement, an attempt has been made to trace the development of the division of the German labor movement from its beginning down to the eventful January of 1919. This division resulted from the growth of various factions within the Social Democratic Party. These factions advocated different political policies for the SPD on the basis of their own philosophy of the party's mission, of the working class within the bourgeois state, and of the methods to be

---

Dr. Bracher states: "An examination of the literature concerning the development after the first World War reveals that, besides a wealth of memoirs and political tracts, only legalistic discussions about constitutional and administrative questions . . ., showed any activity which, however, never transcended the most restricted specialists' circles. On the other hand, scientific attempts of historians, sociologists, economists, and political scientists who after all are of considerable consequence for the over-all evaluation of the development as well as for the formulation of political views, are still less numerous." (*Ibid.,* p. 70.)

Some well-known German historical accounts, such as that of Bruno Gebhardt, *Handbuch der Deutschen Geschichte* (2 vols.; Stuttgart-Berlin-Leipzig: Union Deutsche Verlagsgesellschaft, 1931) do not even mention the January Uprising. Others, such as Erich Eyck, *Geschichte der Weimarer Republik* (Vol. I; Erlenbach-Zuerich and Stuttgart: Eugen Rentsch, 1934) treat this event in a very superficial manner.

employed in bringing about socialism. The anti-war issue had also worked within the Social Democracy to break up the unity of the party.

In November of 1918, when the war-weary German soldiers and substantial parts of the disillusioned urban population seized the initiative in order to end hostilities, the various factions of the German socialist movement attempted to superimpose their respective political aims upon the revolutionary developments. This writer has concluded that the socialist movement, because of its traditional position of opposition to the Imperial authorities and because of its ability to provide the masses with an alternative political myth, could have given form and aims to the revolution beyond the immediate objectives of ending the war and removing the Imperial government. The German socialists failed in this task because of their own disunity and their refusal to compromise with each other. The Majority Socialists, possibly with such noted exceptions as Noske and others who had completely accepted the values of the "bourgeois" state as superior to the ideals of socialism, were no less sincere in the pursuit of their evolutionary policies toward the ultimate goal of socialism, than the leftist groups with their revolutionary approach.

The outcome of the conflict was that none of the socialist factions was able to gain a dominant influence over German political developments. Thus the victor of the internal struggle was not the SPD or KPD but the nationalistic, reactionary forces which, because of the divided labor movement, were able to re-establish eventually their former position of political hegemony.

The Spartacist Uprising as such did not bring about the reorganization of the counterrevolutionary powers, as has been asserted in some interpretations; they were by that time already in the process of being built-up. Contrary to another frequent misconception about the January events, the Free Corps, which constituted the most tangible manifestation of the anti-socialist, anti-democratic, anti-republican forces, did not become involved in the January Uprising until the very end, when the defeat of the revolting workers had already been accomplished by remnants of regular army units and Social Democratic fighting forces. In one important respect most interpretations, including that of this writer, agree: The January Uprising deepened the cleavage within the German labor movement and thereby greatly reduced its overall strength during the period of the Weimar Republic.

This study has also attempted to indicate that a number of specific conceptions relating to this critical phase of the German labor movement are incorrect. For example, the Spartacist League (and subsequently the KPD in its early phase) and the center of international Communism were independent organizations. This study has sought to demonstrate that the alleged direction of the German Communists by Moscow was non-existent during the period under discussion.

This fact is important because it explains the foundation for the later criticism of Luxemburgism, the German ideological deviation from Marxism-Leninism, by the Communist International. It is also significant because it disproves the charges that the Spartacist Uprising was ordered and directed by the Russian Bolsheviks.[5] Apparently the only official representative of the Russian "brother" party during this eventful period was Karl Radek. The personalities of Rosa Luxemburg and Karl Liebknecht, leaders in their own right who could not easily be persuaded by foreign direction, also made for the independence of the young KPD.

Last but not least, the findings of this study confirm, in the case of Germany, the validity of assertions made by such leading experts in the field of Communism as Franz Borkenau and Hugh Seton-Watson, that during the first phase of international Communism from 1918 to 1920, foreign revolutionary movements were not directed by Moscow.[6]

---

[5] See, for example, Bernstein, *op. cit.*, pp. 145, 188. Bernstein even has Russians participating in the uprising.

[6] Seton-Watson, *op. cit.*, p. xii; Borkenau, *op. cit.*, pp. 32-33.

Summary

IN NOVEMBER of 1918, the socialists came to power in Germany in the wake of the German Revolution which was started by a spontaneous mass uprising of war-weary sodiers, sailors, and large parts of the urban civilian population. Spontaneous mass actions, beginning with a mutiny of German sailors at Kiel and spreading rapidly over the rest of Germany, had as their major aim the ending of the hopeless and costly war. As a secondary objective, the masses were determined to abolish all those institutions which they regarded as obstacles for obtaining peace from the Allies. A growing majority of the German people had come to believe that the Emperor himself was one of the main obstructions, and that he had to be removed, together with the Imperial government and the Supreme Command of the military forces. Both of these institutions had lost the people's confidence, largely because of the military defeat.

The German socialists formed a revolutionary, provisional government in spite of the fact that the German Revolution was definitely not inspired by socialist ideas. They were able to assume power simply because the masses believed that for over two years they had been opposed to a continuation of the war and had been working toward the conclusion of an early armistice. Consequently, the socialists were the only organized political groups acceptable to the majority of the people because presumably they — and only they — could bring peace, the major objective of the mass uprising.

At the end of the war, the German socialist movement was comprised of two mass parties, the Majority Socialists (SPD —

217

the successor to the former Social Democratic Party of Germany) and the Independent Social Democratic Party of Germany (USPD). The movement also included several other political factions, of which the Spartacist League and the Revolutionary Shop Stewards were the most important. When the Majority Socialists took over the government from the last Imperial Chancellor, Prince Max von Baden, they were uncertain as to the strength of their influence among the people. They did not know whether the workers' and soldiers' councils — the real power factors in Germany at the moment, which were created spontaneously wherever the revolutionary masses removed the Imperial and state authorities — were willing to cooperate with the new Reich government. It was thought possible that the councils might consider a Majority Socialist cabinet as undesirable competition to their own revolutionary ambitions. In order to broaden its base among the people, the Majority Socialists invited the Independents to participate in the government on the basis of parity. For over a month, Germany was ruled by a socialist coalition cabinet, which, in the interest of appealing to the revolutionary forces, had assumed the radical-sounding name of Council of People's Commissars. It was a fragile coalition, however, because both parties attempted to impose their respective political concepts on the revolutionary changes. The dissension which developed within the cabinet was further aggravated by a number of bloody clashes between the Majority Socialists, who were supported by remnants of the regular army, and the left wing radical workers. This led to the withdrawal of the Independents from the government in December, 1918. From that time until the formation of the so-called Weimar Coalition (SPD and a number of democratic "bourgeois" parties), which took place after the general elections in January, 1919, the Majority Socialists occupied a position of political monopoly in the Reich cabinet.

The fight among the socialist factions for a dominant position in order to influence the development of the German Revolution was also carried on within the revolutionary agencies created by the mass uprising, the workers' and soldiers' councils. The latter had formed a pyramidal structure which reached its apex at the Reich level in the so-called Central Council, the permanent executive committee of the First Reich Congress of Workers' and Soldiers' Councils. (Prior to the First Reich Congress of Councils, held December 16-24, 1918, the Berlin Workers' and Soldiers' Council with its Executive Council had usurped authority for all of Germany.) Within the council system, the Majority Socialists succeeded in occupying the controlling positions after the Independents' refusal to participate in the Central Council because of their opposition to the Majority Socialists' program endorsed by the Reich Congress. Thus the two parallel governmental structures — the old state apparatus headed by the Provisional government, the Council of People's Commissars, and the new council system with the Central Council at its helm — cooperated effectively in most localities throughout the Reich. The general tendency was to shift more and more governmental functions to the traditional agencies and to consider the councils as supervisory or controlling organs of the revolutionary masses.

The Majority Socialists, who considered themselves only as trustees of the people until general elections could be held, used their power to consolidate the political, social, and economic gains made in the course of the German Revolution. These efforts of the Majority Socialists were in complete agreement with their ideological concepts and with their confidence in the superiority of evolutionary and democratic reform methods in achieving improvements for the lower social classes. They were effectively supported by the influential trade union leaders; they were violently opposed, however, by the left wing radical forces such as the Spartacist League, the Revolutionary Shop Stewards, and the Berlin organization of the USPD.

A severe crisis in the socialist movement had already started during the war as the result of factional differences in matters of ideology and policies. The strong anti-war attitude of the leftist opposition elements, which openly defied SPD policies supporting

the war, had led to a division of the party in April, 1917. This
ended the formal monopoly position of the SPD within the socialist movement. A second Social Democratic mass party, the
USPD, entered the political stage. However, the advent of the
German Revolution brought these two socialist parties together
for a short time. Factional strife concerning the aims of the revolution aggravated earlier tensions. The Majority Socialists accused the left wing radicals, especially the Spartacists, of plotting
to overthrow the Provisional government and of intending to
erect a proletarian dictatorship in the form of a government by
councils. The left wing radicals, in turn, charged the moderate
socialists with betraying the proletarian revolution by attempting
to arrest its developments and by making common front with the
avowed enemies of socialism. In January, 1919, the mounting
tension between the two hostile camps within the socialist movement burst into open hostilities. Berlin witnessed a general strike
combined with an armed uprising lasting from January 6 to 13.
This event is usually referred to as the Spartacist Uprising, in
spite of the fact that an *ad hoc* revolutionary committee which
charged the workers in Berlin to overthrow the Majority Socialist
government was dominated not by the Spartacists but by the
Revolutionary Shop Stewards.

This study attempted to investigate the nature of this crisis in
the German socialist movement in the light of contemporaneous
power relations and to determine its influence upon the further
course of the German Revolution of 1918-19. A re-examination
of the evidence appeared desirable because most of the available
interpretations are either based on erroneous factual premises or
are highly influenced by the political views of their authors.

To provide a basis for conclusions concerning the nature of
this insurrection, an attempt has been made to trace the growth
of those political concepts of the left wing which have a direct
bearing upon the theories guiding the left wing radicals, primarily
the Spartacists, in the formulation of their policies and actions.
Contrary to the assertion of the moderate socialists, the political

doctrines of the Spartacists did not envisage the use of a *coup d'état,* a violent overthrow of the government by a determined minority, as a method of acquiring political power. The political concepts of the Spartacist leaders, Rosa Luxemburg and Karl Liebknecht, stressed that only when the "revolutionary proletarian party" had succeeded in obtaining the support of the majority of the proletariat would the party, as the vanguard of the workers, assume political power from the bourgeois or quasi-bourgeois government and establish the dictatorship of the proletariat. Both Rosa Luxemburg and Liebknecht emphasized that this situation had not been realized in Germany at the end of 1918 or the beginning of 1919. The revolutionary party had just been founded. The masses of workers still followed the alleged treacherous SPD leaders. Therefore, they believed the main task of the young KPD was to educate the workers and make them understand that their interests were being betrayed by the SPD and USPD and that only the KPD was working consistently for the socialist revolution.

An examination of the events leading to the January fighting does not support the second assertion either. One of the most convincing arguments that the Majority Socialists did not intentionally start the series of events is the almost complete lack of physical forces available to the government at that time. When the position of power began to change in favor of the Majority Socialists, however, the determination to settle the basic issue with the revolutionary troublemakers won the upper hand.

Thus, contrary to the widespread assumption that the January Uprising was the product of a premeditated plan (by either the Majority Socialists or the left radicals), this study has indicated that it was an outgrowth of the tensions which existed between the highly antagonistic camps within the socialist movement. It was a violent outburst resulting from the sharp hostility between the socialist factions. Its immediate cause, the Eichhorn incident, would probably have failed to produce a similar serious political crisis in a different situation.

The defeat of the insurgents in Berlin is often credited with having ended the opportunity for the extreme left to prevent the consolidation of the German Revolution. Following the January crisis the revolutionary organizations were considerably weakened, and the government, by contrast, had the newly-formed military force, the notorious Free Corps, at its disposal to deal forcefully with the leftist opposition elements.

The outcome of the violent conflict was that none of the socialist factions was able to gain a dominant influence on German political developments. The real victor of the struggle was neither the SPD nor the KPD, but the nationalistic and reactionary forces which came to the assistance of the Majority Socialist government. Because of the divided labor movement, they were able to survive the German Revolution and eventually to re-establish their former position of political hegemony. This was most certainly one of the major contributing factors to the growth of German Fascism and the ascendance of National Socialism.

This study has also provided some insight into the early phase of the German Communist movement. Among other things it has revealed a German Communist position completely independent in ideological and tactical matters from that of the Russian Bolsheviks. (The Communist International was not founded until March, 1919.)

The events of the German Revolution of 1918-19 still play an important part in contemporary Communist propaganda in Germany. The Socialist Unity Party (SED) of Eastern Germany emphasizes that the working class grows in proletarian wisdom by studying the effects of past theories and tactics. The SED points out that the most significant lesson to be learned from the German Revolution is the need for a united working class led by a revolutionary Marxist-Leninist party. The catastrophe which befell the German labor movement under National Socialism is related directly to the divided socialist movement. Thus, at the end of World War II, when a Socialist Unity Party was proposed by the German Communists and the Soviet Military Administration, this new idea found favorable response among some of the German Social Democratic leaders and some of the rank-and-file members of the SPD. When these well-meaning Social Democrats awakened to the fact that the new party was not the product of a merger of the SPD and KPD on a co-equal basis but a continuation of the KPD under a different name, it was too late to do anything about it.

Bibliography

I. Primary Sources

1. Books (including Memoirs and Treatises)

Barth, Emil. *Aus der Werkstatt der deutschen Revolution.* Berlin: A. Hoffmann's Verlag, 1919.

Beckmann, E. *Der Dolchstossprozess in Muenchen vom 19. Oktober bis 20. November 1925.* Muenchen: Verlag der Sueddeutschen Monatshefte, 1925.

Bernstein, Eduard. *Die Internationale der Arbeiterklasse und der europaeische Krieg.* Tuebingen: Mohr, 1916.

Braun, Otto. *Von Weimar zu Hitler.* 2d ed. New York: Europa Verlag, 1940.

Daeumig, Ernst. *Der Aufbau Deutschlands und das Raetesystem.* Berlin: Verlag Der Arbeiter-Rat, 1919.

David, Eduard. *Die Sozialdemokratie im Weltkriege.* Berlin: Verlagsbuchhandlung Vorwaerts, 1915.

Eichhorn, Emil. *Eichhorn ueber die Januar-Ereignisse. Meine Taetigkeit im Berliner Polizeipraesidium und mein Anteil an den Januar-Ereignissen.* Berlin: Verlagsgenossenschaft Freiheit, 1919.

Fischer, Anton. *Die Revolutions-Kommandantur Berlin.* (printed as manuscript) [Berlin, 1922].

Froelich, Paul. *Rosa Luxemburg, Gedanke und Tat.* Hamburg: Verlag Friedrich Oetinger, 1949. (Reprint of 1939 Paris edition.)

_____. *Zehn Jahre Krieg und Buergerkrieg.* 2d ed. Berlin: Vereinigung Internationaler Verlags-Anstalten, 1924.

Grotewohl, Otto. *Dreissig Jahre spaeter. Die Novemberrevolution und die Lehren der Geschichte der deutschen Arbeiterbewegung.* 4th ed. Berlin: Dietz Verlag, 1952.

Grzesinski, Albert C. *Inside Germany.* Translated by A. S. Lipschitz. New York: E. P. Dutton & Co., 1939.

Haase, Hugo. *Hugo Haase, sein Leben und Wirken.* Published by Ernst Haase. Berlin: E. Laubsche Verlagsbuchhandlung, 1929.

Kautsky, Karl. *Die Internationale und der Krieg.* Berlin: Buchhandlung Vorwaerts, 1915.

————. *Die proletarische Revolution und ihr Programm.* Berlin: Buchhandlung Vorwaerts, 1922.

Keil, Wilhelm. *Erlebnisse eines Sozialdemokraten.* 2 vols. Stuttgart: Deutsche Verlags-Anstalt, 1948.

Ledebour, Georg. *Der Ledebour Prozess.* Berlin: Verlag Freiheit, 1919.

Lenin, Vladimir I. *One Step Forward, Two Steps Back.* London: Lawrence & Wishart Ltd. [1941].

————. *The Collapse of the Second International.* Moscow: Foreign Languages Publishing House, 1949.

————. *The Proletarian Revolution and the Renegade Kautsky.* New York: Internationl Publishers, 1934.

————. *Two Tactics of Social-Democracy in the Democratic Revolution.* New York: International Publishers, 1935.

————. *What Is To Be Done?* Moscow: Foreign Languages Publishing House, 1947.

Lensch, Paul. *Drei Jahre Weltrevolution.* Berlin: S. Fischer Verlag, 1917.

Levi, Paul. *Unser Weg wider den Putschismus.* Berlin: A. Seehof & Co. Verlag, 1921.

Liebknecht, Karl. *Ausgewaehlte Reden, Briefe und Aufsaetze.* Berlin: Dietz Verlag, 1952.

————. *Reden und Aufsaetze.* Published by Julian Gumperz. Hamburg: Verlag der Kommunistischen Internationale, Verlagsbuchhandlung Carl Hoym Nachf. Louis Cahnbley, 1921.

Luettwitz, Walther Freiher von. *Im Kampf gegen die November-Revolution.* Berlin: Vorhut Verlag, 1934.

Luxemburg, Rosa. *Ausgewaehlte Reden und Schriften.* 2 vols. Berlin: Dietz Verlag, 1951.
The following selections from this collection are of particular pertinence to this study:
Die Krise der Sozialdemokratie (1916), I, 258-399.
Massenstreik, Partei und Gewerkschaften (1906), I, 157-257.
Rede zum Programm (1919), II, 655-88.
Sozialreform oder Revolution? (1899), II, 126-37.
_____. *Die Russische Revolution.* [Berlin:] Verlag Gesellschaft und Erziehung, 1922.
_____. *Koalitionspolitik oder Klassenkampf?* Berlin: Vereinigung Internationaler Verlagsanstalten, 1922.

Mueller, Hermann. *Die November-Revolution.* 2d ed. Berlin: Verlag der Buecherkreis, 1928.

Mueller, Richard. *Der Buergerkrieg in Deutschland. Geburtswehen der Republik.* Berlin: Phoebus-Verlag, 1925.
_____. *Vom Kaiserreich zur Republik.* 2 vols. Vienna: Malik-Verlag, 1925.
_____. *Was die Arbeiterraete wollen und sollen.* Berlin: Verlag Der Arbeiterrat, 1919.

Niemann, Alfred. *Kaiser und Revolution.* Berlin: August Scherl Verlag, 1922.
_____. *Revolution von oben—Umsturz von unten.* Berlin: Verlag fuer Kulturpolitik, 1927.

Noske, Gustav. *Erlebtes aus Aufstieg und Niedergang einer Demokratie.* Offenbach a.M.: Bollwerk-Verlag K. Drott, 1947.
_____. *Von Kiel bis Kapp.* Berlin: Verlag fuer Politik und Wirtschaft, 1920.

Prinz Max von Baden. *Erinnerungen und Dokumente.* Stuttgart: Deutsche Verlags-Anstalt, 1927.

Radek, Karl (pseud. Arnold Struthan). *Die deutsche Revolution: oder trau, schau, wem?* Moskau: n.p., November 1918.
_____. *Die Entwicklung der Weltrevolution.* [Moscow:] Westeuropaeisches Sekretariat der Kommunistischen Internationale [1920].

————. *Proletarische Diktatur und Terrorismus*. Hamburg: Verlags-buchhandlung C. Hoym Nachf. Louis Cahnbley [1919].

Scheidemann, Philip. *The Making of New Germany*. 2 vols. New York; D. Appleton & Co., 1929.

Severing, Carl. *Mein Lebensweg*. 2 vols. Koeln: Greven Verlag, 1950.

[Social Democratic Party of Germany.] *Nichts getan? Die Arbeit seit dem 9. November 1918*. [Berlin:] Arbeitsgemeinschaft fuer staatsbuergerliche und wirtschaftliche Bildung [1919].

Stampfer, Friedrich. *Die ersten 14 Jahre der Deutschen Republik*. 2d ed. Offenbach a.M.: Bollwerk-Verlag K. Drott, 1947.

Troeltsch, Ernst. *Spektator-Briefe. Aufsaetze ueber die deutsche Revolution und die Weltpolitik 1918/22*. Tuebingen: Verlag von J. C. B. Mohr (Paul Siebeck), 1924.

Ulbricht, Walter. *Der Zusammenbruch Deutschlands im ersten Weltkrieg und die Novemberrevolution*. Berlin: Dietz Verlag, 1951.
————. *Zur Geschichte der deutschen Arbeiterbewegung*. 3 vols. Berlin: Dietz Verlag, 1953.

Weber, Max. *Gesammelte Politische Schriften*. Muenchen: Drei Masken Verlag, 1921.

Westarp, Kuno Graf von. *Das Ende der Monarchie am 9. November 1918: Abschliessender Bericht nach den Aussagen der Beteiligten*. Berlin: Helmut Rauschenbusch Verlag, 1952.

Wrisberg, Ernst von. *Der Weg zur Revolution, 1914-1918*. Leipzig: Verlag von K. F. Koehler, 1921.

Zehn Jahre deutsche Geschichte, 1918-1928. 2d ed. Berlin: Otto Stollberg Verlag, 1928.

2. COLLECTIONS OF DOCUMENTS

Astrow, W., Sleopkow, A., Thomas J. *Illustrierte Geschichte der russischen Revolution 1917*. Berlin: Neuer Deutscher Verlag, 1928.

Buchner, Eberhard. *Revolutionsdokumente. Die deutsche Revolution in der Darstellung der zeitgenoessischen Presse*. Vol. I.

Berlin: Deutsche Verlagsgesellschaft fuer Politik und Geschichte, 1921.

Drahn, Ernst und Friedegg, Ernst (ed.). *Deutscher Revolutions-Almanach fuer das Jahr 1919.* Hamburg/Berlin: Hoffmann & Campe, 1919.

Drahn, E. and Leonhard, S. *Unterirdische Literatur im revolutionaeren Deutschland waehrend des Weltkrieges.* Berlin: Verlag fuer Gesellschaft und Erziehung, 1920.

Hohlfeld, Johannes (ed.). *Deutsche Reichsgeschichte in Dokumenten.* 2 vols. Berlin: Deutsche Verlagsgesellschaft fuer Politik und Geschichte, 1927.

Illustrierte Geschichte der Deutschen Revolution. Berlin: Internationaler Arbeiterverlag, 1929.

Kommunistische Partei Deutschlands. *Spartakusbriefe.* Berlin, 1920.

Marx, Heinrich. *Handbuch der deutschen Revolution 1918-1919.* 2 vols. Berlin: A. Gruebel Nachf., 1919.

Meyer, Ernst (ed.). *Spartakus im Kriege. Die illegalen Flugblaetter des Spartakusbundes im Kriege.* Berlin: Vereinigung Internationaler Verlagsanstalten, 1927.

Sozialistische Einheitspartei Deutschlands. *Dokumente der Sozialistischen Einheitspartei Deutschlands. Beschluesse und Erklaerungen des Zentralsekretariats und des Parteivorstandes.* 2 vols. Berlin: Dietz Verlag, 1952.

Taegliche Rundschau. *Kriegs-Rundschau.* Vol. V, *Vom Kriegsende bis Friedenschluss.* Berlin: Verlag der Taeglichen Rundschau, 1920.

3. ARTICLES AND OTHER PUBLICATIONS

Arbeitswissenschaftliches Institut der Deutschen Arbeitsfront. *Die Streiks im 1. Weltkrieg 1914-1918.* Berlin: Deutsche Arbeitsfront, 1943.

Daeumig, Ernst. *Der Aufbau Deutschlands und das Raetesystem.* Korreferat und Schlusswort auf dem II. Raetekongress in Berlin (8-14 April, 1919). Berlin: Verlag "Der Arbeiter-Rat," 1919.

Freiheit. *Der Mord an Karl Liebknecht und Rosa Luxemburg.* Berlin: Verlagsgenossenschaft Freiheit, 1920.

Kautsky, Karl. "Aussichten der Revolution," *Deutscher Revolutions Almanach fuer das Jahr 1919.* Edited by Ernst Drahn und Ernst Friedegg. Hamburg/Berlin: Hoffmann & Campe Verlag, 1919, pp. 26-31.

Kommunistische Partei Deutschlands (Spartakusbund). *Bericht ueber den Gruendungsparteitag der Kommunistischen Partei Deutschlands (Spartakusbund) vom 30. Dezember 1918 bis 1. Januar 1919.* Berlin, 1919.

Lenin, Vladimir I. "The War and Russian Social-Democracy," *Selected Works.* Vol. V. Moscow/Leningrad: Co-operative Publishing Society of Foreign Workers in the U.S.S.R., 1935, pp. 123-30.

Liebknecht, Karl. *Ausgewaehlte Reden, Briefe und Aufsaetze.* Berlin: Dietz Verlag, 1952.

The following selections from this collection are of particular pertinence to this study:

"An den Vorstand der sozialdemokratischen Reichstagfraktion, Berlin" (1914), pp. 284-85.
"An die Proletarier aller Laender" (1918), pp. 476-80.
"An die Zimmerwald Konferenz" (1915), pp. 315-17.
"Antimilitarismus" (1915), pp. 318-35.
"Begruessungsschreiben an den Gruendungsparteitag der KP Polens" (1918), pp. 496-98.
"Das, was ist" (1918), pp. 472-75.
Der Hauptfeind steht im eigenen Land [illegal leaflet, 1915], pp. 298-301.
"Der neue Burgfrieden" (1918), pp. 468-71.
"Die Krise in der USP" (1918), pp. 521-24.
"Die Dezembermaenner von 1915" (1916), pp. 336-43.
"Dr. Karl Liebknecht zu den Thesen Dr. Eduard Davids" (1915), pp. 308-14.
"Ein schwarzer Tag im Reichstag" (1916), pp. 343-45.
"Fuer den Politischen Massenstreik" (1906), pp. 98-104.
"Gegen den Reformismus" (1910), pp. 168-78.
"Gegen die Nationalversammlung — Fuer die Arbeiter—und Soldatenraete" (1918), pp. 503-04.

"Kampf um die Partei" (1916), pp. 388-83.
Klassenkampf gegen den Krieg (1915), pp. 292-95.
"Liebknechts kleine Anfrage" (1916), pp. 345-51.
"Nicht die alte Leier, sondern das neue Schwert" (1916), pp. 448-53.
Ruestung der Revolution" (1918), pp. 499-502.
"Ueber den politischen Massenstreik" (1905), pp. 89-90.
"Ueber den politischen Massenstreik" (1913), pp. 267-71.
"Trotz alledem!" (1919), pp. 526-30.
"Was ist zu tun?" (1918), pp. 481-95.
"Was will der Spartakusbund?" (1918), pp. 505-20.
Zur Kriegssitzung des Reichstages [illegal leaflet, 1914], pp. 281-83.

Luxemburg, Rosa, *Ausgewaehlte Reden und Schriften*. 2 vols. Berlin: Dietz Verlag, 1951.

The following selections from this collection are of particular pertinence to this study:

"Auf die Schanzen" (1918), II, 635-39.
"Das Versagen der Fuehrer" (1919), II, 698-702.
"Der Acheron in Bewegung" (1918), II, 617-21.
"Der Anfang" (1918), II, 594-98.
Die Lehre des 24. Maerz [illegal leaflet, 1916], II, 551-57.
"Der politische Massenstreik" (1913), II, 442-49.
"Der Weg zum Nichts" (1918), II, 622-24.
"Der Wiederaufbau der Internationale" (1915), II, 517-32.
"Die Nationalversammlung," (1915), II, 517-32.
"Die Ordnung herrscht in Berlin" (1919), II, 708-14.
"Die Revolution in Russland" (1905), II, 213-16.
"Die Wahlen zur Nationalversammlung" (1918), II, 651-54.
"Eberts Mamelucken" (1918), II, 645-50.
"Eine taktische Frage" (1899), II, 60-64.
Entweder—oder [illegal pamphlet, 1916], II, 533-50.
Hundepolitik [illegal leaflet, 1916], II, 558-62.
"Kartenhaeuser" (1919), II, 703-07.
"Liebknecht" (1916), II, 567-71.
"Militarismus, Krieg und Arbeiterklasse" (1914), II, 491-504.
"Nach dem ersten Akt" (1904/1905), II, 217-23.
"Nationalversammlung oder Raeteregierung" (1918), II, 640-44.

"Rede auf dem Internationalen Sozialistenkongress zu Stutt-gart" (1907), II, 308-10.

"Reden auf dem Jenaer Parteitag der Sozialdemokratischen Partei Deutschlands im Jahre 1905," II, 236-46.

"Reden auf dem Londoner Parteitag der SDAPR" (1909), II, 274-307.

"Reden auf dem Mannheimer Parteitag der Sozialdemokra-tischen Partei Deutschlands im Jahre 1906," II, 256-61.

"Sozialdemokratie und Parliamentarismus" (1904), II, 189-200.

"Um den Vollzugsrat" (1918), II, 630-34.

"Versaeumte Pflichten" (1919), II, 693-97.

Was ist mit Liebknecht! [illegal leaflet, 1916], II, 563-66.

"Was machen die Fuehrer?" (1919), II, 689-92.

"Was weiter?" (1910), II, 324-37.

Wofuer kaempfte Liebknecht und weshalb wurde er zu Zucht-haus verurteilt? [illegal leaflet, 1916], II, 572-80.

Spartakusbund [Karl Liebknecht]. *Arbeiter und Soldaten!* [Leaflet, November 8, 1918]. Published in Karl Liebknecht, *Ausge-waehlte Reden, Briefe und Aufsaetze.* Berlin: Dietz Verlag, 1952. Pp. 466-67.

Spartakusbund. *Was will der Spartakusbund?* (Berlin, December 1918). Published in *Illustrierte Geschichte der Deutschen Revolution.* Berlin: Internationaler Arbeiterverlag, 1929. Pp. 259-63.

Stampfer, Friedrich. "Nationalversammlung und Sozialdemokratie," *Deutscher Revolutionsalmanach fuer das Jahr 1919.* Edited by Ernst Drahn und Ernst Friedegg. Hamburg/Berlin: Hoffmann & Campe Verlag, 1919. Pp. 73-84.

Vollzugsrat des Arbeiter- und Soldatenrates. *Die buergerliche Presse arbeitet gegen die Revolution* [Leaflet]. Berlin: December 17, 1918.

Wollenberg, Erich. "Der Apparat—Stalins Fuenfte Kolonne," *Ost-Probleme,* 3. Jahrgang, No. 19 (May 12, 1951), 575-89.

II. *Secondary Sources*

1. BOOKS

Amonn, Alfred, *Die Hauptprobleme der Sozialisierung.* Leipzig: Verlag von Quelle & Meyer, 1920.

Bartel, Walter, *Die Linken in der deutschen Sozialdemokratie im Kampf gegen Militarismus und Krieg.* Berlin: Dietz Verlag, 1958.

Bergstraesser, Ludwig. *Die Geschichte der politischen Parteien in Deutschland.* Muenchen: Isar Verlag, 1952.

Berlau, A. Joseph. *The German Social Democratic Party 1914-1921.* New York: Columbia University Press, 1949.

Bernstein, Eduard. *Die deutsche Revolution.* Berlin: Verlag fuer Gesellschaft und Erziehung, 1921.

Beyer, Hans. *Von der Novemberrevolution zur Raeterepublik in Muenchen.* Berlin: Ruetten & Loening, 1957.

Borkenau, Franz. *Der Europaeische Kommunismus. Seine Geschichte von 1917 bis zur Gegenwart.* Bern: Francke-Verlag, 1952.

Brinkmann, Karl. *Soziologische Theorie der Revolution.* Goettingen: Vandenhoeck & Ruprecht, 1948.

Carr, Edward Hallett. *German-Soviet Relations Between the Two World Wars, 1914-1939.* Baltimore: The Johns Hopkins Press, 1951.
_____. *Studies in Revolution.* London: Macmillan & Co. Ltd., 1950.

Cole, G.D.H. *The Second International, 1889-1914.* (A History of Socialist Thought, Volume III, Part I.) London: Macmillan & Co., 1956.

Conze, Werner. "Die Weimarer Republik 1918-1933." *Deutsche Geschichte im Ueberblick. Ein Handbuch.* Published by Peter Rassow. Stuttgart: J. B. Metzlersche Verlagsbuchhandlung, 1952-53. Pp. 616-665.

Coper, Rudolf. *Failure of a Revolution: Germany in 1918-1919.* Cambridge: University Press, 1955.

Durbin, Evan Frank Mottram. *The Politics of Democratic Socialism, An Essay on Social Policy.* London: G. Routledge & Sons, Ltd., 1940.

Ebenstein, William. *The German Record. A Political Portrait.* New York/Toronto: Rinehart & Co., Inc., 1945.

Erpenbeck, Fritz. *Wilhelm Pieck—ein Lebensbild.* Berlin: Dietz Verlag, 1952.

Eyck, Erich. *Geschichte der Weimarer Republik.* Vol. I. Erlenbach-Zuerich/Stuttgart: Eugen Rentsch, 1954.

Fainsod, Merle. *How Russia is Ruled.* Cambridge: Harvard University Press, 1953.

————. *International Socialism and the World War.* Cambridge: Harvard University Press, 1935.

Fischer, Louis. *Men and Politics. An Autobiography.* New York: Duell, Sloan and Pearce, 1941.

————. *The Soviets in World Affairs. A History of the Relations between the Soviet Union and the Rest of the World, 1917-1929.* 2 vols. Princeton: Princeton University Press, 1951.

Fischer, Ruth. *Stalin and German Communism.* Cambridge: Harvard University Press, 1948.

Flechtheim, Ossip Kurt. *Die KPD in der Weimarer Republik.* Offenbach a.M.: Bollwerk-Verlag K. Drott, 1948.

Fraenkel, Ernst. *Military Occupation and the Rule of Law. Occupation Government in the Rhineland,* 1918-1923. London/New York/Toronto: Oxford University Press, 1944.

Gay, Peter. *The Dilemma of Democratic Socialism; Eduard Bernstein's Challenge to Marx.* New York: Columbia University Press, 1952.

Gebhardt, Bruno. *Handbuch der Deutschen Geschichte.* Vol. II. 7th ed. Revised and published by Robert Holtzmann. Stuttgart/Berlin/Leipzig: Union Deutsche Verlagsgesellschaft, 1931.

Gerth, Hans and Mills, C. Wright. *Character and Social Structure. The Psychology of Social Institutions.* New York: Harcourt, Brace and Co., 1953.

Goerlitz, Walter. *Der Deutsche Generalstab. Geschichte und Gestalt 1657-1945.* Frankfurt a.M.: Verlag der Frankfurter Hefte, 1950.

Gordon, Harold J., Jr. *The Reichswehr and the German Republic, 1919-1926.* Princeton: Princeton University Press, 1957.

Gyorgy, Andrews. *Governments of Danubian Europe.* New York: Rinehart & Co., 1949.

Haenisch, Konrad. *Die deutsche Sozialdemokratie in und nach dem Weltkrieg.* 2d ed. Berlin: C. A. Schwetschke, 1919.

Halperin, S. William. *Germany Tried Democracy. A Political History of the Reich from 1918 to 1933*. New York: Thomas Y. Crowell Co., 1946.

Heidegger, Hermann. *Die deutsche Sozialdemocratie und der nationale Staat, 1870-1920*. Goettingen: Musterschmidt-Verlag, 1956.

Heiden, Konrad. *Der Fuehrer. Hitler's Rise to Power*. Translated by Ralph Manheim. Boston: Houghton Mifflin Co., 1944.

Inkeles, Alex. *Public Opinion in Soviet Russia — Study in Mass Persuasion*. Cambridge: Harvard University Press, 1950.

James, Cyril Lionel Robert. *World Revolutions 1917-1936. The Rise and Fall of the Communist International*. London: Martin Secker & Warburg Ltd., 1937.

Kautsky, Karl. *Terrorismus und Kommunismus*. Offenbach a.M.: Bollwerk-Verlag K. Drott, 1947.
————. *Wie der Weltkrieg entstand*. Berlin: Verlegt bei Paul Cassirer, 1919.

Klein, Fritz. *Die diplomatischen Beziehungen Deutschlands zur Sowjetunion 1917-1932*. Berlin: Ruetten & Loening, 1952.

Kochan, Lionel. *Russia and the Weimar Republic*. Cambridge: Bowes & Bowes Publishers Ltd., 1954.

Kuczynski, Juergen. *Der Ausbruch des Ersten Weltkrieges und die deutsche Sozialdemokratie; Chronik und Analyse*. Berlin: Akademie-Verlag, 1957.

Kunina, A. E. *Proval amerikanskikh planov zavoevaniia mirovogo gospodstva v 1917-1920 gg*. Moskva: Gosudarstvennoe izdatel'stvo politicheskoi literatury, 1951.

Lamprecht, Kurt. *Regiment Reichstag. Kampf um Berlin Januar 1919*. Hamburg-Bergedorf: Fackelreiter Verlag, 1931.

Laski, Harold J. *Reflections on the Revolutions of Our Time*. London: George Allen & Unwin Ltd., 1952.

Lutz, Ralph Haswell. *Fall of the German Empire 1914-1918 Documents of the German Revolution*. Stanford University, California: Stanford University Press, 1932; 2 vols.

Mammach, Klaus. *Der Einfluss der russischen Februarrevolution und der Grossen Sozialistischen Oktoberrevolution auf die deutsche Arbeiterklasse, Februar 1917—Oktober 1918.* Berlin: Dietz Verlag, 1955.

Mehring, Franz. *Geschichte der deutschen Sozialdemokratie.* 4 vols. 4th ed. Stuttgart: J. H. W. Dietz Nachf., 1909.

Mendelsohn-Bartholdy, A. *The War and German Society.* New Haven: Carnegie Endowment for International Peace, 1938.

Mohler, Arnim. *Die Konservative Revolution in Deutschland 1918-1932.* Stuttgart: Friedrich Vorwerk Verlag, 1950.

Mueller, August. *Sozialisierung oder Sozialismus? Eine kritische Betrachtung ueber Revolutionsideale.* Berlin: Verlag Ullstein & Co., 1919.

Muenzenberg, Willi, *et al. Karl Liebknecht: Ein Gedenkbuch.* Berlin: Verlag der Jugendinternationale, 1931.

Obermann, Karl. *Die Beziehungen des amerikanischen Imperialismus zum deutschen Imperialismus in der Zeit der Weimarer Republik (1918-1925).* Berlin: Ruetten & Loening, 1952.

Oelssner, Fred. *Rosa Luxemburg: Eine kritische biographische Skizze.* Berlin: Dietz Verlag, 1951.

Oertzen, F. W. von. *Die deutschen Freikorps 1918-1923.* 2d ed. Muenchen: F. Bruckmann A. G., 1937.

Paquet, Alfons. *Der Geist der russischen Revolution.* Leipzig: Kurt Wolf Verlag, 1919.

Pettee, George Sawyer. *The Process of Revolution.* New York: Harper & Brothers, 1938.

Pieck, Wilhelm. *Probleme der Vereinigung von KPD und SPD.* Berlin: Verlag Neuer Weg, 1946.

Plamenatz, John Petrov. *German Marxism and Russian Communism.* London/New York: Longmans, Green and Co., 1934.

Plievier, Theodor. *The Kaiser Goes: The Generals Remain.* Transl. from the German by A.W. Wheen. London: Faber and Faber Ltd., 1933.

Postgate, Raymond William. *The International During the War.* London: The Herald, 1918.

Prager, Eugen. *Geschichte der U.S.P.D.* Berlin: Verlagsgenossenschaft Freiheit, 1921.

Roemer, Wilhelm. *Die Entwicklung des Raetegedankens in Deutschland.* Berlin: Verlag von Emil Ebering, 1921.

Rosenberg, Arthur. *A History of the German Republic.* Translated by I. F. D. Morrow and L. M. Sieveking. London: Methuen & Co., Ltd., 1936.
_____. *Die Entstehung der deutschen Republik.* 2d ed. Berlin: Ernst Rowohlt Verlag, 1930.

Rudin, Harry R. *Armistice 1918.* New Haven: Yale University Press, 1944.

Runkel, Ferdinand. *Die deutsche Revolution.* Leipzig: Verlag von Grunov, 1919.

Schmidt-Pauli, Edgar von. *Geschichte der Freikorps 1918-1924.* Stuttgart: Robert Lutz Nachfolger Otto Schramm, 1936.

Schorske, Carl E. *German Social Democracy, 1905-1917; the Development of the Great Schism.* Cambridge: Harvard University Press, 1955.

Schreiner, Albert. *Zur Geschichte der deutschen Aussenpolitik, 1871-1945.* Vol. I. Berlin: Dietz Verlag, 1955.

Seton-Watson, Hugh. *From Lenin to Malenkov. The History of World Communism.* New York: Frederick A. Praeger, 1953.

Sforza, Count Carlo. *Europe and Europeans. A Study in Historical Psychology and International Politics.* London: George G. Harrap & Co., Ltd., 1936.

Simkhovitch, Vladimir G. *Marxism Versus Socialism.* New York: Ginn & Co., 1912.

Strobel, Heinrich. *The German Revolution and After.* Transl. by H. J. Stenning. New York: Thomas Seltzer, 1923.

Stuemke, Bruno. *Die Entstehung der deutschen Republik.* Frankfurt a.M.: Verlag von Willy Ehrig, 1923.

Taylor, A. J. P. *The Course of German History. A Survey of the Development of Germany since 1815.* London: Hemish Hamilton, 1951.

Thiele, Wilhelm. *Zum kommenden Raete-Gesetz. Wesen und Aufgaben der Arbeiter-Raete.* Berlin: Verlag Lindendruckerei (1919).

Tormin, Walter. *Zwischen Raetediktatur und sozialer Demokratie. Die Geschichte der Raetebewegung in der Deutschen Revolution 1918/19.* Duesseldorf: Droste-Verlag, 1954.

Valentin, Veit. *Geschichte der Deutschen Revolution von 1848-49.* Berlin: Ullstein [c. 1930-33].

_____. *The German People — Their History and Civilization from the Holy Roman Empire to the Third Reich.* New York: Alfred A. Knopf, 1946.

Varain, Heinz Josef. *Freie Gewerkschaften, Sozialdemokratie und Staat; Die Politik der Generalkommission unter der Fuehrung Carl Legiens (1890-1920).* Duesseldorf: Droste-Verlag, 1956.

Volkmann, Erich Otto. *Der Marxismus und das deutsche Heer im Weltkriege.* Berlin: Verlag Hobbing, 1925.

_____. *Revolution ueber Deutschland.* Oldenburg: Gerhard Stalling Verlag, 1930.

Waite, Robert G. L. *Vanguard of Nazism. The Free Corps Movement in Postwar Germany 1918-1923.* Cambridge: Harvard University Press, 1952.

Das Werk des Untersuchungsausschusses der Verfassunggebenden Deutschen Nationalversammlung und des Deutschen Reichstages 1919-1930. (Vierte Reihe.) Die Ursachen des Deutschen Zusammenbruches im Jahre 1918. (Zweite Abteilung.) Der Innere Zusammenbruch. 12 vols. Berlin: Deutsche Verlagsgesellschaft fuer Politik und Geschichte, 1928-30.

Wheeler-Bennett, John W. *The Nemesis of Power. The German Army in Politics 1918-1945.* London: Macmillan & Co., Ltd., 1953.

Winnig, August. *Das Reich als Republik.* Stuttgart/Berlin: J. G. Cotta'sche Buchhandlung Nachf., 1930.

Wolfe, Bertram D. *Three Who Made a Revolution.* Revised ed. Boston: Beacon Press, 1948.

Zebenko, M. D. *Die reaktionaere Ideologie der Rechtssozialisten im Dienste des amerikanischen Imperialismus.* Berlin: Dietz Verlag, 1953.

2. ARTICLES

Bracher, Karl Dietrich. "Zum Verstaendnis der Weimarer Republik," *Politische Literatur* (Frankfurt a.M., 1952). No. 2 and 3, 69-74, 108-112.

Brjunin, W. G. "Klaus Mammach: Der Einfluss der russichen Februarrevolution und der Grossen Sozialistischen Oktoberrevolution auf die deutsche Arbeiterklasse Februar 1917," a book review in *Zeitschrift fuer Geschichtswissenschaft,* 4. Jahrgang, Heft 2 (Berlin [Soviet sector], 1956), 402-406.

Einhorn, Marion. "Zur Rolle der Raete im November und December 1918," *Zeitschrift fuer Geschichtswissenschaft,* 4. Jahrgang, Heft 3 (Berlin [Soviet sector], 1956), 545-559.

Froelich, Paul. "Wie die SED Rosa Luxemburg ehrt," *Der Kochel-Brief* (Kochel, Oberbayern). 4. Jahrgang, No. 1-2 (January-February 1953), 5-11.

Haenisch, Konrad. "Die Ursachen der deutschen Revolution." *Handbuch der Politik.* Edited by Gerhard Anschuetz, Fritz Berolzheimer, *et al.* Vol. II, *Der Weltkrieg.* Berlin: W. Rothschild, 1921.

Kleen, Walter, "Ueber die Rolle der Raete in der November-Revolution," *Zeitschrift fuer Geschichtswissenschaft,* 4. Jahrgang, Heft 2 (Berlin [Soviet sector], 1956), 326-331.

Maehl, William. "The Triumph of Nationalism in the German Socialist Party on the Eve of the First World War," *Journal of Modern History,* XXIV, No. 1 (March 1952), 15-41.

Matern, Hermann. "Die Politik der KPD und der SPD in der Zeit der Weimarer Republik," *Forum,* Wissenschaftliche Beilage (Berlin, September 15, 1952).

Meinecke, Friedrich. "Die Revolution; Ursachen und Tatsachen," *Handbuch des Deutschen Staatsrechts.* Edited by Gerhard Anschuetz und Richard Thoma. Vol. I. Tuebingen: Mohr, 1930. Pp. 95-119.

O'Boyle, Lenore. "The German Independent Socialists during the First World War," *The American Historical Review,* LVI, No. 4 (July 1951), 824-31.

Paulus, Guenther. "Zur Verfaelschung der Geschichte des zweiten Weltkrieges in der westdeutschen Geschichtsschreibung," *Zeitschrift fuer Geschichtswissenschaft,* 1. Jahrgang, Heft 3 (Berlin [Soviet Sector], 1953), 445-65.

Snell, John L. "Socialist Unions and Socialist Patriotism in Germany 1914-1918," *The American Historical Review,* LIX (1953/54), 66-76.

Index

—, Executive Council endorsing the national assembly, 134
Workers' and soldiers' councils, 76f, 85f

Zebenko, M. D., 209n
Zetkin, Clara, 11, 27, 44n, 57, 101, 186
Zickler, Artur, 194n
Zimmerwald Conference (first), September, 1915, 51

Zimmerwald Conference (second), Keinthal, Easter, 1916, 51
Zimmerwald Conference (third), Stockholm, September, 1917, 52n
Zimmerwald International, 52n
Zimmerwald Left, 51
Zinoviev, Gregory, 49